Nov. 26

50

The United States in Puerto Rico

1898-1900

The United States in Puerto Rico

1898-1900

by

Edward J. Berbusse, S.J.

The University of North Carolina Press · Chapel Hill

1416184

Acknowledgments

To acknowledge is to recognize, and I do admit indebtedness to many persons in the labors of gathering materials and of evaluation in the writing of this book. So many have helped that I shall omit all names, lest someone be forgotten. But let it be said that I am most indebted to the gracious personnel of the National Archives in Washington, D.C., to members of the faculty and staff of the University of Puerto Rico, Georgetown University, and Fordham University.

Having set as a principle a "nonrecognition" of names, let me violate it with one exception. I recall with gratitude many hours of learning from the now deceased Monsignor Mariano Vasallo, who for many years was Chancellor of the Diocese of San Juan. His knowledge of the history of Puerto Rico at the turn of the century and his wisdom of insight helped me to see more clearly.

Acknowledgment

Contents

Introduction

The years 1898 to 1900 represent a change from the autonomous constitution that Spain had granted Puerto Rico in 1897 to the civil government that the Congress of the United States legislated in 1900. This period is marked by essential changes in political, social, religious, and educational life. In order to understand the cultural status and political reaction of Puerto Ricans upon entering the territorial system of the United States, it is necessary to present a survey of the islanders' striving for political home-rule during the nineteenth century. This will explain in good part the tensions that characterized the relations of the United States and Puerto Rico from the first days of change of sovereignty in 1898. It is highly significant that at the moment of occupation by the United States, the island was possessed of a significant degree of administrative autonomy and that this autonomy represented long years of labor in the nineteenth century.

The coming of the United States to Puerto Rico was first regarded by the Puerto Ricans as an opportunity to participate in Anglo-Saxon political life and legal procedures. But the days of enchantment were shortened, for the military governments were exacting and did not extend the full political and legal rights of continental United States to the island. Even when the first civil government was instituted under the Foraker Act of 1900, the hallmark of colonial dependence was most apparent, and the Puerto Ricans expressed their disappointment.

In attempting to understand this political disillusion, one must know something of the many cultural strands that blended into a unity and comprised the Puerto Rican tradition. The strongest fiber in this tradition was the philosophy of the individual and of his rights in society. This heritage was deeply rooted in a past inherited from Spain; moreover, it had felt the influence of the Americas, where independence from Europe had become a reality and where new ideas were being molded. Puerto Ricans had long desired self-determination and representative government. Alongside this political goal was a religious status: the Puerto Rican's traditional adherence to Catholicism. In this he retained much of the cultural shell of revealed religion, along with the substance of its code of moral living, but lost contact with a great part of the philosophical and theological foundations of the Catholic faith.

More harmful to Christian life than such nominal Catholicism was the practice of royal patronage which placed control of ecclesiastical affairs in the hands of the crown. By 1898 there had been four centuries in which clerical appointments, financial control, and supervision of church operations had pertained to the Spanish throne. This identity of church and state was a constant source of conflict. The church lost its vigorous independence. The ''new thought'' of the eighteenth- and nineteenth-century liberals was passionately opposed to church influence and voiced a strong anticlerical propaganda. Its expression was strongly reflected in educational circles. At the turning into the twentieth century, the church also encountered an opposition from the Protestant evangel that accompanied the military forces of the United States. The proselytizing efforts of Protestant sects, as well as their significant position in public education, soon convinced Puerto Ricans that these religious efforts were part of the new regime, and so religious tension became a part of the conflict in understanding between the United States and Puerto Rico.

This book seeks to emphasize the tensions and essential changes that occurred during the last years of Spain's hegemony and the first years of United States sovereignty. The first two chapters describe the conflict in ideas that the nineteenth century brought to Puerto Rico, as well as the growth of their political institutions. It is a sketch of the evolution from colonial servitude to assimilation into Spanish citizenship and the peninsular party system and finally to a type of administrative autonomy. These chapters are extended in order to inform readers from the continental United States of the political evolution in Puerto Rico. Succeeding chapters review the operation of the United States military governments in Puerto Rico from 1898 to 1900 and analyze the pressures that affected Congress in its drafting of a civil government for Puerto Rico. Thereupon we study the beginnings of civil government under the Foraker Act.

It was originally proposed that two final chapters be written on church-state relations and educational problems in nineteenth-century Puerto Rico. Wiser counsel and reflection have urged the following of a chronological order and the incorporation of such special topics into the time-order telling of Puerto Rico's story of change in sovereignty from Spain to the United States. A last chapter presents the religious and educational conflicts in the first years of United States occupation of Puerto Rico.

This book is directed primarily to those in the continental United States who are uninformed on the history of Puerto Rico, a free associated state (commonwealth) of the federal union. Though this writing is entitled *The United States in Puerto Rico, 1898-1900,* the author has sketched the nineteenth-century backgrounds in Puerto Rican history. It is hoped that this will serve as an insight into the ideas and institutions that came into conflict upon the entrance of the United States into Puerto Rican life. It is by no means an exhaustive treatment of the period but only aspires to open up an area of history for further investigation.

PART ONE

Puerto Rico
within the Spanish Colonial Empire
during the Nineteenth Century

I

Evolution of Ideas and Institutions in Puerto Rico during the Nineteenth Century

The cultural and spiritual contribution of Spain's colonizing in the New World has been much debated. Some writers have exaggerated the greatness of her cultural and civilizing influence; others have over-stressed the severity of her colonial policy. Whatever may be the truth, it cannot be denied that Spain left an indelible impression on the cultural forms of Hispanic America. Any attempt to erase what is an essential part of the thought and institutions of the Hispanic American world is futile. Nevertheless, Spain failed to produce a dynamic evolution of her ideological and cultural influence, and this ultimately led to the breaking of the political bonds. This failure can be attributed to a blindness in seeing that the colonials were sons of Spain with the same inherited individualism and love of self-government that characterized the peninsular Spaniards. Her policy of sending *peninsulares* to govern well-educated *criollos* and *mestizos*[1] was the static attitude that produced a new crop of colonials whose thinking and action were set on the forging of independence.

Puerto Rico, like other colonial areas of Spain, experienced this same urge for reform. While the masses of the people consumed

[3]

their days in supplying basic needs, the intellectuals or political
leaders were the ones who argued their rights and labored for institutional changes. The categories of reform were in the political, social,
economic, and educational areas. The political changes were of three
possibilities: assimilation into Spain as a province, an autonomous
charter that would give extensive local administration, or complete
independence. Under the heading of social problems came such
matters as slavery, the class structure, and regulations for the migration of peoples to Puerto Rico. The economic problem included
foreign trade (free or bound by the principles of mercantilism), a
system of internal taxation and the budget, the development of varied
crops, and the extention of transportation facilities that would connect all parts of the island, bringing produce to the ports. Education
was a constant subject of grievance, and illiteracy rates were high.
Spain had granted few secondary schools and had rejected the appeal
for a university in Puerto Rico. The right of students to be educated
in foreign countries was not always approved; nor were scholarships
generously granted to good students of the poorer classes. Lastly,
the right of the church to take its place in education, or rather to
continue it, was subject to strong opposition when the leaders of the
"new thought" expressed their anticlericalism. It is chiefly in the
nineteenth century that we see these problems come into focus; it is
then that annoyance with Spain's reactionary policy became most
vocal. A survey of these relations between Spain and Puerto Rico is
necessary as a background to an understanding of this island's relations with the United States following the occupation of 1898.

POLITICAL AND ECONOMIC ISOLATION OF PUERTO RICO

As a key to the Caribbean Sea, Puerto Rico had a major role in
the controlling of traffic that moved back and forth to Spain. Against
the invasions of major European powers that sought to crack Spain's
colonial empire, she reared mighty fortresses. El Castillo del Morro
and San Cristóbal stand in Puerto Rico today as memorials to the
engineering skill of Spain who dominated the world in the sixteenth
century, held her own in the seventeenth, and gradually fell from
power in the eighteenth and nineteenth centuries.

In Spain, the nineteenth century saw a fluctuation that swung
between the extremes of absolutist monarchism and anarchic separatism. Between these two were many shades of moderate political
thought. Spaniards were disgusted with Charles IV (1788-1808) and

his chief minister, Godoy, who had been duped by Napoleon. The latter had convinced the monarch that he should resign his throne and surrender the right of succession of his son, Ferdinand VII. In July of 1808, Napoleon set up his brother, Joseph Bonaparte, as king of Spain; and from then on many Spanish colonists used the title of "legitimacy" as a lever to pry themselves away from Spain. While giving lip-service to Ferdinand, their hearts desired independence. In Spain, the revolutionary juntas rose in the spirit of a new nationalism, a deliverance from the foreign despot, and increased political rights. The military junta of "legitimacy" in Spain wrote its ideas into the Constitution of 1812 which resembled the French Constitution of 1791. This liberal constitution declared sovereignty as residing in the nation; individual rights were proclaimed; and the Cortes was made their protector. The ideals of this constitution became the model for the liberals on the point of revolt in Latin America, as well as for the liberal constitutions that were formulated thereafter in southern Europe. The spirit came out of the minds of the bourgeoisie, intellectuals, theorists, and army officers; they were the class that was bred by the enlightenment and the philosophers of the French Revolution. In the colonies, the people rose in the name of the new freedom that not merely rejected Napoleon but also the peninsular Spaniards who dominated colonial government.

In the light of this, Spain sought to isolate her colonies from the revolutionary ideas that were awake in Europe and from the economic interests of competing powers. She might well have succeeded in this if she had been realistic enough to grant ever-expanding intellectual and political rights to her subjects. But, as a once mighty power, she lived in the land of memories; and of such recollection came a static approach to the increasing demands of the colonies. In response to the enthusiasm of her insular subjects for self-rule, she gave an arbitrary rule of peninsular military men. When education was requested, she often regarded it as the opening of the window to new and dangerous ideas that might ferment and beget independence. In refusing to understand the new thought, she engendered irritation in her colonists, who not only began to speak in terms of the rights of Spaniards and of provincials with their particular *fueros* (code of laws), but also in terms of emancipated America. The ever-progressing North American power was sprung upon Spain as a model; the ideals of Simón Bolívar were expressed in barely cloaked language. It was time for Spain either to make concessions to a growing Puerto Rican people or to crush out the spirit of growth. She did neither fully. She rather attempted concessions and then withdrew them. This infuriated a people who were normally noted for their faithful and pacific attentions to the mother country.

Puerto Rico was also of economic concern to Spain. As the eastern-most rib of the Greater Antilles, she caught the trade winds of the Atlantic on the mountain tops that ran along the center of the island. The northern slopes and valleys were wet and ever verdant. Rich soil in a wet tropical climate made it a center for tobacco, sugar, and coffee cultivation. The southern slopes of the island were deprived of the rains and, in the hot dry climate, became cotton centers. Diverse crops were cultivated throughout the island; and a little labor would reward greatly, as long as population centers did not overcrowd or the hurricanes did not cut a swath of destruction. Both reduced the food supply and required imports from the outside world. The system of mercantilism prevented international trade with the island and even the trade of Spanish colonies among themselves. Often it was either starvation or a smuggling of the necessities of life. Periods of economic necessity engendered interest in the outside world and often brought profits that induced the desire of further gain. For some time, especially during the nineteenth-century period of wars between France and England, the iron grip of mercantilism (which considered colonies as dependencies to be exploited for the benefit of the metropolis) was relaxed. Trade outside the nation grew, especially with the United States. For instance, in 1803, the Puerto Rican export of sugar to the United States rose to a high of 263,200 pounds.[2]

Along with this spirit of political and economic independence came the desire for wider education and the opening of a university. What Spain fully realized might produce greater demands for autonomy and even independence, the colonists saw as necessary to progress. They knew something of their constitutional heritage with its political rights—a heritage that antedated the centralized bureaucracy of the Hapsburgs and Bourbons. This was a tradition of strongly defined local rights that were incorporated in the *fueros* and written into the Laws of the Indies. They had heard of the great Spanish jurists, Francisco Vitoria and Francisco Suárez, whose treatises on the state and international law are classics in the literature of government.[3] They had seen the successful struggle of the

North Americans against a colonial power of Europe. In other sections of Latin America, they saw the beginnings of revolt under Francisco Miranda and Simón Bolívar. Spain's attempt to restrict Puerto Rico in her desire for some form of self-determination was destined to meet with reluctant submission.

Concomitant with this political stress was the formation in Latin America of economic societies of liberals who primarily concerned themselves with a study of new methods of agriculture and industry but who also became the seed-bed of the new political philosophies.[4] In Puerto Rico, the Sociedad Económica de Amigos del País was founded in 1813, and by permission of the Spanish Cortes, it was allowed to promote the development of industry, transportation, and agriculture.[5] This, it must be remembered, occurred during the short constitutional period of 1810-14, when the Cortes expanded its ideas of representative government and when Puerto Rico was given the status of a Spanish province, with the right of representation in Spain's revolutionary Cortes. However, all was undone in 1814 when the restored and absolutist monarchy of Ferdinand VII dissolved the Cortes and annulled all of its constitutional acts.

In the intellectual upheavals of the nineteenth century, the church, which had controlled education and influenced thought during three centuries, was severely tried. By the early nineteenth century, Puerto Rico had passed through three centuries of inadequate religious instruction and a weakened practice of the faith, in part because of a limited clergy and a widespread population that was difficult to reach over mountainous terrain and few roads.[6] Modern philosophies had battered the church badly, and it was often a static church that met its antagonists. The church, moreover, was wholly dependent upon a state that shifted easily from a conservative to a liberal political practice. It was caught in the midst of the political conflict and threatened with ambivalence. It found the conservative position less violative of its creed and metaphysic but just as dominating as the liberal. Consequently, it frequently aligned itself with the conservative element that was destined to lose power in Puerto Rico's evolution of ideas. An exception to this is found in the early nineteenth century when the bishop of Puerto Rico, Juan Alejo de Arizmendi, participated with his clergy in the ceremony of receiving the liberal Spanish Constitution of 1812 and when he exhorted the people to respect the law of the state.[7]

CONSTITUTIONAL RIGHTS VERSUS DICTATORSHIP, 1808-1819

In the Puerto Rico of the nineteenth century, three political factions began to evolve: the Conservatives, who favored unconditional submission to Spain; the Liberals, who were willing to be assimilated as a province into Spain, but only upon the assurance of a great deal of local administrative autonomy; and the Separatists, who believed that Puerto Rico had arrived at a period of development that would permit them to form a sovereign political unity. For the last group, revolution was to become the only instrument of separation. In the face of an ever-growing demand for increased home-rule, concessions were grudgingly given by Spain and arbitrarily withdrawn. This reactionary policy caused increasing resentment. For instance, on September 4, 1810, the Council of the Regency promulgated a royal order that gave the governor of Puerto Rico dictatorial powers that would prevent the spread of the Venezuelan revolt to the island. It is to be noted that the council's decree of emergency powers had been given without awaiting the convening of the Cortes. The reaction of the Separatists was a satirical verse nailed to the door of the house of the council's commissioner: "This people, sufficiently docile to obey the authorities that it recognizes, will never allow a single American to be taken from the island to fight against its brothers in Caracas."[8] About this same time, Don Ramón Power represented Puerto Rico in an extraordinary session of the Spanish Cortes. At its convening, a trend toward liberal legislation was apparent; and Don Ramón was responsible for the setting up of a subtreasury in Puerto Rico. This creation of the Intendencia de Hacienda was a splitting off of treasury powers from the office of the governor general; it also delegated to the intendant (subtreasurer) the handling of the accounting office, the fixing of prices, and the adjudication of finances. And so financial matters were separated from the absolute power of the governor. The first intendant was Don Alejandro Ramírez, a capable man who, in order to create a better climate of economic life, established the Sociedad Económica de Amigos del País. This group sought to promote the development of industry, transportation, and agriculture, and to increase the spreading of useful knowledge.[9]

In February of 1813, the governor of Puerto Rico proclaimed that the Constitution of 1812 become operative in the island; that a representative to the Cortes be elected; and that a Provincial Assembly be created. It was the first expression of representative government in a long while, and the Liberals were exultant. The assembly was a corporation of a semirepresentative character and with administrative powers, consisting of nine members who owned property. Their principal functions were to levy taxes; examine the accounts of the town councils; invest public funds; propose works for the common good; protect pious and beneficent establishments; encourage agriculture, industry and commerce; and increase public education. In accord with this new and representative institution's purpose, the crown lands were divided, and increased trade with the United States—especially in sugar—was fostered. Rigid mercantilism began to yield to some aspects of free trade. Though the duties realized from trade with the United States had risen to 100,000 pesos annually by 1811, they soon sharply declined as a result of the War of 1812 between the United States and Great Britain.

This period of liberalism in Puerto Rico was short-lived because of the return to the throne of Ferdinand VII, who quickly abolished the Constitution of 1812. By decree of May 24, 1814, the Provincial Assembly was suppressed, and Puerto Rico returned to the status of a colony. The Conservatives rejoiced; the Liberals were disgusted but remained pacific; the Separatists were forced to remain passive because of the failure of Bolívar's revolt in Venezuela. In order to assuage the feeling of his loyal subjects in Puerto Rico, Ferdinand VII made large concessions in the economic area. Accordingly, on November 10, 1815, Governor Salvador Meléndez published a royal order, La Cédula de Gracias, that provided for a fostering of immigration, commerce, industry, and agriculture in the island. Foreigners who were born of friendly nations, and who professed the Catholic faith, were admitted. Free commerce between Puerto Rico and the island possessions of foreign powers in America was allowed in the case of emergency, under determination of the governor general and the intendant. Customs of from 12 to 15 per cent were to be paid on goods imported from these possessions.

The study of immigrants to Puerto Rico at this time is an interesting one. Some came from war-torn Haiti and, on arrival in Puerto Rico, tended to favor the Conservative cause. Others came from Louisiana and Florida in the period following United States occupation. Still others came from Venezuela, Guiana, and Martinique, in order to escape the slave revolts or the conflicts between Bolívar and Spain. There were those who favored reaction and those who sought to arouse Puerto Rico against the mother country. Among the heterodox were those who ridiculed the dogmas and authority of the Catholic church. In their intellectual baggage were copies of the Koran, the Talmud, and the tracts of Martin Luther. The works of Voltaire, Rousseau, Diderot, and other leaders of the enlightenment were brought, and in the secrecy of the Masonic lodges, new political and philosophical ideas were discussed.[10]

While the concessions in immigration and trade were approved by the Antillean Conservatives and Liberals and had the effect of moderating tensions, the Separatists were in Mexico plotting the independence of Puerto Rico, Cuba, Mexico, and Santo Domingo. For it was in 1815 that Simón Bolívar was contemplating an invasion of Cuba and Puerto Rico. None of these attempts succeeded; but in 1820, the Riego Revolt broke out in Spain. Ferdinand VII was forced to restore the Constitution of 1812 and to swear to uphold it. In fact, all Spaniards were required under pain of death to swear to uphold the constitution, and the Jesuits were again suppressed. It became an instance in the history of the intolerance of the Liberals, which often matched the intolerance of the Conservatives.

In evaluating the educational situation of Puerto Rico during the period ending with the Riego Revolt of 1820, we note that Article XII of the Constitution of 1812 provided for the establishment of elementary schools in cities and villages. Its curriculum included reading, writing, arithmetic, and catechism. It is notable that, whereas the previous centuries had recognized education as a function of the church, the nineteenth placed it in the hands of the state.[11] There were special conditions in this century that urged increased education while actually preventing its implementation. It was a century of rapidly increasing population. The census of Marshall Alejandro O'Reilly (chief engineer of the coastal defenses in the Spanish Antilles and former captain general in Cuba) in 1765 showed a population of only 44,833 persons, but that of 1803 revealed 174,902. In 1815 the population leaped up to 220,892.[12] To meet the growing needs of education, two groups were organized in 1813: the Provincial Assembly (a local, socio-economic consultative body of Puerto Rico representation) and the Sociedad Económica de Amigos del País (a local society for the advance of commerce, education, etc.). Governor Salvador Meléndez had already ordered the expenditure of public funds for schools and their official inspection.[13] Reporting on primary education of Puerto Rico in 1819, he stated that it was "almost unknown in the interior villages of the island." Others complained that there was general illiteracy throughout the island and that for many years the education of youth had been almost abandoned.[14] As early as 1818, Don Pedro Tomás de Córdoba was lamenting the lack of secondary education in Puerto Rico. Though the Dominican and Franciscan fathers were teaching on the secondary level, it was chiefly for the benefit of those who were preparing for the priesthood.[15]

REPRESSION AND REVOLT IN PUERTO RICO, 1820-1833

In mid-May of 1820, Governor Juan Vasco Pascual of Puerto Rico proclaimed the restoration of the Constitution of 1812 in the island. The Liberals were again exultant and proceeded to initiate a Liberal society called Liberales Amantes de la Patria that was to help formulate party policy. Preparations for an election were already underway at the time of the arrival of new Governor Don Gonzalo Aróstegui. Attesting his devotion to the constitution and to liberty, he supervised the election of the representative to the Cortes and of the members of the Provincial Assembly. The provisional deputy was Marshal Demetrio O'Daly de la Puente, selected as candidate of the Liberals and elected on August 20, 1820. He was instructed by the Assembly to strive in the Spanish Cortes for continued trade with foreign countries; the ending of the costly visits of armed ships from Spain; the foundation of a charity hospital, a hospice, and a *lazareto* (pest house); and lastly the establishment of more primary and secondary schools, along with the opening of a university.

In 1821, the electoral junta of Puerto Rico again selected a Liberal representative to the Cortes in the person of José María Quiñones. He presented some fifteen suggestions of reform to the Cortes, and these were received in Spain with some few amendments. The substance of the reforms was the use of funds collected from Puerto Rico's internal and external revenues for the benefit of the island, and the granting of increased discretionary powers to the Provincial Assembly. The proposition that was a step in the direction of autonomy was made along with Don Félix Varela, the distinguished delegate from Cuba. The delegate from Puerto Rico to the 1823 Cortes was Dr. Ildefonso Sepúlveda, a Liberal and parish priest from Moca. His election and that of the delegates to the Provincial Assembly was well carried out, save for an incident in Añasco, in which the parish priest was jailed for having refused to explain the constitution from the pulpit. He was finally released by the governor's order.

All hopes for greater self-government were suddenly ended when, on October 4, 1823, Ferdinand VII announced the abolition of the constitution and the restoration of his absolute power. Puerto Rico returned to a non-representative status, and the Liberal political societies were abolished. The hope of the Separatists for a union with Bolívar also had to be abandoned for, by 1827, England and Spain had patched up their differences; in addition, the United States had opposed the plan of Bolívar. The lodges of the Freemasons were dissolved, the nightly meetings in the cafes ended, and curfew was called at ten.[16] Strict obedience to the king became the order; and Governor General Don Miguel de la Torre obeyed. Though political life was restricted in the island, large strides were made in trade, especially with the United States.[17]

Governor de la Torre had further problems that were endemic to the Caribbean in those days: naval visits from the United States, filibustering expeditions, and slave revolts. A squadron of United States naval vessels, under the command of Robert Spence and David Porter, arrived at San Juan while on a tour of duty and in search of pirates, and some slight friction arose in that port. But a more critical incident occurred at Fajardo in 1824, when Commodore Porter exacted swift justice of a pirate ship.[18] At the same time, there were reports of filibustering expeditions—stimulated by the Separatists— setting out from New York and Boston with the intent of attacking Puerto Rico.[19] Spain feared that the United States was seriously interested in the islands of Puerto Rico and Cuba. The spirit of expansion was widespread, and much territory had already been acquired by the United States under the Adams-Onis Treaty (1819) with Spain. The United States had also given recognition to the independence of the new Latin American republics and had proclaimed to the world in 1823 that the United States would not tolerate interference by Europe in the political or territorial *status quo* of the Americas. On the matter of Cuba and Puerto Rico, Secretary Henry Clay made clear that the United States was pleased with its trade relations with Spain's Caribbean colonies and continued to recognize Spanish sovereignty.[20] Clay saw no need of these islands at the moment, but many an American saw them as acquisitions of the future. The governor general had good reason to be concerned.

Amid the many revolts of the time, Luis H. du Coudray Holstein, a Swiss adventurer, sought to produce a revolt of the slaves in Puerto Rico in 1822. He had set out from the United States and was waiting in Curaçao for the right moment to attack Puerto Rico and set up the Republic of Borinquen. He planned to disembark at Añasco, but his plot was revealed to General Miguel de la Torre, who prepared his forces and executed some of the conspirators, and Du Coudray was forced to abandon his planned invasions. In 1825, there were attempts at a slave revolt in Ponce; these attempts were charged to conspiracies originating in Santo Domingo and Haiti. These and other slave revolts brought vigorous regulations.[21]

While the Liberals were in power in Spain from 1820 to 1823, the church schools were closed down, and no adequate substitutes were provided. The Sociedad Económica attempted to assist education by setting up chairs of mathematics, drawing, jurisprudence, and grammar in 1822, and during the succeeding years, it added courses in languages, physical science, and mathematics. In 1825, the church schools were allowed to reopen, and from this time on, the educational system of Puerto Rico was directed under the auspices of the church and the Sociedad Económica. In 1832, a Diocesan Seminary was opened by Bishop Gutiérrez de Cos, which served both as a seminary and a Latin School. The first years were preseminary studies, and boys of twelve years of age were admitted. Many of these boys did not choose to continue on to priestly studies and in withdrawing took with them a good preparation for university studies. It was on the lower floor of the seminary building that the Sociedad Económica held its classes. From this school of church and state came some of Puerto Rico's most able professional men.[22] They witnessed the passing of a decade that was marked with repression and political unrest. In 1833, Ferdinand VII died, and Puerto Rico had no reason to regret his passing.

MARÍA CRISTINA VERSUS CARLISTS AND LIBERALS, 1833-1854

From the marriage of Ferdinand VII with María Cristina of Naples in 1830, Isabel II was born. The king legalized her succession to the throne by abolishing the Salic Law of the Bourbons that had excluded female accession to the throne. On the king's death in 1833, the queen mother became regent for the minority of Isabel. Under Prime Minister Martínez de la Rosa, an attempt to strengthen the throne was made by the granting of concessions to the Liberals. A form of representative government was also allowed by royal statute in 1834. This divided the national legislature into two bodies: the Próceres, a group of peers who were selected by the crown from among the bishops, grandees, and favorites of royalty; and the Procuradores, a representative body set up in accord with the electoral law. Puerto Rico was allowed to send two delegates to the latter body. Though the Puerto Rican Liberals were disgusted with the functioning of this law under the rigid General de la Torre, they elected delegates and instructed them to petition for Puerto Rico a reform government that would guarantee the rights of the individual and property. They further asked for free trade, restricted taxation, the expansion of agriculture and industry, the increase of public instruction, and the encouragement of white immigration. Lastly, they were to request the restoration of the Provincial Assembly and elective town councils.

Few concessions were made by the crown, and when the regent dismissed the Procuradores in 1836, a revolt broke out; whereupon the queen was forced to restore the Constitution of 1812. This new assurance of reform was incorporated into the Constitution of 1837. On the basis of Puerto Rico's loyalty to the crown during the Carlist Wars (1833-40), greater reforms were again requested for the island. A revolt in Puerto Rico was only prevented by a change of ministry in Spain. The governor in Puerto Rico was Marshall Miguel López de Baños (1837-40), an absolutist who held power by sheer force in a time when revolutionary forces were in preparation.

His successor, Governor Santiago Méndez Vigo (1840-44) was a little better. He introduced a bit of humor into political life on February 4, 1841, by ordering that no one, save the military, was to use a mustache or goatee. It was his impression that this tonsorial style was used by conspirators. The wall of enmity between Spain and the Antilles was built in 1837 when Spain expelled the overseas representatives from the Spanish Cortes.

The years of 1843-54 in Spain marked the period of rule by the Conservatives. Among the governors of Puerto Rico during that period, the following stand out for the strictness of their rule. General Prim y Prats (1847-48) imposed severe codes against the Negroes, took jurisdiction away from the local courts, and restricted the press. His successor, General Juan de la Pezuela (1848-51), though a member of the Spanish Royal Academy of Languages, opposed the use of funds for the establishment of a central school in Puerto Rico.

He believed that such instruction had lost the Americas to Spain and added that, if they sought education, they might very well go to Spain. The period ended with two other governors who sought to get colonial peace through the distraction of the public from political issues by means of fiestas and dances. When the press criticized the government, it was suppressed, as was *El Ponceño* in 1854.[23]

In partial explanation of Spain's dictatorial rule in the Caribbean islands, it must be remembered that at this time, the filibustering expeditions of Narciso López were starting out from the United States. It was also in this period that the United States, in the spirit of Manifest Destiny, was set on the political and economic domination of the Western Hemisphere. Spain's ambassador to Washington, Angel Calderón de la Barca, distrusted the government in Washington; along with Britain's Lord Aberdeen, he was determined to prevent the seizure of the islands of Cuba and Puerto Rico by the United States. In 1848, President Polk completed the acquisition of extensive territory from Mexico, and when President Pierce had executive power in 1853, he made it clear that "our attitude as a nation and our position on the globe render the acquisition of certain possessions not within our jurisdiction eminently important for our protection." His ministers to London, Madrid, and Paris revealed, through the "Ostend Manifesto," the aggressive policy of the United States. This manifesto suggested that if Spain did not accept a price for Cuba, "we shall be justified in wresting it from Spain."[24] It was clear that if Cuba was necessary for the security of the United States, Puerto Rico would be regarded as another step in "self protection."

Since education was very limited in Puerto Rico at this time, boys of wealthy families were sent abroad for their studies, and some of them went to the United States. Remembering the expansionist policies of the United States during this time and the fears of colonial revolt, one can readily understand why the United States was considered a dangerous place for the higher education of the youth of Puerto Rico. It was also remarked that life in the United States removed enthusiasm for Spanish customs and that dangerous ideas were acquired. Partly for this reason, some advanced studies in accounting, geography, English, civil architecture, French, music, history, and botany were offered in Puerto Rico from 1845 to 1854.[25] In the waves of democracy that swept across the Western Hemisphere, the Antilles necessarily felt its influence. Liberal concessions in economic and political self-government might well have endeared

Spain to Cuba and Puerto Rico and could have preserved the political ties.

The church, also, despite its consistent loyalty to the government of Spain, suffered from these oppressive governments in Puerto Rico. Governor López Baños, in 1839, ordered the priest Nicolás Antonio Díaz to leave the country, and when the capitular vicar (acting administrator of the diocese in the absence of the bishop) attempted to aid the exiled priest, he was threatened with a like penalty.[26]

The state's religious policy was intolerant from the beginning. Article 8 of the Royal Decree of August 10, 1815, denied the admission of non-Catholics to Spain's territories. In 1846, the president of the Board of Commerce and Industry requested of the Overseas Ministry in Madrid the abrogation of this religious requirement. He argued that a more liberal policy would introduce new capital into the island and would foster greater trade and industry. By tolerance, he said, conversions to the Catholic faith would be increased. This opinion was sustained by the governor, the treasurer, and the city councils of San Juan, Ponce, Mayagüez, and Aguadilla. In opposition, the bishop, the magistrates of the territorial court, and the fiscal (attorney general) of the crown wrote that diversity of religious practice would make for political disorder and eventually produce the political independence of the island. The attorney general stated, as a universal principle, that unity of religious belief makes for political unity and that every government must seek to preserve such unity. Since the Catholic religion, he argued, is the only bond that links this island with Spain, to admit other religious beliefs would undoubtedly lead to independence. Bishop Fray Francisco la Puente who had been appointed in 1846 to the bishopric of Puerto Rico, maintained that only the sentiments that derive from the true faith can extinguish the desire of independence. He charged Protestantism with inciting to disobedience and rebellion, while Catholicism stimulates its members to true love of one's country. The petition of the president of the Board of Trade was doomed to failure; in 1849, the government in Madrid replied by sustaining the opposition and ordered that the religious provision in Article 8 of the Royal Decree of 1815 be strictly enforced.[27]

While religious intolerance continued, there was some improvement in primary public education but none in the secondary. Private schools on the primary level increased notably. It was during this second quarter of the nineteenth century that the Spanish school law was drafted, creating school commissions in the province, district, and town. The commissions were composed of civil authorities, the clergy, and a few heads of families, and their duties were the supervision and encouragement of primary school education. This Law of 1834 was applied to Puerto Rico in 1838, but its small success can be attributed to political upheavals and epidemics. The period ended with little political, social, or economic reform—and much public dissatisfaction.

FROM FAILING REFORMS TO THE REVOLT AT LARES, 1855-1868

In the year 1855, an epidemic of cholera broke out on the island, leaving in its wake over thirty thousand victims. So terrible was the death toll that in Caguas the dead were left unburied for a time because of want of those able to bury them.[28] Though the insular government of Marshal José de Lemery aided the victims, it did nothing to advance self-government. An occasional voice was raised in the Cortes requesting administrative autonomy for Cuba and Puerto Rico. Though the Constitution of 1837 had promised "Special Laws" for greater self-government, nothing had resulted. In 1858, Don Julián Blanco Sosa petitioned these laws and was banished from Puerto Rico. The organization of secret societies, such as that of Ramón Emeterio Betances in Mayagüez, with the intent of securing the independence of Puerto Rico was punished. At the same time, José Francisco Basora was preparing to transfer to New York in order to consolidate his efforts with the Separatists of the Cuban junta, groups working together for the emancipation of the slaves and the independence of Puerto Rico.[29]

In the sixties, the Separatists were again urging a revolt under the inspiration of the upheaval that was fostered by Gregorio Luperón and José María Cabral in Santo Domingo. Spain had been ceded the country by the local Antillean government on March 18, 1861, and it was not until January 7, 1865, that Spain gave up this hopeless attempt to reassert her sovereignty there. Though the sympathetic revolt did not succeed in Puerto Rico, it became obvious to the minister of the colonies, Antonio Cánovas del Castillo, that concessions must be made to the islands of Cuba and Puerto Rico. He thereupon called representatives of these peoples to Madrid in order to discuss their social, economic, and political problems, and to propose a set of "Special Laws."[30] The convening body consisted of forty-four members; of these, twenty-two were appointed by Cánovas, and the rest represented the colonies. The Puerto Rican delegates who were elected by the town councils of San Juan, Ponce, San Germán, Arecibo, and Mayagüez represented both the Conservative and Liberal parties.[31]

When the junta met in October of 1866, under the new minister of colonies, Alejandro de Castro, both economic and political problems were discussed. Slavery was to be abolished; commerce between Spain and the Spanish Antilles was to be free; and foreign ships were to be allowed free registration. In the presentation of political considerations, José Morales Lemus of Cuba spoke for both islands. He asked that the same individual rights be granted to the colonials as were enjoyed by the peninsular Spaniards. The Puerto Rican request was for a civil governor who was to co-operate with a Provincial Assembly that was composed of a representative body and a senate. The island was to be divided into the three districts of San Juan, Mayagüez, and Ponce; each was to have its own subgovernor, council, and representative body. The basic unit of the island's government was to be the municipality that was "to obey and guide the ideas and wishes of the citizens"; this was to be governed by the town council, an elective body; and it was the municipality that was to handle all matter of taxation, budget, and finance. The tying in of the island's government with that of Spain was to be through the elected representatives to the Cortes, and representation was to be on the basis of one deputy for each 45,000 inhabitants. The office of intendant (subtreasurer) was to be retained.

After thirty-six sessions, the special junta adjourned on April 27, 1867. Cuba and Puerto Rico had presented a good case for social, political, and economic reforms. They had argued that Spain's past policy had produced the revolutions of the greater part of Hispanic America; that overcentralization had resulted in many ills; that the United States was showing a very neighborly attitude; that other provinces of Spain had long enjoyed special privileges not resulting in separation from Spain; and lastly that Cuba and Puerto Rico were well prepared for a completely liberal system of government. The recommendations, however, were rejected in May, 1867, by Spain's Narváez Cabinet. New taxes were imposed by the local intendant. Public criticism was strong, but quickly suppressed by Governor General Marchesi. Two of the leaders of the opposition, Segundo Ruiz Belvis and Dr. Ramón Emeterio Betances of Mayagüez, fled to New

York where they united with other revolutionists in the formation of the Sociedad Republicana of Cuba and Puerto Rico which plotted the independence of the two islands. Centers of separatism were formed in Puerto Rico, and the spirit of independence was manifested in a musical composition known as *La Borinqueña*.

During this period of intense desire for reform, the United States was engaged in civil war and in subsequent reconstruction. Consequently, the threat of competition of Louisiana sugar to the Puerto Rican crop was ended. In 1865, the sugar production of Puerto Rico rose to 121,053,963 pounds because of the liberal laws that Madrid had passed for the benefit of the island's agriculture and the high prices that sugar earned in the markets of the United States. The production of cotton, tobacco, and coffee also showed increases. Yet positive benefits did not result for the island because of the increased cost of Spain's two recent wars—with Morocco in 1860 and with Santo Domingo in 1864. The Antilles were forced to share the cost of Spain's war burdens. It seemed that Puerto Rico could not succeed in either her political or economic relations with the mother country.

In the year following the special assembly in Spain, a revolt broke out in west-central Puerto Rico on September 23. It raised the glamorous cries of "Death or Liberty," and "Long Life to a Free Puerto Rico," and is known as the "Grito de Lares." A great deal of enthusiasm was aroused in a limited area, and a revolutionary government was set up, but the larger population centers hardly knew of all this. While a priest of the vicinity was forced to offer a *Te Deum* in thanksgiving for the revolt, the more prevalent reaction was a strong protest of loyalty to the government of Spain. When Spain imposed severe sentences, a reaction set in; the women, clergy, and bishop of the island pleaded for, and secured, moderate penalties for the convicted.[32] At about the same time, a revolution against the government of Isabel II had erupted in Cádiz under the triumvirate of General Prim y Prats, Antonio Cánovas del Castillo, and Praxedes Mateo Sagasta. Upon the flight of the queen to France on September 30, 1868, General Serrano set up a provisional government. Thereupon amnesty was granted to the revolutionists of Lares, and Governor Julián Juan Pavía was recalled to Spain.

After 1837 (when Isabel II withdrew the benefits of the Constitution of 1837), and until 1868 (when the Liberal revolt occurred),

Puerto Rico continued in a colonial status of subjection to the absolute decrees of the governor generals sent from Spain. Puerto Rican liberals desired the status of a Spanish province, with the residents enjoying all the rights of peninsular Spaniards, including representation in the Spanish Cortes. When the metropolitan revolt occurred in 1868, new advances in political reform were requested. Before 1870, the existing political factions in Puerto Rico sought differing expressions of assimilation into Spanish political life.

Simultaneous with the agitation on behalf of political reform, there arose a mixed attitude toward the church. In the 1868 uprising of Lares, the revolutionary government required that the pastor of Lares, Don José Gumersindo Vega, offer a solemn *Te Deum* in the church for a successful outcome of the revolt. Upon the priest's refusal to comply, the revolutionaries strongly insisted, and the father acquiesced. He immediately informed Bishop Pablo Benigno Carrión of this action, insisting that he had acted against his own will, under threat, and without knowledge of any precedent in the case. It is interesting to note that, upon the suppression of the revolt, the bishop and his clergy asked that the insurrectionists be pardoned.[33] At the same time, a more heterodox philosophy was being germinated in the Masonic lodges that dotted the island, assisted by the lodges in Cuba, Venezuela, Santo Domingo, the United States, and the French and British Antilles. Though governmental restrictions periodically checked the operations of the Masons, the movement grew. The Grand Lodge of Cuba was the dominant force in Puerto Rico until 1885 when it yielded place to the Sovereign Grand Lodge of Puerto Rico.[34]

Throughout the nineteenth century, the church lost ground to the forces of international masonry. As a counterattack to the "new attitudes," the town council of San Juan, in 1822, had ordered that the teachers conduct their students to the cathedral for a released time program in Christian doctrine. In 1826, the bishop warned the faithful against the agnostic voices; by 1847, it was stated that many of the students of the Sociedad Económica were not attending religious instruction; and in 1868, José Pérez Morís y Cueto declared that the Catholic spirit was suffering much damage in the island. Not only was rationalism on the rise, but also the doctrines of spiritualism were finding their way into the social circles of Puerto Rico.[35] The last half of the nineteenth century was to witness a growth in the spirit of revolt both against the church and the state.

LIBERAL LEADERS IN LATE NINETEENTH-CENTURY THOUGHT:
DE HOSTOS, ACOSTA, BRAU

As the early nineteenth century had seen the rise and fall of interest in the philosophies of the encyclopedists and romanticists, so the end of the nineteenth century saw in Spanish America the impact of a positivistic faith in humanity. It has been asserted that Latin America was in search of a philosophy that would sever all intellectual bonds with Spain. The new leaders believed that the ideas of a static Spain were frustrating the dynamic present of Latin America, and positivism was gaining wide acceptance as the lever that would emancipate Latin America from its past.[36] The tenets of August Comte (1798-1857) became the leading philosophy in several Latin American countries. His "new order" of society built upon the scientific or positivistic state offered a solution. The human mind, he said, had risen to a point at which—emancipated from theology and metaphysics—it believed that it could investigate scientifically and produce reform and progress.[37]

Modern man was to live by a positivistic sociology; that is, through scientific observation and experimentation in human relations, man would arrive at social well-being. The only religion was to be that of humanity at whose shrine man would find truth and give worship. Soon after Comte came Herbert Spencer (1820-1903), whose philosophy offered a series of theses unified through the principle of evolution. The individual, through the interaction of the process of differentiation and integration, was experiencing a newer and better unity. From this evolution, the individual was differentiated from the group and so achieved increased freedom. The state, likewise, must evolve, in order to assist the individual in his quest for freedom and justice. For Spencer, the absolute could not be known. In both Comte and Spencer, we see a thought that conflicted with the metaphysics of scholasticism, as well as with the theological teaching of the Catholic church. This positivistic faith in humanity became prevalent among many intellectuals in Latin America, and its impact on Puerto Rico is found in the writings of such prominent persons as Eugenio María de Hostos, José Julián Acosta, and Salvador Brau.

The Puerto Rican Eugenio María de Hostos (1839-1903) is probably the most outstanding of the Antillean thinkers who, in a long line of Kantians, believed that the world of metaphysics is a land of fancy and illusion. De Hostos regarded the searching for a first cause as useless, since God, he held, was completely inaccessible to the human mind. Following the positivism of Comte, he honored the physical sciences; matter, he regarded, was the only reality that could be known. Hostos saw morality as neither imposed nor ruling conscience, but rather arising from a harmonic relationship between man and nature. Sociology was the study of this ever evolving relationship. In religion, De Hostos was far removed from Catholicism, for he denied the inmortality of the soul; the spirit dies, he said, for it disappears in the matter in which it is contained. Matter, however, does not die, but is continually transformed. Eternal life for De Hostos was an illusion. The theologians, he charged, sought to destroy the secular works of human reason and contemporary civilization. He criticized the *Syllabus of Errors* and the dogmas of the Immaculate Conception and Papal Infallibility. He believed that Protestantism was a more congenial instrument than Catholicism for the development of personality. Though he rejected Catholicism, he could not attack it, arguing that it was still one of the most profound cultural heritages of his people. He hoped for a solution to this inner conflict, when ''a reflecting Pope . . . would make a change from the religion of tradition to that of reason.'' He believed that this religion of reason would espouse a non-imposed moral order and would accord religious with scientific beliefs.

In accord with his positivistic principles, he also rejected the educational theories of the past. As Pedreira describes it: ''The metaphysical and theological tenor of instruction has achieved its purpose, and now has no other interest but historical. The new orientation of the positivist philosophy demands a rapid pedagogical evolution, in accord with the infallible natural law of progress. . . .''[38] From Francis Bacon, De Hostos took the experimental method; from Rousseau, he learned to put the child in contact with nature. In accord with the historical method of August Comte, he believed that Latin America had arrived at a point at which humanity must be considered the beginning and end of all knowledge.[39] He opposed scholasticism, which he believed placed theology over philosophy, and philosophy over reason. Lastly, De Hostos drew from Herbert Spencer the belief that the physical sciences were the best educative experience for youth—mathematical, physical, and natural.

Eugenio María de Hostos consistently applied Spencer's idea of evolution to the independence of Cuba and Puerto Rico. In *La peregrinación de Bayoán,* he states: "The Antilles will be with Spain if there is a granting of their rights; if the epoch of domination continues they will be against Spain."[40] In his desire for greater autonomy, he hoped that the evolution of Spain's treatment would be toward a federation of the Antilles that would include Cuba, Santo Domingo, and Puerto Rico. When he saw that Spain's tendency was toward repression, he allowed his own ideas to turn to full independence.[41] It became quite apparent that the current political thought of Spain would leave little room for an evolution of the "new thought" in the Caribbean Islands. The positivistic thinking of De Hostos was, as a result, to drive him along the road of political separatism.

A contemporary of De Hostos' who felt the influences of the prevailing nineteenth-century philosophies, but who was not fully converted by them, is the Puerto Rican José Julián Acosta. In a most interesting diary, he records his intellectual experiences in Europe. After studying for some time in Spain he went to Germany, and there the attraction of the sciences became very strong. He remarked that Spain could not rival Germany, France, and England in scientific advance; the mother country was retarded in political and intellectual movements as well as in the speculative moral and social sciences. He also observed that the Spanish press was not bringing out books on the new ideas and the advances in science.[42] In Germany, Acosta studied chemistry and, at the home of his professor, met many of the distinguished scholars of the day. This enthusiasm was reflected in his letters, which speak of his desire to continue the intellectual life upon his return to Puerto Rico; he feared, however, that in Puerto Rico he would not find the materials for advanced scientific study. His remark in a letter to a friend that "our race has had more warriors and theologians than naturalists, but despite the shortage there is no lack of fields for the sowing" illustrates the modern influences.

His religious principles were also tested at this time, when he met Don Francisco Aguilera, the Count of Villalobos, who had established a *gymnasium* "in conformity with the principles of Anatomy." In a conversation on religion, the count frankly defined religion as politics. Man, he said, is mere matter, and through matter all phenomena—even the wonders of the intelligence—are explained. Acosta, though shocked by this opinion, remarked that the count was a good man and noted that his foundation for morality did not reside in God but in the force of government that punishes evil. Simultaneously, Acosta was shaken by the death of two of his Puerto Rican companions who had succumbed to the black fever. In grief he turned to his faith and arranged for the reception of the church's sacraments. Acosta soon after returned to Puerto Rico where he became a professor at the Diocesan Seminary. He died in 1891, retaining the conviction that Puerto Rico should not seek separation from Spain nor divorce itself from the Catholic faith. He was convinced that because of its geography, politics, and economy, his island would never become a free and sovereign nation.[43] Instead, he urged the need for scientific progress and the benefits of greater self-government.

Another figure that strides across the last half of the nineteenth century and the beginning of the twentieth is Salvador Brau. He is typical of the leader class, and his philosophy reflects the spirit of revolt that rose up against Spain's despotic rule in the colonies. Of this century, Menéndez y Pelayo writes: "There had passed over Spain a full century of misery and moral decline, of administrative despotism that lacked grandeur and glory, and of shameful impiety." Conscious of this decline, Brau gathered ideas from Dr. Felix García de la Torre, Dr. Ramón Emeterio Betances, and Don Segundo Ruiz Belvis who had been educated in France in the ideas of the revolution of 1848. Their libraries in Puerto Rico were open to him, and he began to feel the influences of Spain's revolution of 1868 and of the Constitution of 1869, which expressed the ideas of pragmatic positivism. In the preface to *Puerto Rico y su historia,* Brau cites Herbert Spencer's *Fundamentals of Sociology* in which society is defined as that which "grows and develops as an organic body, finding its different parts in mutual dependence, and its different activities complementing each other." Brau looked upon man as "a member of this social body, drawn into the impulses and subordinated to the influences of the whole organism." At the same time, he saw the individual as more important than the collectivity: "Society exists for the benefit of its members, not the members for the purpose of society."[44]

In Brau's writings, one finds the ideas that guided his thought. In criticism of Catholic Spain, he wrote: "Torquemada has not conquered Luther; the *Syllabus* has not chained Fulton; there are no gags that suffocate Guttemberg; Washington and Franklin are wrapped in an aureole of light most splendid and more civilizing than the cloud of horrors that surrounded the Duke of Alba and Phillip II. These are my convictions; these are the propositions that give conviction to my pen.''[45]

Convinced of Spain's abuse of his island, he wrote sociological studies that express pessimism and irony, the love of liberty, and an individualistic democracy. Under the pseudonym ''Casimiro Claro'' and through the columns of *El Clamor del País,* he charged the peninsular Spaniards with treating the Puerto Ricans as ''third-class Spaniards'' and regarding the island as an American garrison, not a civil society.[46] Although he loved Spain and its tradition, he resented its suppression of the individualistic spirit.[47] In his criticism of Spain's hegemony, he also expressed the typical anticlericalism of the time. An article, entitled ''El contagio de ultra-tumba,'' discussed at great length the canonical requirements of Christian marriage for Catholic burial, and it charged that the concubines of the poor were denied Christian burial while those of the rich were honored. His conclusion was to urge the secularization of the cemeteries since, he asserted, they belong to the municipalities.[48]

In reading Salvador Brau, as well as other leaders in the last half of the nineteenth century, one is impressed with the impact that French ''liberal thought'' had made upon their thinking. There is a love of abstract political and social ideas, a rigid rationalism, a hatred of the abuses of the past while clinging to many of its ideas. The passwords in their camp were often converted into verbal dogmas that were honored but not too closely scrutinized for meaning. Into such phrases as ''freedom'' and ''self-government,'' ''popular sovereignty'' and ''equal suffrage,'' ''nationalism'' and the ''separation of church and state,'' they poured a content of enthusiasm. It seemed to promise a solution to their social, economic, and political problems. Their short-sightedness, however, became apparent in dealing with opposing ideas and institutions. While believing in their own philosophy of progress and freedom, they simultaneously proscribed all opposing opinions as reactionary and therefore intolerable. In the true spirit of the times, they used rationalism to ridicule the Catholic religion. The new creed was social progress; its morality in the governance of human conduct was secularist; its motivation was the desire to be free, intelligent, and prosperous. Threads of this new thought were evident in Puerto Rico's intellectuals. Against this background they worked for a change that would bring a form of self-government, a beneficial trade policy, and alleviation of the poverty of the masses, and a high rate of literacy. Their ideas of progress were frequently good, but their philosophy was often encompassed by much intolerance.

THE CHURCH'S OPPOSITION TO THE NEW THOUGHT

In nineteenth century Puerto Rico, there was a conflict of scholasticism, the philosophy of the Catholic church, with the ideas of European rationalism. Since there was no university in Puerto Rico, we must look to the secondary schools and to certain intellectual leaders for an expression of this difference in philosophy. Apart from the Diocesan Seminary, which was established in 1832 and granted the power to confer the *bachiller* degree in 1851, there was little secondary school education. At the request of the bishop of Puerto Rico, Most Reverend Pablo Benigno Carrión, and by grant of the Spanish crown, the Jesuits were given charge of the Conciliar Diocesan Seminary in 1858, with the right to conduct a secondary school for lay students in the same building. This was the first stable foundation for secondary education in Puerto Rico. Shortly before the date of their arrival (1858), the Jesuits had been reinstated under the protection of the Spanish government of Queen Isabel II. They were to fight in the vanguard of the church's struggle against the modern philosophies that had rejected Christian revelation. Upon their withdrawal from the island in 1886, the Piarist Fathers (Escolapios) continued this secondary education.

Seminary instruction was based on the scholasticism of the church as expressed by St. Thomas Aquinas; this philosophy was brought to the students through the texts of Don Jaime Balmes (1810-48), philosopher, theologian, and sociologist. He was an apologist who combined profound reasoning ability with a deep awareness of his adversaries' thought. The topical headings of his writings give us an insight into the disputes of the day: "Letters to a Religious Sceptic," "Articles on the Clergy," "Civilization and Society," and "The New French and German Schools of Religious Sentiment." To understand the thought of some Catholics in Puerto Rico at a time when the "new thought" of the nineteenth century had made converts of most of the intellectuals, we must consult the apologetic writings of Balmes.

In his "Letter to a Religious Sceptic," Balmes reasoned that submission to legitimate authority is not servitude and that homage paid to dogmas revealed by God is not slavery but rather the most lofty exercise of our liberty. Scepticism, he said, is a gangrenous growth that fatigues the human spirit, giving no hope to the spiritual needs of man. In discussing the "philosophy of the future" that predicted the prompt death of the church, he argued that it was an unreal philosophy, since it proclaimed, as an absolute law, that society is in constant progression toward perfection. Balmes rejected this generalization, finding in each age its own ills of decay and evolution. Dogmas of a day, he said, are overturned in a day. For instance, he asked, who would dare belong to the schools of thought of the eighteenth century in the nineteenth? The temper of the times, he continued, required that men have ever upon their lips the philosophy of "religious sentimentalism." After a thorough analysis of the thought of Kant, Fichte, Hegel, Schelling, and Cousin, he found that their modernity was no proof of validity. From them he turned to Catholicism, which he saw reaching into the depths of the human spirit through revealed and reasoned truth, while admitting the limitation of human reason. Catholicism, for Balmes, recognized the evolution in man's thought through history, while clinging to the essential truths of man's nature. In his analysis of civilization, Balmes rejected the philosophies of the revolutions of 1848 as extensions of socialist doctrine. He believed them erroneous and inadequate, insisting that the best civilization exists when there coexists (combined in the highest degree and to the greatest extent) the best intelligence, morality, and welfare. The writings of Balmes attest to the voice of the church's philosophy in a world that had turned rationalist and anticlerical.[40]

We know that the works of Balmes were used in the *seminario colegio* of San Juan in 1859 and that theses from his writings were defended publicly. Whether any professors or students of this school developed original ideas in philosophy or published material on the disputed questions of the day is hard to say. The available material is small, though some expression is found in the records of the *Boletín Eclesiástico*. This official publication of the Diocese of Puerto Rico cites at great length the letters of local bishops and of authors whose tracts were reasoned rejections of the various schools of modern philosophy. The fact that this journal and the Catholic secondary school education were sufficiently strong to offset the "new thought," inculcated by the European universities in which the Puerto Rican leaders had studied, is hard to believe. The Puerto Rican writers whose records we have consulted seem to have been largely ignorant of scholasticism. In Salvador Brau's *Ecos de la Batalla*, we find a solitary citation from Aquinas, whom he speaks of as an illuminating thinker on civil government. The passage referred to is from Aquinas' "Treatise on Law" in the *Summa Theologica*, in which he states that "the first condition of every good political system demands that all people have some part in the government, since this is the best way for all to love and defend their constitution."[50] Apart from this passage, Brau shows himself to be antagonistic to scholasticism and a friend of the new philosophies.

The church in Puerto Rico was concerned with this new thought that represented a trend away from religion. In the last part of the nineteenth century, the *Boletín Eclesiástico* carried frequent references to the movement toward secularism and materialism. The bishops in pastoral letters warned both clergy and faithful. In 1864 the *Boletín* remarked that at the end of the last century and during the present, the free-thinkers had stated that religious beliefs had retarded reason; that the pursuit of a future life had been opposed to the evolution of the present. It charged that national education was established in order to spread atheism, that a growth of materialism characterized the new education, and that hatred of the traditions of Catholicism had been engendered.[51] In the following year another article on "Atheistic Materialism" appeared. The author, Don Ramón de la Sagra, maintained that modern democracy was founded on materialistic and atheistic principles; that it was not only opposed to the Catholic world but to real democracy, for it sought to destroy God and the future life.

In 1865, he cited the pastoral letter of the bishop of Lavat (France) to the effect that the revolutions in France had derived from Freemasonry, that their technique was to multiply lodges in all parts and to attract youth, inspiring them with a hatred of Catholic institutions.[52] The following year the *Boletín* carried a letter from the bishop of Orleans (France) which warned against the evil that these doctrines were producing among the youth of Liege, the workers of Geneva, the Freemasons of Paris, and the revolutionists of Italy. The bishop cited a youth who declared that "all men of progress today are materialists; the Revolution is the triumph of man against God." He also cited a remark of Garibaldi's in a speech to the students of Pavía, in which the patriot found it necessary "to destroy the priestly vampire, to exterminate the black robes, to crush the priests against the pavements of our streets.''[53]

The *Boletín Eclesiástico* continued to carry articles on atheistic materialism—drawn from Europe—since the diocesan authorities knew the impact that these ideas were having on the intellectuals of Puerto Rico. Addressing his clergy and the faithful in 1867, Don Pablo Benigno Carrión, bishop of Puerto Rico, warned that the forces of materialism had taken over the scientific, literary, artistic, and economic world and that, though materialism had advanced in the schools and intellectual centers, in the shops and in the stock exchange, it had not and never would grow in the church. The bishop decreed that all priests were to add the prayer, ''Against the persecutors of the Church'' to the Mass. In addition, three days of prayer were to be made successively in the six churches of San Juan, from the second to the nineteenth of February.[54] Conscious of the fight that the church had to wage against the philosophies that sought to destroy it, the bishop was most explicit in warning his clergy to abstain from involving themselves ''in all that has the slightest savor of politics.'' They were ordered to observe meekness and prudence in the performance of their ministry.[55]

While the church was in the throes of conflict with the new thought, the state was planning improved education in the third quarter of the nineteenth century. Under the Plan of 1849, a board of examiners was provided to pass on teacher-applications. The teachers were tested on their knowledge of religion, reading, writing, arithmetic, school management, and methods of teaching.[56] The increase in ''official schools'' is manifest from statistics that reported 29 in 1830 and 122 in 1860. The number of teachers listed in the census for 1860 is 451. They were distributed throughout the island as follows: 99 in San Juan, 37 in Bayamón, 31 in Arecibo, 24 in Aguadilla, 67 in Mayagüez, 80 in Ponce, 65 in Guayama, and 48 in Humacao. It was, also, in this period that Governor General Messina, under order of 1865, divided public education into elementary and superior, with the former made obligatory. He added a new feature, the ''ambulatory school,'' which taught for some months in one village and then moved on to another.[57] This governor had advanced a great deal from the reactionary spirit that characterized Governor General de la Pezuela, who in 1848 had reflected: ''Education brought the loss of America; and, since it is a matter that must be handled with the greatest tact, those who desire to study should go to Spain. . . . The poor had enough in learning to read and write, in sufficient Christian doctrine and in a job; for Spain sought colonies for her glory, not for her destruction. . . ."[58]

Despite the Decree of 1865, which attempted a system of central control, advance was again retarded. The educational interest of the period was geared to political utility. The era of Isabel II (1833-68) saw much arbitrary rule, and the people of Puerto Rico expressed their opposition. While the Liberals submitted with reluctance, the Separatists sought the island's emancipation from Spain. The latter had expressed themselves in a strong proclamation in 1864: "Puerto Ricans: For more than three centuries Spanish despotism has oppressed us, so that even today no son of the country has been called to occupy a post of distinction. . . . The *jíbaros* are poor and ignorant because of the Government that prohibits schools, periodicals, and books; and only recently they denied us the foundation of a university for the poor who cannot send their sons outside of Puerto Rico. . . ."[59] Because of their criticism and inflammatory speech, Governor Félix María de Messina exiled Don Ramón Emeterio Betances, the leader of the Separatists. In the meantime, the new system of education had been ordered. It produced little more than a paper program. As Dean Osuna says, it was rendered impotent by political, social, and economic conditions.[60]

At this time of improving public education, Bishop Benigno Luis Carrión published in the *Boletín Eclesiástico* of October 15, 1860, an announcement of an improved program in the Diocesan Seminary. It consisted of three years of Latin and a year of philosophy which was to include courses in logic, ethics, and psychology; all of these courses were to be taken and passed by examination. When these four years were completed, there were to be three years in sacred theology and sacerdotal rubrics. Examinations in both philosophy and theology, if failed, might be repeated after a couple of months. If there was a second failure, the student was dismissed.[61]

SPAIN RETARDS PUERTO RICAN REFORMS, 1869-1890

In September of 1868, Isabel II was driven from the throne and a constituent assembly of the Cortes was decreed. The period of Liberal reforms in Spain (1870-74) was reflected in the Antilles. Puerto Rico became a Spanish province with representation in the Cortes, and in 1870, the island legally formed its political parties for the first time. The revolutionary government of General Francisco Serrano Domínguez not only promised a fundamental code of rights, but also sent a Liberal governor to Puerto Rico, Don Gabriel Baldrich. From May, 1869, to 1872, three elections were held in Puerto Rico. The members selected to represent Puerto Rico in the Spanish Assembly gave proof of sharp differences existing between the Conservatives and the Reformist Liberals, the former called the party of "unconditional Spaniards." The latter came under the leadership of Dr. Pedro Gerónimo Goyco, the president of the Sociedad Económica de Amigos del País, and in a manifesto of 1870, they expressed their principles of colonial reforms based on the natural rights of man, the abolition of slavery, and administrative decentralization. Within this Liberal party, there developed two factions: one element was led by Goyco who favored the monarchy and preferred assimilation of Puerto Rico into Spain's political system; the other faction was directed by Román Baldorioty de Castro who believed in a republican form of government and sought to obtain insular autonomy (i.e., a wide form of administrative decentralization). Goyco's group was labeled "Monarchical Assimilists," while Baldorioty's group was called "Republican Autonomists." Both, however, joined forces and harmonized differences in their common battle against the Conservatives.[62]

In September, 1873, Governor General Primo de Rivera promulgated a new law in Puerto Rico, which applied Title I of the Spanish Constitution of 1869. It was received with great joy by the Puerto Rican people and was labeled the "Bill of Rights of Puerto Rico" by Rafael María de Labra; José Julián Acosta Calvo proclaimed it "the safeguard of the imprescriptible rights of the human person." With truly liberal feeling, General Primo de Rivera said: "I believe that there is no reason for not governing and administering this province with the same laws that are operative in the Metropolis. There is no reason, no cause for depriving the sons of Puerto Rico of any of the rights that are granted nor any of the duties imposed on those born in the Peninsula." In accord with the new constitution, delegations from the island met in San Juan in order to formulate a petition to be sent to the overseas minister of Spain. Significant among these pleas was one that requested a reduction of duties on imports from the United States in order that the American Union would reciprocate. The petitioners noted that their sugar and molasses, which were chiefly marketed in the United States, had suffered severe discrimination.[63]

The Liberal Reformist party in Puerto Rico had made some significant strides; but the fall of the Spanish Republic in 1874 returned Alfonso XII to the throne, along with royal absolutism. General Rafael Primo de Rivera, governor of Puerto Rico, was replaced by Laureano Sanz whose two periods in office (1868-70 and 1874-75) bred much anti-Spanish sentiment. He dissolved the Puerto Rican militia, the Provincial Assembly, and the town councils. He replaced local teachers with Spaniards, abolished the right of assembly, prohibited literary expression, and persecuted José Julián Acosta and Román Baldorioty de Castro for their Liberal tendencies. Moreover, from 1875 to 1885, there were eight generals who successively took over the role of governor general. This made continuity of effort and constructive administration almost impossible. As we have seen, it was in this period that the Puerto Rican Liberal Reformist party developed two factions: the Asimilistas, a faction of monarchical sympathizers in favor of assimilation into the Spanish political system; and the republican Autonomistas, a faction that urged decentralization and sought Puerto Rican autonomy. It was Rafael María de Labra who represented the Republican autonomist interest of Cuba and Puerto Rico in the Spanish Cortes. He was supported in Puerto Rico by Baldorioty de Castro who spoke through the pages of *La Crónica* in Ponce, and was a most outstanding exponent of Liberal thought in Puerto Rico during his time.[64]

With the restoration of Alfonso XII to the throne, a Conservative ministry under Antonio Cánovas del Castillo was established, and the Puerto Rican Conservatives—called Incondicionales—co-operated with the vigorous Governor Sanz Posse and his successors. The local representative body, the Provincial Assembly, became at this time little more than an advisory body to the governor. In 1876, a new Spanish constitution was under formation, and the article that applied to the government of the overseas provinces was Number 89. This read: "The Overseas Provinces shall be governed by *special laws*. But the Government remains authorized to apply to the same (provinces) the laws that have been promulgated or are to be promulgated, with the modifications that it judges necessary and upon giving an account to the Cortes." This article left much room for diverse interpretations between Cánovas del Castillo, the Conservative, and Práxedes Mateo Sagasta, the leader of the Liberal Monarchical party. The former held that all the laws that were operative in the peninsula were to be applied to the provinces if they were pertinent; in the case of special conditions existing in the provinces, a special law was to be drafted. Sagasta, on the other hand, held that the essential part of Article 89 was that the overseas provinces were to be governed by special laws. But since at the time of the adoption of the new constitution there were no "special laws," the government might bring to the provinces those laws that were operative in Spain with whatever modifications they believed necessary after informing the Cortes.

Rafael María de Labra of the Republican faction of the Liberal Reformists requested in 1879 that the Cortes grant the Antilles political and administrative decentralization on the basis of national unity, along with broader economic privileges. He asked for the termination of export duties, the granting of coastal trade, and the arranging of treaties that would gradually abolish intolerable customs. It was during this time that Puerto Rican sugar interests were suffering from retaliatory tariffs in United States ports. When the Sagasta government came into power, under order of 1881, the Spanish Constitution of 1876 was published in Puerto Rico, but nothing resulted. Again, in 1883, Labra petitioned the Cortes to extend full civil rights, as enjoyed by peninsular Spaniards, to the inhabitants of Puerto Rico and Cuba. This plea was echoed in Puerto Rico during November of the same year when the Liberal Reformist party met in San Juan and petitioned that Puerto Ricans be granted full citizenship, with political and judicial rights equal to those enjoyed in the peninsula, and the right of administrative decentralization.

Though these concessions were again tabled, the new year brought the hope of relief through a trade agreement signed by the Spanish and American governments on January 12, 1884, to become effective on March 1. The government in Madrid authorized the entrance of North American products in Spanish ports at reduced tariffs, while the Washington government suppressed the additional tax of 10 per cent imposed on products from the Spanish Antilles. This agreement was followed in November by a Treaty of Commerce that allowed a good percentage of sugar from Cuba and Puerto Rico to enter the United States duty-free. A 50 per cent reduction in tobacco duties was granted in the American market; foodstuffs, machinery, and cattle from the United States were admitted free to the Spanish markets; and American wheat duties were to be gradually reduced until they reached the same amount paid by foreign wheat. Lastly, North American tobacco was to pay 2 cents per pound. But this Foster-Albacete Treaty was left unratified because the Cortes believed that it handed over the commerce of Puerto Rico and Cuba to the North American Union. Again Labra pointed out that Spain was denying the essential interest of her provinces and thus antagonizing them.[65]

While the problems of Puerto Rican trade were under the continual consideration of the Cortes, there was a simultaneous dispute as to whether or not the autonomic government espoused by a section of the Reformist party was legally compatible with the Spanish constitution. Decisions in the judicial tribunals of Cuba, Puerto Rico, and Spain found that the doctrine of autonomy was legal. The espousal of "autonomist government" came to the fore in 1884, replacing the "assimilist" doctrine that had held control in Liberal circles from 1874 to 1884, under the leadership of Celis de Aguilera. The doctrine of autonomy sought to implement the Reformist ideal of administrative decentralization, and was fostered under the radical leadership of Baldorioty and Labra. On January 3, 1884, Rafael María de Labra, along with four other deputies, asked the Cortes to complete the political organization of the Antilles by the passage of laws that would extend full political and civil rights to them. It also was asked that a new administrative organization be formed, granting the fullest possible administrative and economic decentralization that was compatible with national unity. This latter idea was, in a word, autonomy. In 1884, a part of the Puerto Rican press espoused the new political doctrine. *El Clamor del País,* the official organ of the Central Committee of the Reformist party, was put under the control of Julián E. Blanco, upon the resignation of José Celis Aguilera as president of the Reformist party in September, 1884. The new editor, attempting to prevent a serious party split, wrote in May of 1884: "In reality there is neither Autonomist nor Assimilist, but the old party which is a grand association of all the Liberals who above all desire reform. They strive as Autonomists and Assimilists to live in union and understanding, in order to achieve the Electoral Law of the Península, civil government, along with provincial and municipal reform." During the following year, however, the paper was given over to Salvador Brau who took a definite stand in favor of autonomic government.

A Liberal Autonomist Committee was formed under the presidency of Julián E. Blanco, the secretariat of José Gómez Brioso, and with Juan Hernández López, Francisco Cepeda, Manuel Elzaburu, Manuel F. Rossy, and Manuel Fernández Juncos as voting members (*vocales*).   **1416184**

A next step in the advance of autonomy was achieved in the Assembly of Ponce (1887) where Autonomist members of the Cuban and Puerto Rican Liberal Reformist party met. At this meeting, the Puerto Rican Autonomist party, selected Román Baldorioty de Castro as its president. The constitution of this party, which was signed on March 10, 1887, provided in Article 2 for a political and juridical identity with the party's compatriots in the peninsula and for the achievement of the "greatest possible decentralization, within national unity." The third article allotted to the Provincial Assembly the direct representation of all local interests. Article 5 stated an equality of civil and political rights with the peninsular Spaniards. In Article 6, there is a listing of these so-called "local questions"; among these, to mention but a few, are public works, public instruction, agriculture, banking, police force, customs, and treaties of commerce. Article 7 became so important a matter that it is well to cite it completely: "Conceding the local character of the autonomists union or party, it is left to each one of the affiliates to enter in complete liberty into the political parties of the Metropolis, that may accept or defend the autonomy of the Antilles; and to sustain their own ideas in respect to the form of government."

The Autonomist party of Cuba declared like principles, and a union of both parties was urged in order to realize their common ideals, while leaving to the delegation or to the directory the nature of this union. The platform finally proclaimed that it unanimously accepted "the autonomic plan of the eminent Republican Don Rafael María de Labra" and so proceeded to name him "leader, i.e., guide and principal voice of this party in the Metropolis."[66]

Spain began to fear the growth of the Autonomists' power and, because of a petition of the Puerto Rican Conservatives, sent a reactionary governor to check these advances in self-government. Governor General Romualdo Palacios soon arrived in the island; after placing his military headquarters in Aibonito, he set about the repression of the Autonomists. From all parts of the island came reports of abuse of power. Homes were illegally entered; Autonomist meetings were broken up; and charges were raised against such leaders as Luis Muñoz Rivera, Baldorioty de Castro, Salvador Carbonell, and Herminio Díaz Navarro. Torture to exact information —known as *componte*—was widespread, and communication with Spain was cut off. When word finally reached Madrid through a cable sent from the island of St. Thomas, the government immediately recalled Palacios. His second-in-command, Juan Contreras, took over the government, re-established the constitutional rights of the individual, and released those who had been jailed. The major part of the atrocities were committed in the southern section of the island. Here the anti-Spanish sentiment waxed strong.[67]

By 1890, Puerto Rico had experienced sufficient changes from liberal reform to reactionary repression to be disquieted. Among the Reformist Liberals a growing insistence on political and economic reform was manifest. Spain would have to make large concessions; it was in the last decade of the nineteenth century that this reform was accomplished through an autonomous charter. In the next chapter, we shall outline the steps that brought that form of local self-government.

While Puerto Rico was suffering strong political unrest in this third quarter of the nineteenth century, there was a simultaneous conflict in church-state relations involving education, morality, and religion. In 1871, the *Boletín Eclesiástico* criticized the "modern evils," quoting from the *Boletín Mercantil*, which charged that atheistic literature and seductive works were threatening the foundations of all civilized society.[68] This diocesan publication cited such journals as *L'Univers* and *L'Union*, which were alarmed over a bill presented by the minister of public instruction to the French Chamber of Deputies. The measure sought to prevent autonomous Catholic schools from conferring academic degrees. The articles pointed out that, by this legislation, the principle of equality before the law would be violated and that education would become a monopoly of the state. The proposed law was said to violate the liberty of the religious orders and the concordat with the church. Lastly, it took the right of education away from the parents and imposed a schooling without God.[69] The prophetic character of this writing in relation to Puerto Rico becomes clear when we recall that it was only three years later that a Royal Order set up the Civil Institute of Secondary Instruction. This public agency was empowered to hear the examinations of all students applying for their academic title, and it soon discriminated against students of religious institutions.[70]

In his first pastoral message of 1875, Bishop Puig y Montserrat of Puerto Rico criticized the spirit of rationalism and the denial of all divine and human authority to the "subversion of the whole moral order and the enthronement of pure materialism." He saw in the enemies of the church a determination to prevent religious education in the schools under the pretext of liberty. Again, in 1879, the bishop returned to his theme of the serious deficiency in moral and religious education that had handicapped family life in Puerto Rico. He explained the high rate of illegitimacy by the decline of Christian morality; he insisted that youth could not learn these principles from fathers who had violated God's law so constantly.[71]

In an address before the students and faculty of Colegio San Ildefonso (high school) in 1887, the dean of the cathedral, the Reverend Juan Perpiñá y Pibernat, spoke of the philosophical ills of the times: "The modern world suffers from . . . a lack of solid and true knowledge in the metaphysical sciences of firm and true philosophical ideas. . . . The French Encyclopedia during the end of the last and the beginning of the present century, the mislabeled philosophical ideas of the German Schools . . . which, though admirable in their method of exposition, contain little truth, still exert their pernicious influence in all branches of human knowledge and in the most hidden fibres of society. . . . Human reason is making itself independent of God.'"[72] This address of the cathedral's dean was rich in immediate experience, for it was in 1886 that the Jesuits had withdrawn from Puerto Rico because of religious discrimination.

The Jesuits had begun their educational apostolate in 1858, combining an instruction for seminarians and lay students. In 1878, they had terminated their seminary instruction and were aided by the Provincial Assembly in the setting up of a high school in Santurce. In 1882, their efforts were restricted by a Royal Order that established the Civil Institute of Secondary Education and granted it the exclusive power to confer the degree of *bachiller* on the basis of examinations administered by itself. In these examinations, obstacles were multiplied for the boys who studied at the Jesuit *colegio*. The Liberals, who were then in power by like pressure, brought about the withdrawal of the Jesuits from Puerto Rico in 1886 and the closing of their school, which in 1882 had two hundred students.[73]

The Civil Institute took control of academic secondary education in the island, since accreditation depended upon its approval. Its first director was Don José Julián Acosta who was under the patronage of the Sociedad Económica and of Father Rufo Manuel Fernández. The former, however, tendered his resignation in 1884. Dissension soon arose within the institute, and the charge of political intrigue and scheming for personal profit was brought against it.

Other church schools were the Colegio Asilo de San Idelfonso, which was conducted under the auspices of the Ladies of San Idelfonso from 1860 on. There were two schools for poor children: one founded in San Juan (1865) and another at San German (1883). In Río Piedras, a Protectorate for Youth was established in 1879. In 1880, a secondary school for girls was opened in Santurce by the Religious of the Sacred Heart. Though this school was chiefly attended by girls of the wealthier classes, many scholarships were given to talented girls of poor families.[74]

By 1890, Puerto Rico had experienced many desires for reform in the educational, economic, and political aspects of its life within the Spanish kingdom. She had suffered so many changes from liberal reform to reactionary repression that she was disquieted. Reformist liberals were insisting on greater autonomy; and Spain, in danger of losing her last colonies in the new world, would have to make concessions. It was in the last decade of the nineteenth century that this reform came in the nature of an autonomous charter. In the next chapter, we shall outline the steps that brought this liberal form of self-government.

II

Puerto Rico's
Autonomous Charter

Queen María Cristina conferred on Puerto Rico the encomium of "ever faithful" in May of 1897; the fact is that the relations between Spain and her Puerto Rican colony were for the most part pacific. This tropical island with its lovely skies and sandy shores, its central ridge of green mountains, and its trade-wind climate, seems to have been created for peaceful and temperate living. Though the early decades of the twentieth century in Puerto Rico were to witness much terrible poverty and a quiet submission to suffering, the latter part of the nineteenth century is said to have had its better periods. A report sent to the Colonial Exposition of Amsterdam in 1883 describes the conditions of this dependency of Spain: "That which is called pauperism in Europe is as a general rule unknown in Puerto Rico. For though the richness of the island is inferior to that which its natural elements could produce—considering the great fertility of the lands and the dense population of more than 700,000 inhabitants— the feeling of charity and of hospitality continues developing in a notable degree. In addition to the few necessities that the climate imposes, there is the frugality of the inhabitants, especially of the

poorer classes.'' This report goes on to describe the charitable works
of the St. Vincent de Paul Society, the orphanage in which three
hundred children of both sexes were educated, and an asylum in San
Juan that gave care to more than one hundred old and invalid
poor. There were other hospitals under the care of the bishop and
the military authorities; and there was a corps of seven doctors and
nurses who were paid to visit the sick and the poor in their homes.
Finally, there was a leper colony, and other towns had their small
hospitals and charitable organizations.[1]

This report may very well be exaggerated; some authors find that
the island in the latter part of the nineteenth century was suffering
an economic decline. Among these is James McCormick, a long-time
resident of the island who, in 1880, was commissioned by the Provincial Assembly to give an analysis of conditions. He found that
agricultural production was diminishing and its sale suffering a loss
of price, while real estate was decreasing in value. The landholders
had been ruined, and the leading merchants were in severe straits;
industries found no demand and no profitable market. Commercial
interests had been paralyzed because of insufficient capital, and
foreign capital had been frightened away. The sugar industry was
then producing only half the yield of former years. Another critic
said that the economic depression was caused by: restrictions on the
coastal trade, discrimination against the island in trade with Spain,
high duties on United States flour, export duties, and the annoying
formalities of officials.[2]

In the very next year, 1881, Salvador Brau was writing in the
periodical *El Agente* of the need to establish a sound political economy that ''embarks on the study of the important social interests,
not only in relation to accumulated capital, but also in respect to the
generating principles of this capital, tending toward the destruction
of all antagonism between the proletariat and the propertied class; and
trying to raise the social level by means of the supreme formula:
'Work and Savings, Justice and Liberty.' ''[3] His program aspired
to do away with mercantilism that shut the door on international
trade; he favored the immigration of foreign colonists who would
apply their capital and skill to the fomenting of a sugar industry.
Lastly, he believed that the Puerto Ricans had shown that they were
worthy of exercising the right of Spanish citizenship, as had been
recognized by the Cortes of 1812.[4]

While the standard of economic living could change violently, the social life of the people remained much the same. In reading through the archives of the Interior Department of Puerto Rico, one finds—amid many of the ordinary reports on public health, education, repair of highways, and police activities—the details surrounding public festivities. For instance, the town of Isabela announced its triduum in honor of St. Anthony of Padua in 1890. The first day of celebration began with the band marching through the streets at high noon playing festive music. At 1:00 P.M. prizes were distributed to the school children. Between 4:00 and 5:00 P.M. a troubador's contest was arranged in which the judge presented prizes to the one who sang best and the one who presented the best verses. On the second day, there were horse races and games of skill, with the ladies acting as judges. This day closed with a display of fireworks. On the last day, a Solemn Mass with a panegyric in honor of St. Anthony was sung, and alms were given to the poor. From 2:00 to 4:00 P.M. in the afternoon, there were foot races, obstacle feats, horse races, and games of skill. At 7:00 P.M., there were fireworks followed by a formal dance at 9:00. The poster announcing the activities requested that the people decorate their balconies and display lights in the windows.[5] Apart from other interesting reports on folk customs, there is the frequent entry in the municipal reports of "public peace"; this bears witness to the peaceable nature of the Puerto Rican people.

In the educational system, statistics for the year ending 1897 show that 82 per cent of the population was unable to read and write and that, of the remaining 18 per cent, 4.5 per cent were only able to read. And so, of a total population of 894,302, there were 735,118 who could neither read nor write. The total number of public schools was 538, and the number of private schools was 22. There were 15,108 boys and 7,157 girls in school attendance.[6] It was apparent that a prerequisite to autonomous government must be greater mass education, and this was sought by the leaders who appealed to Spain's government in the last years preceding the granting of the Constitution in 1897.

As one reflects on Spain's political treatment of Puerto Rico during the major part of the nineteenth century, it is difficult to avoid the judgment that it was mostly a policy of reaction. There were certainly enlightened governors, and many of their administrative acts were for the betterment of Puerto Rico, but one is impressed with the fact that a new governor almost every year made for little

continuity in policy. Besides, the inaugural address of the newly
arrived governor was consistently bitter-sweet: sweet in the sense
that they protested a regime of justice for all; bitter in the sense that
the rod of punishment for those who deviated from the governor's
concept of the law was ill concealed. The message of Governor
Segundo de la Portilla in 1875 is a good example of this: "His
Majesty's Government having named me Governor General of this
small but beautiful part of the soil of the Fatherland, I come to
your shores with the sole ambition of adapting in them my love of
justice. Slave of the laws by duty and by habit, I shall take care to
fulfill them. But at the same time I will be inflexible in the demand
that all imitate me in their fulfillment. . . ." After so delivering
himself General Portilla concluded with an expression of paternalism:
"Rest at ease, then, in the belief that your Governor will ever know
how to accomplish that which he promises."[7]

In this century of upheaval, the forces of a Reformist Liberalism
were constantly increasing, and the mother country gave them little
opportunity for political evolution. The peninsular government never
approved of such atrocities as were perpetrated in the *compontes* of
1887 under Governor Palacios; in fact, upon learning of them, it
quickly ordered his recall. On the other hand, like most colonial
powers, the peninsular government was slow to see the inevitable and
tended to listen to the Conservative elements. An index of this
reluctance to change institutions was Spain's tardiness in the abolition of slavery. She seemed not to see that this Liberal agitation was
a strong expression of awakening class consciousness. What the slave
was to the reactionary social and economic elements, the islander was
to the peninsular; if the chains of one were broken, the political bonds
of the other might well be severed. The actual emancipation was not
fully a pure act since the pressure of world powers—chiefly Great
Britain and the United States—had its measure of influence.

Lastly, in the colonies' determination to trade with the United
States and in their constant appeal for better trade agreements, Spain
was slow to make concessions. This was in part because of the pressures of commercial interests in the peninsula and the fear that her
West Indies possessions would be drawn into the expanding grasp
of the United States. Spanish mercantilism was a desperate effort to
isolate her colonies from this danger. She saw in particular forms of
Liberalism—and here the Assimilists and Autonomists were often
confused with the Separatists—an instrument that might pry away

from her these last possessions. In all truth, an old tradition was being measured and challenged by revolutionary ideas.

AUTONOMY IN THE MAKING, 1888-1896

The pressures for greater self-rule occurred during the ministries of two prominent Spaniards: Don Antonio Cánovas del Castillo, a Moderate-Conservative, and Don Práxedes Mateo Sagasta, a Liberal Monarchist. Early in his political career, Cánovas saw the danger of Spain's loss of her colonies and wrote in 1883: "Beg God to preserve for us the decreasing inheritance that we have received from our fathers."[8] As early as 1870, he spoke before the House of Deputies of a nation that had lost its sense of mission and its means of fulfilling its purpose. He found Spain destined to lose its colonies, since it had lost its moral and physical forces. In contrast, he presented the United States since 1810 as a nation that had severed its bonds with England under the law of human progress. Americans had achieved both moral and physical superiority. As an antidote to the Cuban revolt, Cánovas stressed in 1891 the need for superior moral and physical force.[9]

By this time, it had become clear to the Spanish government that concessions had to be made to the new political energies of the colonies. This was confirmed by a letter of the governor general of Puerto Rico in 1889. In writing to the Minister of Overseas, he urged the need for reform in the political and social treatment of Cuba and Puerto Rico. He noted the following:

First, the political parties are, within this Administration, the most effective instruments of Government.

Second, the Government of His Majesty considers that it is of the highest political interest that these parties continue and develop under the same constitutional legality; that they become means of harmony and not of dissension.

Third, that Spanish citizens of Cuba and Puerto Rico should enjoy the same rights and fulfill the same duties as the citizens in the Peninsula. And so the political parties should be allowed to act freely in their right of organization, meeting, and expression of opinion through the press. The press must be free if it is to reflect the judgment of opinions which become the basis of parliamentary governments; while at the same time this freedom is not to weaken the expression of justice, not to prevent the punishment of crimes committed by the press.

Fourth, a reform of the system of tribute is needed, that

the taxes be imposed in just proportion between the ability
of the country and the sacrifice of the tax-payer.

Fifth, a reform in the services of Finance so that justice
and equity may be attained. The budget should not include
anything that does not bring a service of the State to the
security and welfare of the country.

Sixth, agriculture, industry and all means of general wealth
should be fostered; public instruction should be stimulated;
public works should be advanced. The State should fulfill its
obligations to such as those who have defended the country
with their blood.

Seventh, the security of the person and the right of property should be protected. Civil and economic administration
should be corrected so that probity may be the guarantee of
the employed and that will recommend him to the approval
of the country and of His Majesty's government.[10]

From this document, it becomes clear that the Spanish government
in Puerto Rico was aware of the need of reform and that it would be
well for the Home Office to give consideration to the political ferment
that was underway through the political parties.

While Spain was concerned over Puerto Rico and Cuba's demand
for autonomy, the parties in the island of Puerto Rico were engaging
in local politics. With the end of the reign of terror in 1887, the
Autonomists began the reorganization of their party, which lasted
from 1888 to 1890. A difference developed within the ranks of the
Autonomists. Julio Vizcarrondo, Puerto Rican deputy for Ponce in
the Spanish Cortes, opposed co-operative action with Cuba on the
grounds that Puerto Rico should not have to suffer the penalties for
Cuba's revolt: "I do not believe it fitting that Puerto Rico should
follow the good or bad fate of Cuba. . . . We have different inclina-
tions . . . and other aspirations. . . . Let us live in friendly separation.
I, who do not wish to see my island a colony of Spain, but rather
a Spanish province, would never want to see it a colony of Cuba.
The most unhappy slave is the slave of the freeman."

Román Baldorioty de Castro, leader of the Autonomist Liberals,
stressed the difference of interests between Puerto Rico and Cuba:
"The difference between Puerto Rico and Cuba is immense. Here
we have no man of stature, and they have many. Here we would
agree to a municipal life that is fairly reasonable, while they aspire
or are driven on to the life of Canada or Australia. They desire a
Cuban country within or without the national unity; we would agree
to desire the life of a secondary province." With failing health and

POLITICAL PARTIES IN PUERTO RICO, 1870-1900

CONSERVATIVE—organized as a party in 1869 and consisted of governmental officials and peninsular Spaniards who opposed liberalizing reform in the colonial governments. It gradually acquired the pejorative name of "unconditional Spaniards."

SEPARATISTS—a very small group that separated from the Liberal party and sought the complete independence of Puerto Rico.

LIBERAL—was organized as a party in 1870 and desired the extension to Puerto Rico of the reforms of the Spanish Revolution of 1868. It was named the Reformist Liberal party and developed two tendencies: (1) *traditionalist*—assimilation into the political party system of Spain, and (2) *autonomist*—decentralization away from Spanish control and republican.

1870	REFORMIST LIBERAL PARTY⌐	
	↓	↓
1874	Republican Autonomist	Monarchical Assimilist
	↓	↓
1883	Autonomist	Assimilist
	↓	
1885	AUTONOMIST PARTY	
	↓	
1887	Republican Autonomist Monarchical Autonomist	Party Meeting in Ponce Article 7
	↓	
1891	Republican Autonomist Monarchical Autonomist	("Anti-Pact" or "Anti-Fusion") Meeting at ("Pact" or Fusion") Mayagüez
	↓	
1897	PUERTO RICAN AUTONOMIST PARTY Meeting at San Juan	
	↓	
	Autonomist Party ("Historical" or "Orthodox") Liberal Party ("Fusion")	
	↓	
1898	UNITED AUTONOMIST LIBERAL PARTY	
	↓	
	Autonomist Party ("Historical," "Orthodox," or "Pure") Liberal Party ("Fusion")	
	↓	
1899	PUERTO RICAN REPUBLICAN PARTY AMERICAN FEDERAL PARTY	

NOTE: The various meetings of the Liberal party were held in order to arrive at an accord between the two factions that differed on the type of political relation between Puerto Rico and Spain.

The names in quotes refer to names carried in the battle of the press between the differing factions of the Liberal party.

much discouragement, Baldorioty believed that Puerto Rico "will be reduced by misery or emigration; or it will by entreaty gain better conditions of government. Cuba will be an autonomic colony, or it will be lost through the war."[11] The death of Baldorioty brought the end of a significant period in the gradual evolution of the Liberal party and its policies. Younger men were to take up the Reformist struggle and produce the Autonomous Charter of 1897.

One of the leading and younger Autonomist-Liberals was Luis Muñoz Rivera who on July 1, 1890, founded *La Democracia* in Ponce. This paper was dedicated to the securing of a political autonomy for Puerto Rico. It believed in a solidarity of interests and sentiment between Spain and her American colonies. The editor opposed any union with the United States: "Annexation to the United States which appeals to many of the Islanders seems to me ever absurd, because of the incompatibility of the Latin and Anglo-Saxon races; and because of the absorbing character of the politicians in Washington, along with the anemic nature of our people who are apt to be quickly assimilated."[12] In mid-February of 1891, Muñoz Rivera launched a vigorous campaign for union with the Liberal Monarchical party of Spain, under Práxedes Mateo Sagasta. Since this party was liberal-monarchical, in contrast to the conservative-monarchical party of Cánovas del Castillo and since it was to hold power during most of the period from 1885 to 1895, Muñoz Rivera resolved to work with its leaders. He explained his so-called "Pactist" theory as a strong fusion with the Liberal party of Spain whose doctrine would answer Puerto Rico's needs and whose strength would give power in the conflict with the Puerto Rican Conservatives. In reviewing the situation of the Liberals in the Spanish Antilles, he saw four distinct possibilities: first, annexation to the United States, which he believed was rejected by all Puerto Ricans who were proud of their Latin blood; second, a separatist rebellion, which "no one among us defends, and which, considering the conditions of this people, is an unrealizable utopia"; third, "complete autonomy, which does not fit within the Spanish system, and which the Government of Madrid will never grant us"; and lastly, "decentralization, to which we aspire today, and which we will at last achieve without exorbitant sacrifices, as long as we know how to advance firmly and to disdain all sterile romanticism." In order to achieve this type of self-rule, Muñoz was convinced that Puerto Rico would have to unite with the Liberal party in Spain.

Muñoz Rivera described himself and his followers as "men of our age, eminently practical." He dedicated himself to the achievement of political autonomy, while admitting that Cuba might cherish a more radical solution. Puerto Rico, he said, is "absolutely dependent upon the Castilian metropolis; and from it—or from annexation to a foreign country, which is a crime—we must hope for all." He then proceeded to contrast his people with the Cubans: "We are lacking in the strength of the people because of the ignorance of the country population. We are without a militant youth because of the apathy and laissez-faire attitude of our youth. We are wanting enriched personalities, because they greatly fear creative statesmanship (*la política romántica*); and are motivated by an unpardonable selfishness. It is necessary to educate the first group, to stimulate the second, and to attract the third class."[13] The Cubans, on the other hand, he found, had "received a baptism of blood in a war of ten years" and were marshaling their forces to impose their will upon the parties in Spain or to achieve their goals by revolution. In view of these factors and constrasts, Muñoz Rivera was convinced that Puerto Rico could not evolve a parallel policy to that of Cuba; instead she must wed herself to the Liberal Fusionist party of Sagasta. In analyzing this position of Muñoz, historians of Puerto Rico are at odds. Some maintain that he even favored incorporation into the Sagasta party during the years of 1891-96; others hold that Muñoz Rivera sought a pact but finally had to accept a fusion with Sagasta's party as the best offer of the time. The difference between pact and fusion was to produce the split in the Autonomist party.[14]

It was this difference that came into clear focus in the Autonomist party meeting that was held in Mayagüez from May 15 to 18, 1891. The meeting was held under the presidency of Francisco Mariano Quiñones, with José de Diego, José Gómez Brioso, and Salvador Brau acting as secretaries. Muñoz Rivera immediately offered his plan, i.e., an agreement with a Liberal Spanish party. De Diego offered an amendment that specified a pact with only the Republicans of Spain. Here began the open conflict of the Republican Autonomists with the Monarchical Autonomists. Both plans were rejected; and the compromise of Fernández Juncos was offered. It became the much discussed Article 7 that read: "The Delegation, along with the Leader [Labra] of the Party, and by means of the commissioners that it designates . . . is empowered to come to an agreement and to accomplish an understanding or alliance of the Puerto Rican Autonomist Party with the Peninsular democrats that accept or defend the autonomic-administrative system of the Antilles.''

This Article 7 was adopted by the party at Mayagüez; but immediately it became a matter of differing interpretation. The Republicans understood it to mean: first, that the two factions within the Puerto Rican Liberal party were to retain their distinct personality; and, second, that any alliance realized with the peninsular democrats would be a pact, not a fusion, and would achieve an autonomous administrative system of the Antilles. Muñoz Rivera, on the other hand, read the article as supporting an elastic authority to form a fusion with a Peninsular party that would commit itself to give political autonomy to Puerto Rico.

A new directory was elected, with Julián Blanco as political director, Juan Ramón Ramos as legal director, Manuel Fernández Juncos as economic director, and Salvador Brau as secretary. This directory informed the Leader of Puerto Rican interests in the Spanish Cortes, Rafael María de Labra, of the proceedings at Mayagüez and instructed him to form an alliance ''with the group or groups of the great Peninsular Republican party, as his renowned patriotism and outstanding judgment might advise.'' This authorization, it is to be noted, limited interpretation of the phrase, ''the democratic parties of the peninsula,'' to mean the Republican party and accordingly rejected any alliance with the Monarchical party of Sagasta. This was a challenge to Muñoz Rivera who took up the battle in *La Democracia* by favoring fusion with the Sagasta party. He was answered by Don Francisco Cepeda Taborcias, a Republican Autonomist, through the pages of *La Revista de Puerto Rico*. The battle grew to white heat; and the best efforts of Julián Blanco failed to bring an understanding. Through a manifesto on December 19, 1891, the directory attempted to draw some general lines of the party's program and to divorce itself from ''the extreme statements of certain members.'' This brought a strong reply from Muñoz Rivera, who asked if the directory's statement was intended as an attack on *La Democracia*. A special meeting of the party's two factions was held in order to settle differences, and while Muñoz refused to accept the explanation of the manifesto, the delegation ratified its former reading of the ''alliance'' to mean a pact with the peninsular Republican party. José Celso Barbosa, who was soon to become the leader of the Puerto Rican Republicans, agreed with this interpretation; the conflict was thus set between the Republicans (called "anti-Fusionistas") and the Monarchical Autonomists (called "Fusionistas").

At this time of conflict within the Autonomist party of Puerto Rico, the *Gaceta Oficial* carried a decree pertinent to the oncoming elections of 1893. It required that electors be Spaniards, twenty-five years of age, and that a minimum fee of 5 pesos be paid in Cuba, while a minimum of 10 was required in Puerto Rico. Since this was a decree of the Sagasta government, the directory with its anti-Sagasta tendencies issued a proclamation on February 10, 1893, urging all members of the Autonomist party to refrain from voting. Julián Blanco issued a statement in mid-summer which, while criticizing the discrimination against Puerto Rico, urged all to vote in the interest of the economic good of the country. Dr. José Celso Barbosa took a stand against Blanco, pointing out that this might bring about a third party. The Puerto Rican Autonomist party was seriously weakened during the years of 1893-95 by misunderstandings, differences of doctrine, and personal attacks through the press. Many meetings were held to attempt to unite the party, but without success. In a meeting on March 2, 1895, in Aguadilla, three factions appeared in the Autonomist party: first, those who desired association with the Spanish centralist Republicans and who were led by Fernández Juncos and Matienzo Cintrón; second, those who sought a pact on the basis of regional union with Cuba and who were under the control of Rossy, Barbosa, Veve, and Gómez Brioso; and third, those who wanted accord with the Spanish Liberal party and who accepted Muñoz Rivera's viewpoint.

In May of 1895, Muñoz Rivera went to Spain to visit with the principal Spanish statesmen and to discuss Puerto Rico's problems and the possibility of an understanding with some of the peninsular parties. He visited with such statesmen as Moret, Castelar, Sagasta, Pi y Margall and others but avoided a visit with Rafael María de Labra, the leader of the Puerto Rican Autonomists and their representative in the Cortes. While praising Labra for his personal and public virtues, he found him easily annoyed with those who spoke out in opposition: "I admit that I am almost incompatible with his Olympian pride." The real reason for not visiting with Labra, however, seems to be that Labra was strongly opposed to any union with the Sagasta party, believing that the Antilles should preserve a grand cordiality with the Republicans in Spain but not fuse with them. He was convinced that the Autonomists should prepare for the establishment of a democratic regime that would be able to confront any bureaucracy or oligarchy. On returning from Spain, Muñoz Rivera saw little possibility of convincing the Autonomist party of his plan to fuse with the Sagasta party. In an assembly held in San Juan during the following month, his plan was voted down, and this determined Liberal thereupon left the Autonomist party.[15]

While this dispute was going on within the ranks of the Puerto Rican Autonomists, the Cuban revolt had broken out again because of the failure of the Pact of Zanjón (1878). A group of Puerto Ricans in New York then took up the cause of Puerto Rico's complete independence from Spain. These Puerto Rican Separatists held an assembly in "Chimney Hall" at Sixth Avenue and 27th St., New York City, on December 22, 1895. And so the Puerto Rican section of the Cuban Revolutionary party was founded; officials were elected from the sixty members present. This group continued to function until it was dissolved on August 2, 1898. It is well to remember that while José Martí wrote the "bases" for the Cuban Revolutionary party, organized a chain of local organizations into a functional unity, and emphasized the identity of the Cuban and the Puerto Rican causes, there was little contact with Puerto Rican centers before July 25, 1896. Roberto H. Todd, a prominent member of the Puerto Rican section of the Cuban junta in New York, writes that "on December 1, 1895, none of the six members elected to the Directory were in contact with any revolutionary center in Puerto Rico."[16] Todd found the work of the junta difficult, since Puerto Ricans, unlike Cubans, had few traditional resentments that could prompt a rebellion. Nor were the revolutionary clubs widespread in Puerto Rico. The only reference Todd makes to island-interest is that of Pedro J. Fournier, who in 1896 was commissioned by the leading Autonomists—Luis Muñoz Rivera, José Gómez Brioso, Federico Degetau, and Rosendo Matienzo Cintrón—to have a conference with Dr. Henna, in regard to a projected invasion of Puerto Rico.[17]

Little agreement existed between the Autonomist party of Puerto Rico and the Puerto Rican Revolutionary junta in New York. An unpublished letter of Dr. José C. Barbosa to Roberto Todd denied that the Autonomists had become instruments of the Spanish government ("unos gubernamentales"). He added: "From New York all seems very easy, but it is necessary to be here in order to be able to judge the situation." He was convinced that some time would have to pass before "there could be any hope of action worthy of a virile people." As for himself, Barbosa said, he would continue in his obligations to the Autonomist party. Gerardo Forrest, a member of the Revolutionary junta in New York, had an unauthorized and imprudent interview with the American press, in which he spoke of the coming revolution in Puerto Rico. He also made a secret visit to Puerto Rico in order to discuss the situation with the leaders of the Autonomist party. Roberto Todd gives a report of a letter from Barbosa in which he cites Dr. Barbosa's statement in an interview with Forrest: "In all the country, it would be difficult to find ten men who have sufficient valor to sacrifice themselves for the idea that you propose." In the same month of July, 1896, Forrest had an interview with Luis Muñoz Rivera who reported it as follows: "My position is this, Mr. Forrest: I am a partisan of independence as an ideal. All have to be free. Nevertheless I consider that the independence of my country is absolutely impossible. Our masses are even lacking in a complete civic education. They never fought and will not fight with the power of the Cuban masses. To attempt force is the equivalent of making a useless sacrifice. After 25 years of titanic struggle, Cuba has not been able to succeed. Puerto Rico would succumb without success and without glory. . . ." Muñoz then explained that the delegation of the Autonomist party, after a meeting in Caguas, appointed a commission to present their cause in Madrid; and that if autonomy is not achieved: "I do not know what they will do. But I can assure you on my word that I will return to Puerto Rico by way of New York; and I will turn to you . . . with arms in hand, in order to liberate our land or die in the attempt.[10]

AUTONOMIST MISSION TO SPAIN: 1896-1897

In a meeting in Caguas, on July 27, 1896, the Autonomist party's delegation appointed a commission to represent its political goals in Spain. The members of this commission were: José Gómez Brioso, political director and head of the party; Rosendo Matienzo Cintrón, a representative of the delegation; Federico Degetau and Luis Muñoz Rivera, journalists; and Rafael María de Labra, the leader of the party. The instructions to the commissioners, which seem to have met the approval of all, were: first, the commission was to visit the head of the Spanish government in order to inform him of the purpose of the Puerto Rican Autonomist party; second, it was to get information from the chiefs of the peninsular democratic parties; third, the commission was authorized to make an alliance with the party that

promised to defend now and to develop when in power the full
Autonomist plan as expressed in the party's constitution; fourth, the
solemn promise of acceptance was to be made by the chief of the
Peninsular party in the presence of the Cortes or by public document;
and fifth, the understanding might better be made with a party that
has the surest possibility of soon becoming the government party.[19]

On September 16, 1896, the commissioners set sail for Spain. The
first sign of sharp difference of opinion appeared in a letter of
Gómez Brioso who wrote on the high seas of the extended discussions
and who feared party friction, despite the agreement of Caguas. He
reported that Muñoz Rivera was set on joining forces with Sagasta,
while Degetau was determined on a strict "republican" interpretation of the instructions. On arrival in Spain, Muñoz Rivera immediately began discussions with the coalition party of Sagasta, while
the other commissioners had their formal talk with Cánovas del
Castillo who was prime minister and head of the Monarchical Conservative party. This Conservative leader showed himself well
informed on Puerto Rico, believed that the reform law of Puerto
Rico could precede that of Cuba, and spoke at length of universal
suffrage, jury trial, and other reforms. There were also many confer-
ences with the Sagasta party and with the leading Republicans. From
mid-November on, Gómez Brioso began to turn toward an understanding with Sagasta. Apart from the matter of universal suffrage and
jury trial—which Sagasta found to be imprudent because of the
recently emancipated Negroes—Gómez Brioso reported that his position offered no difficulty. He quoted Sagasta as saying: "You are
authorized to announce that the Liberal party over which I preside
will implant in the Island of Puerto Rico, as soon as it has power, the
reform laws voted by the Cortes in the sense of the most broad
administrative decentralization. . . . And I will add to this all the
political rights that are enjoyed in the peninsula. . . ." It is to be
noted that the promises of Sagasta were identical with those of
Cánovas; but because of the Cuban crisis, it was most likely that the
Cánovas government would fall from power and give place to the
Sagasta Party. [20]

In seeking the approval of the Puerto Rican Autonomist Directory,
Gómez Brioso was checked by the opposition of the party's leader,
Rafael María de Labra, who saw the Centralist Republicans as the
only party disposed to accept the Autonomist platform of the
Puerto Ricans. Since the Republicans were out of power, the com-

mission had but two alternatives: first, to labor for the revision of the Cánovas Reforms, which would culminate in a form of self-government; or second, to continue the search for a formula of accord with Sagasta, which would lead to an alliance tending toward the attainment of autonomy. On December 31, 1896, the Cánovas government published the *Abarzuza Decrees,* which brought into effect in Puerto Rico the reforms that had been passed March 15, 1895, and then suspended because of the insurrection in Cuba. The texts of these reform decrees were not approved by the commissioners; moreover, they did not find them in accord with the Ley Maura. This action set the mind of Gómez Brioso on the side of Muñoz Rivera and Matienzo Cintrón, and the three men proceeded to work out a formula with Sagasta.

The resultant formula drafted by Gómez Brioso states: "The Commission of the Autonomist party of Puerto Rico, in the name of the delegation and by virtue of the powers with which it has been invested, declares that it will offer its support to the Liberal party over which Don Práxedes Mateo Sagasta presides, both in its general and local politics, since the ideals of the Program of Ponce in 1887 will be realized by said collectivity." It can be seen from this formula that, while a pact was being made with the Sagasta party, it was also to be made on the basis of the 1887 party platform. After studying this formula, Sagasta offered a substitute that read: "Since this party in evolving the bases of reform . . . will grant to the Antilles . . . the greatest decentralization possible within the national unity, in the care and management of its own municipal and provincial interests; and will satisfy the democratic principles, always in the ideal of a perfect equality of rights between the citizens of the Antilles and their peninsular brothers—both equally Spaniards. . . ." The vagueness of this clause was immediately apparent to the commission; Degetau refused to approve it, and the others registered their disappointment.

In the meantime, Labra criticized the commission's discussions, on the grounds that colonial autonomy would be ruined by the conversion of the Puerto Rican Autonomist party into an "exclusively monarchical party." While Labra was expressing his disappointment to the secretary of the party, Luis Sánchez Morales, Gómez Brioso was writing to Dr. José Barbosa that since an agreement with Cánovas had failed and since the Republic was non-existent, he had agreed to a formula with Sagasta. This formula is extensive, but must be quoted, since it is the basis of the future split in the Autonomist party of Puerto Rico. It reads:

> The commission of the Autonomist party of Puerto Rico . . . declares that it will support the Liberal party of Don Práxedes Mateo Sagasta, both in its general and Antilles politics, since this party, on evolving the bases of reforms in the broadest spirit and the most liberal judgment, will grant to the Antilles . . . the greatest decentralization possible within national unity, so that the initiative and management of its local interest . . . may completely belong on them. . . . And with the cessation of all distinction between the Spaniards, the inhabitants of Puerto Rico are to enjoy the same rights as the peninsulars, as the surest means of giving satisfaction to the democratic principles proclaimed by all.
>
> And since the incorporation of the Autonomists of Puerto Rico into the ranks of the Liberal party [of Spain] is necessary for unified proceedings, the commission will submit to the general assembly of the party [in Puerto Rico] such *incorporation* in order to constitute in the island a single Liberal party, in submission to the discipline of the peninsula as its prolongation in that overseas province.

This formula was signed in Madrid on January 12, 1897. I have italicized the word *incorporation* in order to bring out the conflict that it offered both to Article 7 of the Constitution of the Puerto Rican Autonomist party (as amended in the Assembly of Mayagüez in 1891) and to the instructions given at Caguas in July, 1896.[21] The commission had finished its work without the approval of Commissioner Degetau and its leader, Labra. It was to face further difficulties in San Juan.

The returning commission, after a warm welcome in the port of San Juan, addressed the Autonomist Assembly which held its sessions in the San Juan theater on February 12 and 13, 1897. The history of the commission's discussions with the various peninsular parties was given; and then the arguments on the *Formula Sagastina* were presented. Muñoz Rivera made much of the point that by entrance into the so-called "Fusionista" party of Sagasta, the Puerto Rican Autonomists would be empowered to influence all the official acts of this party when it became the government party. Matienzo Cintrón defended the change of plans as the only means of realizing the Autonomist party's ideals. In the midst of the discussion and in order to avoid a party split, the opponents of the *Formula* presented to the assembly a compromise proposition that praised the commission's work, but which, under Article 4, stated that, "the Assembly agrees to support every Peninsular party that realizes our program, in that which is exclusively related to the development of the regional political status." This proposition was objected to by the commissioners, Gómez Brioso, Matienzo Cintrón, and Muñoz Rivera; and they threatened to leave the assembly if the proposition were not withdrawn. It was accordingly withdrawn, and the debate continued. During the third session, the *Formula Sagastina* was offered for vote to the 131 delegates present. The vote showed seventy-nine in favor of the plan, twenty-four opposed, and twenty-eight abstaining from a vote. Thereupon Dr. Santiago Veve Calzada and Dr. José Celso Barbosa reiterated the Autonomist creed; and Barbosa spoke the final words of the defeated faction: "I carry with me the Autonomist banner which with my friends we shall continue to wave." Manuel F. Rossy left the presidency of the assembly and, with the others who had opposed the *Formula Sagastina,* withdrew from the hall.

With this division of the Autonomist party came the birth of the two parties that remained separated, save for very brief periods. The Liberal Fusionists ("Pactistas") were brought under the leadership of Luis Muñoz Rivera, while the Historical Autonomists ("Ortodoxos," or "Puros") followed the presidency of Manuel Fernández Juncos. This latter party was organized by the Manifesto of February 16, 1897. On the following day, through the periodical, *El País,* the Ortodoxos contrasted the two positions. The party of the Pactistas, the writer said, might be called "practical" and would lead to immediate but ephemeral results. For himself, he preferred a policy of "idealism" that esteems rights and educates the people to liberty, in the belief that a future day will bring autonomy.[22] The two schools of thought became rivals for public support. One stressed the need for adjusting party principles to the practical realities of life; the other stressed the holding to inviolable political principles.

Muñoz Rivera became enthusiastic about the possibilities of the pact with Sagasta and saw no danger of revolt against Spain in Puerto Rico. He expressed his loyalty to Spain through a letter to a friend, on April 14, 1897:

> My propaganda of six years prepared the minds, and the war in Cuba completed the work. And today, no man of judgment thinks of uprising or revolutions. Peace and liberty with Spain as the sovereign are desired. Without this, not even the most outright autonomy would be accepted by us. . . .

The country is Spanish, and it will ever be so. Even if
Spain maltreats and deceives her, she will not descend to the
abyss in which Cuba is ruining herself and will be lost. In
our evolution . . . Puerto Rico will develop into a section of the
country, and the Puerto Ricans into real Spaniards, the same
as you, Sagasta and Cánovas. I do not doubt that the Liberal
leader will fulfill his promises. . . .

This same idea of loyalty to Spain appeared in another letter of
Muñoz Rivera during the following month when he wrote to Don
Antonio Maura: "Your advent to power and support of us in the
administration of Puerto Rico will bring Spain not a single defection.
The revolutionary tendency that existed only in germ will remain
ended; and there will not be the slightest shadow of danger for the
future."[23] In June of 1897, even another letter states: "a year ago
one could observe the beginnings of revolutionary movements. . . .
These were directed from New York and Paris by the Doctors Henna
and Betances who presided over the Separatist organizations. But
today this tendency is disappearing. The island is with us, and we are
with Spain."[24]

THE AUTONOMOUS CHARTER PROCLAIMED IN 1898

On August 8, 1897, Cánovas del Castillo was assassinated, and on
October 4, the liberal government of Práxedes Mateo Sagasta came
into power. By November 25, 1897, the new prime minister had
secured the autonomous charter for Puerto Rico. This gave the island
a quasi-dominion status, along with the retaining of its representation
in the Cortes. The charter provided a bicameral legislature: the
Council of Administration consisting of fifteen members, eight of
whom were elected and the remaining seven appointed by the
governor general; and the Chamber of Representatives, which was
elective on the basis of one representative for every 25,000 inhabitants.
This insular parliament was empowered to legislate on local matters,
to provide for the island's budget and revenue, to regulate tariffs, and
under the approval of the peninsular government to negotiate commercial treaties with foreign governments. The Insular Cabinet
(Council of Administration) consisted of a president, a secretary of
government and justice, and secretaries of the treasury, education,
public works, and agriculture. The assembly was limited to purely
local matters, while broader legislation on political, civil, or judicial
matters was handled by the Cortes in Spain. The town councils

(*ayuntamientos*) were declared autonomous in local matters; and universal suffrage for males over twenty-five years of age was decreed. Lastly, the governor general was named by the queen and had the power of commander-in-chief of the army and navy. In civil and political matters, he was not to intervene unless authorized by the cabinet. He was, however, granted supreme powers in times of emergency.[25]

Puerto Rico's *Gaceta Oficial* announced on January 12, 1898, that new Governor General Andrés González Muñoz would come to proclaim the autonomous charter. In a first message, he praised the virtues of the Puerto Rican people, but on the following day, he died and was succeeded by interim Governor General Ricardo Ortega.[26] It was not until February 9, 1898, that Governor General Manuel Macías inaugurated the new government; and on February 12, the officers of the Insular Cabinet took the oath of office before the governor. This body represented both factions of the former Autonomist party. The Sagasta Liberals (Fusionistas) were Luis Muñoz Rivera, secretary of government; Juan Hernández López, secretary of public works; and José M. Quiñones, secretary of agriculture. The Historical Autonomists (Puros) were Francisco M. Quiñones, president; Manuel Fernández Juncos, secretary of treasury; and Manuel F. Rossy, secretary of education. Only for a brief period—from mid-February to mid-March of 1898—were these two parties welded into the Union Autonomista Liberal, a coalition party presided over by Manuel C. Román. It was an attempt to get the new charter off to a successful start.[27]

The enthusiasm for self-government was best expressed by San Juan's new newspaper, *El Liberal*. It introduced its first issue by identifying itself with liberty and with the Liberal party that "fosters autonomous and decentralized government." This party, they insisted, will show the world that Puerto Rico is worthy of liberty, is able to govern, and is discreet in the exercise of power. The paper requested an extensive program of public works, including new highways and railroads, in order to join agriculture with commerce; a university for the capital and schools throughout the island were also requested. Lastly, the new government was asked to function on the basis of democratic principles and judicial responsibility. While eager for self-government, the editor protested his loyalty, asserting that "we have incontrovertible proofs of the absolute support of our people and of our party." This Liberal party was undoubtedly devoted to Spain and opposed to intervention by the United States. When war seemed imminent with the latter power, *El Liberal* spoke clearly: "When Yankee wealth attempts to measure its strength against the glory of Spain . . . we do not here have to defend doctrines nor political proceedings. We have to defend our race, our history, our religion, our language, and our honor. The country is our only doctrine; to die or conquer is our sole procedure."[28]

On March 27, 1898, the Puerto Ricans went to the polls to elect their Insular Assembly. The results showed twenty-six seats for the Liberal Fusionistas, four seats for the Historical Autonomistas (Puros), one for the Conservatives ("Incondicionales"), and one for the Oportunistas.[29] This newly elected body, however, did not hold its first session until July 17, 1898. The tardiness of convening was a result of the war situation that had developed between the United States and Spain. Under emergency powers, Governor Macías appealed to the loyalty of Puerto Rico and proclaimed that, in accord with Article 37 of the *Ley de Extranjería,* "none of those whom this law considers foreigners shall be subject to military service." On April 17, 1898, he announced a public subscription of one million pesos for the public defense. Within the same week, the secretary of justice and government, Luis Muñoz Rivera, urged the mayors of the municipalities to increase agricultural production against an emergency and warned the press that the spreading of false rumors might bring action under the Penal Code.

Governor Macías decreed the suspension of certain constitutional guarantees on April 22, and on April 23, he invoked his powers as lieutenant general of the army and captain general of the District of Puerto Rico in order to declare a state of war and to forbid the export of cattle. While the members of the cabinet made a strong appeal to the people to defend "the flag that protected our cradles and will protect our tombs," they also regretted the temporary withdrawal of the Autonomous Charter. They stated that they were even more loyal under the new constitution.[30]

PRESSURES IN THE UNITED STATES BRING A WAR

During this period in which Puerto Rico was seeking to convince Spain that its right to an autonomous constitution was long overdue, and while the battle of political ideals and interests became sharp in the island, there was an ever-growing struggle in the United States between the forces of those who urged and those who opposed an active intervention in the Spanish colonial struggle. The domestic conflict in the United States revolved around a series of interests, and the retelling of the events of these days has evoked much dispute among historians. Manifest Destiny, national defense, business interests, political duplicity, humanitarianism, yellow journalism, and a diplomacy of *real-politik* have been advanced as the explanation of the changing attitude of the United States toward Spain in the days preceding and following the explosion of the United States warship *Maine*. The degree of cause that each of these contributed to the making of war will ever remain a matter of dispute among historians.

Manifest Destiny is a very old "drive" in the history of United States' expansion; it has, in fact, its theological origins in the Calvinism that came with the settlers and was expressed by many of the founding fathers. Practical politicians used it in the conflict of sectional interests; and it reached a high point of expression in 1859 when, through the unratified McLane-Ocampo Treaty, the United States reached its ultimate in land aggression against Mexico.[31] With the coming of the Civil War and the aftermath of Reconstruction, this aggressive doctrine lay dormant. It was resurrected, however, in the 1890's when public opinion and the press became vigorously nationalist and when the United States government took a strong stand on such issues as the Venezuela boundary dispute with Britain. While the imperialists saw the United States in danger of not developing its power, and—as Theodore Roosevelt said—of not realizing that "all the great masterful races have been fighting races," certain members of the Protestant clergy saw the hand of God in a missionary war against Spain.[32]

Stemming in part from the doctrine of self-defense in "natural law," and also from a belief in national destiny, was the determination to advance the national defense. The Monroe Doctrine of 1823 contained more self-defense and economic evolution than high idealism, and it was consistently summoned in the protection of new interests. Cuba's recurring revolts against a weakened Spain, and Puerto Rico's strategic position of entrance through the Mona Straits to the Caribbean, were problems that bore relations to the defense of the United States. They were not to be left available for seizure by a strong European power; and since Spain was too weak to hold them, they would be better secured under United States protection. So argued the imperialists who saw the necessity of naval

bases in strategic areas and the need of colonies for the production of
raw materials and the marketing of manufactured goods. Politicians
who had domestic scandals to worry about were also glad to see public
opinion turned to international issues. Moreover, they saw in it a
good vote-getting issue in a public that was again feeling its nationalism and looking for more colonies.

The place of business interests in the production of the Spanish-
American War has been seriously discussed by many writers. Professor Beard made much of these facts: in 1898, about 95 per cent of
Cuba's export to the United States was sugar; much American capital
had been poured into Cuban sugar enterprises; and President Cleve-
land's Message to Congress on December 7, 1896, stated that "the
industrial value of the Island (Cuba) is fast diminishing and that
unless there is a speedy and radical change in existing conditions, it
will disappear altogether." Beard pointed out that up to $50 million
of American capital was invested in Cuba and the volume of trade
with Cuba had reached the high point in 1893 of $103 million. His
conclusion was that "the American interests associated with Cuban
industry and trade derived practical benefits from forcible intervention and expanded under the rule of law later established in
virtue of the Platt Amendment."[33] Professor Pratt's study of
business journals comes to more precise and demonstrable conclusions.
They may be summarized briefly:

> It seemed safe to conclude that American business in the
> winter of 1897-1898 was opposed to war and either opposed to
> colonial expansion or oblivious to the existence of the prob-
> lem. . . .
> After the battle of Manila Bay, American business became
> definitely imperialistic—that is, if a wish to retain the Philip-
> pines is an evidence of an imperialistic attitude. . . .
> The conversion of business opinion was accomplished by the
> combination of a European threat against the freedom of the
> American market in China. . . . In one paper, the New York
> *Journal of Commerce,* there appears . . . the shift of position
> induced by the action of the European Powers in China. In
> November 1897, against all schemes of colonial or naval expan-
> sion; in December, for a canal, Hawaiian annexation, and a
> big navy; in May and thereafter, for retention of the entire
> Philippine archipelago and aggressive assertion of American
> rights in China. . . .
> In the Caribbean, business interests not only insisted that
> the United States needed Porto Rico for its strategic and
> commercial value, but suggested that it might prove impossible

to adhere to the Teller Amendment, which had pledged the United States not to annex Cuba.[34]

In this article, Professor Pratt stresses the fact that business interests, before the European threat to American markets in the Far East, enjoyed advantageous trade relations in the world markets and were unconcerned with colonies; a form of free trade was also being advocated by certain business interests.

Of far greater seriousness as a cause of the war was the propaganda of the yellow press. Taking advantage of the human reaction to atrocities, the yellow journalists of the late nineteenth century set out to manufacture horrors. This had the double effect of raising newspaper circulation and of precipitating a war. Joseph E. Wisan presents the sordid picture of the efforts of the American press to win public interest through glaring headlines and sadistic stories. He cites William Randolph Hearst's reply—as publisher of the New York *Journal*—to his artist Remington's complaint that there was no war in Cuba: "You furnish the pictures; I'll furnish the war."[35] The battle for circulation between Hearst's *Journal* and Pulitzer's *World* was well geared to circulation and not to the formation of mature public opinion. In the absence of such modern media of communication as radio and television, it is apparent that the press could be irresponsible and largely blameworthy for rushing a people down the road to war.

While these factors were at work, the United States government continued its diplomacy of non-intervention. On April 4, 1896, Secretary Olney asked Spain to give a rapid solution to the Cuban problem. In urging that Spain give administrative reforms to the islands, he pointed out that the proximity of the United States to the same forced her to take interest.[36] While in President McKinley's annual message of 1897 he had found that forcible annexation of Cuba was outside of "our code of morality," powers were at work to force his hand. They consisted of a small group of journalists, intellectuals, and politicians who came of old line Anglo-Saxon families; the most prominent were Henry Cabot Lodge, Albert J. Beveridge, Whitelaw Reid, Theodore Roosevelt, Albert Shaw, and Walter Hines Page. Their aggressive plan advocated the building of a navy, an isthmian canal, naval bases and colonies in the Caribbean and the Pacific for the protection of the canal, and the annexation of Hawaii and Samoa.[37] In the last days before the war, when the queen of

Spain was willing to make many concessions to prevent war and when the American ambassador in Madrid was pleading for patience, President McKinley signed the declaration of war. It combined a recognition of "duty under God" with political expediency.

It was at the end of April, 1898, that the United States Congress declared war on Spain, and by mid-May, Admiral Sampson was at the gates of San Juan. After a two-and-a-half hour bombardment of the fortresses of El Morro and San Cristóbal, and after learning the strength of these bulwarks, he withdrew.

Co-operating with the war effort of the United States was the Puerto Rican section of the Cuban Revolutionary party, with its headquarters in New York. In early 1898, Dr. Henna began to correspond with Senators Lodge, Cullon, Morgan, and Murphy, in order that when the question of Cuba was brought up in the Senate, Puerto Rico might also be considered. In March of the same year, Dr. Henna moved to Washington, and by means of letters of introduction from the Cubans Gonzalo de Quesada and Ricardo Díaz Albertini—the chargé d'affaires and secretary of the Cuban Legation respectively—was able to arrange an interview with Henry Cabot Lodge, the senator from Massachusetts and a member of the Senate's Committee on Foreign Relations. The senator "had a true interest in the concerns of Puerto Rico, [and] promised to consider the island in the Senate, if Dr. Henna would give him information." The interview concluded with Senator Lodge's giving him a letter of introduction to Assistant Secretary of the Navy Theodore Roosevelt, "who had in his hands the preparation of all the details in case of war." Dr. Henna offered his services and those of the New York junta in order to aid in the emancipation of his country; he also provided maps and information, and proposed himself for the job of civil commissioner with the United States troops that were to invade Puerto Rico.[38]

In his ever-growing contacts, Dr. Henna received a letter from Roosevelt on March 15, 1898, in which this expansionist wrote: "I have no doubt that the description of Puerto Rico which you have sent me will be of the greatest use. Certainly all that which you have given us so far has proved very useful. I believe that in the case of hostilities we will be able to use you and your friends to great advantage, precisely as you suggest; and I will insist that it be so." The reference to the aid given was the map and other military information such as the location of roads and fortifications and the number of soldiers in each village.[39] On March 21, Dr. Henna had an interview with President McKinley; he reported it as follows: "Puerto Rico has the same motives of complaint as Cuba, and ought to secure the same fate as she. To secure the independence of Cuba and to leave Puerto Rico with Spain would bring upon the United States the same disturbances that Cuba occasions today. We have not yet raised up a revolt; not because we have not desired to, but because we have been unable. If Spain leaves Cuba and remains in Puerto Rico, she will continue to be a threat to Cuba, the United States, and all America.... The United States can save us, making us independent. And the majority of the people will determine in the future whether or not to ask annexation to the American Union."

At the time of the invasion of Puerto Rico by the United States, Dr. Henna was confined to bed with pneumonia. General Stone, however, interviewed Dr. Henna in New York on May 25, proposing that he accept the position of surgeon on the General Staff of General Miles. This Dr. Henna rejected, since he preferred going as "an ordinary Puerto Rican and with his known position of representative of the revolutionists." He was, however, still applying for the position of civil commissioner; but since this was a civil matter, it was left to the determination of President McKinley. As late as July 14, 1898, Dr. Henna was still offering his serices in this civil capacity. Appended to his letter was a manifesto, a rather extravagant document; it reads in part: "From the status of miserable Spanish colonists . . . at this moment you climb to the famous heights of full citizenship. From today onward you will constitute a FREE STATE (*estado libre*). . . . Puerto Rico . . . rises as a State or nation in the shadow of the greatest Federation. . . . You will not be the booty of conquest; but there will be left to your own free initiative the organization of yourselves under your own form of government." This document was written by Eugenio María de Hostos and Dr. Henna and signed by the leading members of the New York junta. It was never circulated in Puerto Rico. According to Roberto Todd, both Henna and Hostos acted in good faith and attempted to convince those who doubted that the United States would leave the island to its own political determination once the war was over.[40] Hostos was set on preventing the annexation of Puerto Rico to the United States; and the Separatist leader, Betances, wrote from Paris to Dr. Henna in opposition to annexation. He suggested that the North American forces be met by those of Puerto Rico who were to fight under the banner of independence and that United States' co-operation be used only to attain the island's liberty. For, he added, "if Puerto Rico does not act rapidly, it will be an American colony forever."

PUERTO RICAN REACTION TO THE AUTONOMOUS CHARTER AND
TO UNITED STATES OCCUPATION

During the days of threatened invasion by the United States, the new autonomous government began to function. On July 17, 1898, Governor General Manuel Macías summoned the Insular Assembly into session. Following the governor's address, the assembly set about its first work on July 19 of reducing the cabinet posts to four. Accordingly, on July 22, all cabinet officers resigned; and the Governor gave approval to the new appointment. Luis Muñoz Rivera became president of the cabinet and secretary of government; Juan Hernández López was appointed secretary of justice, Julián E. Blanco y Sosa became secretary of interior, and Salvador Carbonel was made secretary of industry.[41] Muñoz Rivera had a homogeneous cabinet, and he urged a program of economy and finance before the assembly. He invited the Historical Autonomists (Puros) to assist in the deliberations, he considered the hunger problem to be the assembly's first consideration, and he categorically declared Puerto Rico's loyalty. With a dramatic touch, he said: "We are Spaniards and wrapped in the Spanish flag will we die."[42]

The economic crisis had by this time produced widespread poverty. In Sabana Grande, the poor were said to have only bad water, a little salt, and some green mangoes. While Secretry Muñoz Rivera was urging the immediate solution of the hunger problem, *El Liberal* was making a strong plea for effective use of Articles 557 and 558 of the Penal Code against the merchants who were exploiting the people through abnormally high prices.[43]

On July 25, the troops of the United States approached the southern coast of Puerto Rico and invaded at Guanica. What little there was of military action is most interestingly described in *The Chronicles of the Hispanic-American War in Puerto Rico* by Angel Rivero. An amusing testimonial to Puerto Rico is left by an American sergeant, Karl Stephens: "The women of Puerto Rico are either very pretty or very ugly; there is no in-between. The men don't become intoxicated, nor do they mistreat their wives. At the hour of repast and siesta they avoid business. They neither swear nor use other profane words. In a word they show more interest in a sonnet than in the price of a barrel of salt pork. For both men and women in Puerto Rico, life is a rose, a cigarette, a song, a laugh, a kiss, and a tomorrow.'' When they approached Yauco, Mayor Francisco Mejía came out to meet the American forces and gave the following welcome: ''Fellow citizens, long life to the United States of America! Hurrah for its valiant troops! Viva Puerto Rico Americano!''[44] Before the capital city of San Juan was seized, an armistice had been signed between the United States and Spain. It was a brief campaign of nineteen days and was described by Angel Rivero as a model of modern, humanitarian warfare. The customs, laws, and religion of the people were respected; and this invasion took on something of a triumphal procession.

By August 13, 1898, Ponce was occupied by the forces of the United States, and on August 17, an armistice was proclaimed. Governor Macías, in accord with Article 42 of the Autonomous Charter of 1897, granted a generous reprieve to political prisoners. Shortly before this, Queen María Cristina had ordered a commission to arrange the details of Spain's evacuation of Cuba and Puerto Rico; this was in accord with Article 4 of the Washington Protocol. In these last days, the governor general made many appointments to offices in public works and in the school system, as determined by Article 43 of the Autonomic Charter. He dissolved the national subscription for the prosecution of the war, and he also decreed the end of the publication of the *Gaceta Oficial* and of the Bureau of Census. The last issue of the *Gaceta Oficial* under the seal of Spain appeared on October 16; the first publication under the seal of the United States was on October 18. The official announcement of the cession of Puerto Rico to the United States was made by Governor Macías on September 29, 1898,[45] and on September 30, he officially ordered the cessation of the constitutional powers of the Spanish judges in favor of United States sovereignty.[46]

In discussing the public reaction to the United States' occupation of Puerto Rico, one must consider that it occurred during the first days of the operation of the Autonomous Charter. It was a sudden shock to the enthusiasm for self-rule when the island was invaded by a people who displayed the intrepid and impudent philosophy of Manifest Destiny, along with a magnificant achievement in material progress. For a moment, the Puerto Rican was stunned. A first reaction was in favor of the tradition that was Spain—its language and culture, law and politics, philosophy and religion. Besides, the

Autonomous Charter was getting under way, and despite sharp party conflicts, it offered promise. A second reaction was the hope that the much admired progress of the United States would come to Puerto Rico, that the laws and constitution of the northern republic would become a reality in the island. The last shock came when Puerto Ricans realized that they were to share in neither the privileges of the American Constitution of 1789 nor in the Spanish Autonomous Charter of 1897. It made a poor basis for love of the United States.

Antonio S. Pedreira, in his *Insularismo,* gives us some reflections on those days: "The year 1898 found us placing our people under the protection of an autonomist constitution; and this we were hardly able to establish. In the very moment of beginning a new political life, the Spanish American War defeated (*malogró*) our purpose, and our normal development suffered a quick end (*síncope*). From a European polarization we passed without realizing it to that of North America."[47] Cayetano Coll y Toste, speaking of the same issue during the fourth centenary celebration of the Christian colonization of Puerto Rico, said in 1908:

> The famous Laws of the Indies, the Fuero Juzgo, the Fuero Real, the Siete Partidas, the Novísima Recopilación, the honored Constitution of '12, and all those after '37, along with the Leyes Especiales, the Códigos Nacionales . . . and finally the Autonomous Charter of 1897 have been the politico-social canons of our people.
> Here is the Puerto Rican country, formed by the enriching care (*al calor benéfico*) of Spain, the Mother Country. The four centuries that have transpired from 1508 to 1908 have little by little been forming our Antillean characteristics. . . . People who change nationality have to suffer deep political, social, and economic upheaval. This is the law of History. . . . Of necessity the antagonisms of each people will appear: one of Saxon origin, the other of Latin roots.

His conclusion is an expression of bitterness: "Our autonomous constitution is abolished and the Puerto Rican people changed—in fact, but without right—into a political orphan that is at the mercy of the American Congress."[48]

From the pen of another Puerto Rican who is also a jurist, we garner further insight: "While indeed, this once famous and now almost forgotten Spanish decree of 1897 has been the object of much adverse commentary and bitter criticism . . . yet when viewed in a dispassionate and calm spirit of justice, it cannot be denied that it contained some very liberal provisions. . . . Had Spain twenty-five years earlier given this same organic act both to Puerto Rico and to Cuba . . . there would have been in all probability no real occasion for the intervention of the United States in the destinies of these two islands."[49] In Enrique Calderón's *El Dolor de un Pueblo Esclavo,* there is an impassioned expression of the value of the autonomous constitution as "an opening for the two countries of the Antilles to achieve independence." All this, he concludes, was frustrated by the United States' invasion which was "one of the greatest violations of all principles in international law."[50]

As we page through the Puerto Rican press of these last days of autonomic government and first days of invasion by the United States, we find much strong expression. Mariano Abril, writing in the Liberal paper, *La Democracia,* charged the United States with a history of aggression against the Indian territories, Mexico, Hawaii, and Spain. After asserting that "Yankee expansionism" is an inheritance from Britain, the editorial concluded: "If the United States would bring war to Puerto Rico, I am sure that Puerto Ricans would defend themselves to the death, shedding their blood in the defense of Spain."[51] At the end of June, 1898, Luis Muñoz Rivera was interviewed by *La Correspondencia.* After expressing it as the wish of the Liberal party that the two chambers of the legislature be summoned under the Autonomous Charter, he stated that "there are two principal matters: the defense of the country and the defense of autonomy." When the insular parliament was finally summoned, Mariano Abril looked upon July 17 as a day that "will go down in our history as the line that divides two epochs: the slave colony from the free." In the governor's act of taking an oath to the Autonomous Charter in the presence of the representatives of the country, there was "the submission of all the colonial power of four centuries before the right of a people."[52]

In this period of rapid change, the church also had its point of view. In March, 1898, various pastors throughout the island asked the Reverend Buenaventura Bea, administrator of the diocese of San Juan, if they should take an active part in the election of deputies to the Cortes and of representatives to the insular legislature. The administrator gave a masterly reply that combined priestly zeal with prudence: "It is certain that we ought to interest ourselves in the welfare of the people and we cannot be indifferent to their fate." He then asked them to resolve his doubts as to those who are best fitted to contribute to the morality of the island, to the providing of Christian instruction and work for the laborers. "Where," he asks, "are these good friends of the people that are so praised but so poorly aided?" He exhorted them to remember that they, as priests, must be as fathers to all men, that they must separate themselves from political conflicts and dedicate themselves to the mission of bringing all men to God. In May, the *Boletín Eclesiástico* carried another message from the administrator of the diocese. This time all the churches of the island were ordered to give thanks to God for relief from the siege of San Juan by the naval forces of the United States on May 12.

Soon after, the Yankee forces were invading the southern shores of the island, and the *Boletín Eclesiástico* on August 6, 1898, announced the end of publication because of a lack of workers, the interruption of the mails, and the breakdown of communications between the capital and the outlying parishes. In the midst of the enemy invasion, the secretary, Dr. Rafael Pijoán, extended the canonical faculties of the country vicars and urged them to a faithful fulfillment of their duties for the good of the church and the state. The secretary warned the pastors that the labor of the church is alien to all political conflicts and that they must embrace all nationalities and races in order to win them to Christ.[53]

RELIGIOUS EDUCATION: 1890-1899

During the last years of Spanish hegemony, the church in Puerto Rico had encountered many serious problems. In 1890, the rector of the Piarist school for boys in Santurce addressed the student body on the growing religious indifference and immorality. He said:

> After the rationalism of the Encyclopedists of the past century came the Reign of Terror with its rivers of blood. After the materialistic and sensualistic culture of our times, one may hear the threatening voice of Socialism and of Anarchism. . . .
> Among the moderns consider Voltaire and Feuerbach; they have science, but no education. . . . If it is impossible to separate instruction from education . . . if the merit of a man lies in the sentiments that affect his heart and in the virtues that ennoble his soul, it is likewise impossible to separate education from religion. Education that doesn't proceed from religious principles is without meaning, for it has at its base no better motive than mere utility and expedience. It is nothing when it is founded on the forgetfulness, disdain, ignorance or indiffer-

ence to the intrinsic laws . . . that mark the natural dependence of man upon the Supreme Creator; when it is based on the opposition or forgetfulness of the order of relations that bind the creature to His Creator.[54]

In 1894, Bishop Toribio Mingüella y Arnedo addressed his flock on the serious needs of the church in Puerto Rico, especially in regard to family life and the necessity of accord between church and state. Again, in 1895, he pointed to the many women abandoned with their children without any means of support by unfaithful husbands. He continued: "Without a legitimate union blessed by God, there is no family; without a family, there is no society; and without legitimate marriages there could be no hope of a healthy society, a cultured people, or a practical Catholicism." This forceful bishop stated that the vice of drug addiction had appeared at some places in the island. This, he charged, upset the nervous system, stultified intelligence, and paralyzed all good action. He found a twofold slavery: that of ignorance and that of the passions that had degraded woman. He urged that no means were more effective than the Gospel and the teaching of the Catholic church—in proclaiming the unity and indissolubility of marriage—to raise the dignity of the woman.

On the widespread lack of education, he said: "The abandonment of education brings with it a lack of instruction, because many parents do not teach, nor can they teach their children that which they don't know. Nor do they attempt to bring their children to the schools. It is well known that among a people whose homes are spread here and there over a rugged terrain, it is impossible for all children to attend school, and difficult for many. . . ." But, the bishop continued, since the municipalities have at great sacrifice increased the budget for education, there is no justification for the high rate of illiteracy that is reported in the official statistics of 1888. He cited the fact that "less than 14 per cent of the population could read and write, while more than 86 per cent lacked even elementary instruction." The growing crime rate was also a matter for criticism. The bishop noted that it was not more alarming only because of the good nature and gentleness of character of the Puerto Rican. He lastly decried the Catholic who, while bragging of his faith, lived in contradiction to its teachings. This, the bishop charged, gave grounds for the unbelievers to criticize, the latter being unwilling to recognize that bad Catholics are so because they do not practice as true Catholics.

Throughout his pastoral letter of 1897, this vigorous bishop again returned to the criticism of abuses that existed in his diocese. He saw the basic evil as "religious indifference" that is "the infirmity that kills and the sepulchre that entombs innumerable souls." This indifference, he believed, had its roots in incredulity; its admission of all religions as good was reductively to reject all. He found many Catholics living in complete spiritual indolence, as manifested by the nonobservance of the law of God and the laws of the church. He continued: "Doubtless there are many intelligent men in our diocese who are Christians of belief and works. But it is also true that there are others who are more or less informed in other fields of knowledge, while very ignorant in their religion. This ignorance is the mother of indifference, for that which is not believed is not practiced; and that which is not known is not believed. . . ."

Shortly after this, Bishop Mingüella returned to Spain, in order to become bishop of Sigüenza. His farewell message found him leaving Puerto Rico with a heart full of gratitude and sorrow. Bad health "and perhaps even more a lack of zeal have convinced me that we might do little good to the diocese." His final word of advice was to "love God above all things"; then, "love Spain that has given you her name, blood, language, civilization and Faith"; finally, "love true and reasoned liberty, liberty that is founded on order, that ennobles, that is a gift of God and a part of well-being and of glory."[55]

The matter of better moral and religious education was raised by Antonio Daban, the governor general of Puerto Rico, in the official *Gaceta* of April 28, 1896. He urged the pastors to visit the public schools frequently, in order to observe and report to the municipal boards the status of moral and religious education. They were ordered to report directly to the governor's office any significant matter relating to education. Within a year, the *Boletín Eclesiástico* was publishing certain laws in the Spanish regulation for schools. Significant among these are the following:

Art. 37: The study of doctrine and the religious practices in the primary schools shall be under the immediate inspection of the pastor, or of the church representative on the local commission.

Art. 38: The moral and religious instruction shall occupy the first place in all of the school's classes.

Art. 39: There is to be a short but daily lesson in Christian Doctrine, along with Bible History. In this the practice of the applied principles is to be explained, in accord with the capacity of each class.

Art. 42: In towns where there is the praiseworthy custom of having the teacher accompany his students to Sunday Mass, this is to be continued. Where it is not the practice, the teachers are to introduce it.

Art. 48: In order that good habits and religious principles —acquired in the schools—may not be endangered by bad example in the home, the teachers should contact the parents in order to secure their cordial co-operation.[56]

It is to be noted that simultaneous with the steady growth of population in Puerto Rico, the number of clergy was decreasing. Whereas the number of priests in 1870 approximated 200, in 1880 there were less than 160. The *Ecclesiastical Guide* for the latter year listed 128 parish-clergy, 23 attached to the cathedral, and a few others in chaplaincies. By 1897, the *Gaceta Oficial* of Puerto Rico was requesting permission for more missions in the island and pointing out the serious shortage of priests. It further noted that the priests were exempt from military service. By Royal Order of February, 1897, Juana Díaz with its 25,000 Catholics was raised to the level of a parish after having received the bishop's approval. The governor general spoke of it as one of the richest and most productive sections in the province. This is an example of the crown's fulfilling its obligation under the *patronato real* of supplying a pastor and increasing the church's income. Another appeal of the bishop is significant. On May 5, 1897, he was allowed by the civil authorities to arrange for religious instruction in the public secondary schools.[57]

Fray Francisco Valdés was named by the Overseas Ministry on March 1, 1898, to succeed to the bishopric of Puerto Rico, but his installation did not take place because shortly thereafter the forces of the United States entered the island.[58]

Within a year after the occupation of Puerto Rico by the United States, a new look was proposed by a new breed for Puerto Rican education. Gumersindo Rivas, writing in *La Democracia,* advocated a "modern philosophy" of education and described the opening of a new American kindergarten that was well ventilated, spacious, and hygienic. He reflected that the school is something more than the religious temple; and the professor . . . consecrated to it is worth more than the priest who is dedicated to a cult that is more or less certain, but always harmful to the health of the soul that ought to live amid the clear and the splendid. . . . The school is the scientific truth . . . the church is the indecisive obscurity. . . . The school is tomorrow; the religious temple is yesterday. If the latter were closed, humanity would continue unperturbed along the road to the future."⁵⁹ The influence of modern educationists in Puerto Rico at the time of the change of sovereignty was not slight. In the "Carroll Report" of 1899, the testimonials of quite a few persons reveal this. When Dr. Henry K. Carroll, special United States commissioner to Puerto Rico, was visiting in Ponce, a Dr. Vidal, identifying himself as a free-thinker, bitterly criticized the religious processions of Lent. When asked if there were many free-thinkers in Puerto Rico, he answered: "All men who have studied at all are free-thinkers, and most of the doctors studied in France and got their ideas there."

In the town of Guayanilla, Mayor Eustaquio Torres assured Dr. Carroll that "persons of the highest culture in the island—generally free-thinkers—will receive with good will the principle of religious liberty which separation of Church and State brings about." Don Celestino Domínguez, mayor of Guayama, spoke even more strongly:

> No person of any degree of education in this country, if asked his opinion on the matter, would deny the great advantages of a separation of church and state. The clerical power in every country in the world has been a drag on progress, and nobody ignores the fact that Spain owes her decadence to this. . . . In this island the clerical influence has been so powerful, so strong and so oppressive that when the American troops arrived, everyone thought their influence would be destroyed, and rejoiced accordingly. The hunger for liberty was so great that the country has seen and will see with pleasure the disappearance of clerical influence.

At the time of the American occupation, the lines between the free-thinkers and the Catholic church were sharply drawn; the differences centered chiefly on civil marriage, cemeteries, church property, and support of the clergy. Father Montañez of Guayama strongly contested the statements of the free-thinkers. Father Juan Perpiñá y Pibernat, capitular vicar of the diocese of Puerto Rico, in asking that the United States support the clergy in the interim of finding sources of revenue, stated that "if the municipalities are asked to contribute to the church they will refuse to do so." Almost four months later, the vicar of the diocese again pointed to the source of trouble. He charged that the town councils "are bad ones, put in by Muñoz Rivera . . . and they are working against the church." It would seem that most of the leaders of Puerto Rico at the time of the change of government were in ideological conflict with the church;

their theories had been in evolution for many years. An amazing contradiction in all this is, as Father Montañez asserts, that ''even the free-thinkers themselves, when they are going to die, call for the priest.''[60]

The nineteenth century in Puerto Rico had felt the impact of the European philosophies of the enlightenment, romanticism, and positivism. Realization of this gives better understanding to the ever-recurring problems of conflict of church and state. It helps explain the anticlericalism among the intellectuals and political leaders. Lastly it provides a background that clarifies the misunderstandings of the early governors—both military and civil—who came from the United States to Puerto Rico. There was an irreconcilable conflict between the ''new thought'' that was intolerant and the church that offered no new dynamic expression of Christianity.

When the Spanish flag was lowered forever from above the fortresses of El Morro and San Cristóbal and replaced with that of the United States on October 18, the people of Puerto Rico must have felt mixed sentiments. They were deeply Spanish in tradition and had been ever loyal to Spain. A large percentage of the people, in agreement with the Liberal party of Muñoz Rivera, had come to believe that the Autonomous Charter of 1897 would realize the political ideals for which they had searched. Their reception of rule by the United States was filled with the fear that it might bring all the things that Spaniards had come to hate in the Anglo-Saxon. Though they had experienced hard and arbitrary rule by Spain over a long period, they wondered about the United States with its different religion, social prejudices, political ideals, and aggressive trade policies. They hoped that their political autonomy would be augmented by this democratic nation of the north, but they were secretly concerned about the superiority that the Anglo-Saxon might feel toward the Latin. Where there was no room for self-determination, there was the hope that a high level of territorial status would be granted them. It was with such mixed feelings that the Puerto Ricans saw the troops from the north set up barracks in their island and issue military orders to their civil tribunals. They neither fought the Americans as they entered, nor did they welcome them without fears. Colonialism was ever suspect to a people who had lived under its rule for four centuries.

PART TWO

Puerto Rico's Early Years
within the United States
Territorial System

III

United States Military Governments
in Puerto Rico, 1898-1900

We have said in the previous chapter that many Puerto Ricans hoped that the annexation of Puerto Rico to the United States would bring an improved political status. Writing in 1898, Juan B. Nieves, in his *Annexation of Puerto Rico to the United States*, stated that it had never occurred to him to think of his country as independent. He was convinced that his country depended on the world outside, that while he always favored a broad degree of autonomy, he did not favor independence. The latter, he believed, would make of Puerto Rico "a seed-bed of internal discord, and in the future a victim of Santo Domingo or Cuba." A further statement that would have been rejected by many—possibly by a majority of the population—was that "we have proved on a hundred occasions that we lack a politico-social education, that we are unprepared (*inhábiles*) to live the life of free peoples."[1] Whatever may have been the complexity of his reasons for favoring annexation to some democratic power, he certainly was one of those who furthered the already established idea of the United States' occupation authorities. It was a simultaneous conviction of the military leaders from the United States that a well-disciplined control was to be one of their contributions to Puerto Rico.

There are two aspects to this study of the years 1898 to 1900: the action of the military governors in administering to immediate needs; a study of the commissions that made reports to Washington on conditions in the island. The latter aspect gives insight into the gradual formation of United States policy, and it will be treated in the next chapter.

The period of military dominance in Puerto Rico was begun by Major General Nelson A. Miles who, from July 25 to August 14, 1898, possessed full civil and military control of the island. He withdrew, leaving the command with Major General John R. Brooke who, along with Rear Admiral W. S. Schley and Brigadier General William W. Gordan, met with General Ricardo Ortega to discuss the withdrawal of Spanish forces. On October 18, 1898, when the last Spanish forces had withdrawn, General Brooke became the military governor. He held this post until relieved by Major General Guy V. Henry on December 9 of the same year. Henry was replaced by Brigadier General George W. Davis on May 9, 1899, and the latter ended his term of duty as governor when the first civil governor, Charles H. Allen, was inaugurated on May 1, 1900.

From a legal point of view, this period of the United States' occupation can be divided into three parts. The first is the time of military action that ended with the peace protocol of August 14, 1898. The second is the interim that terminated with the exchange of ratifications of the Treaty of Paris on April 11, 1899. During the first two periods, it was the duty of the United States to further the military aims under international law. In the last period, the United States, under terms of the Treaty of Paris, was bound to determine the civil rights and political status of Puerto Rico. This obligation was complicated by the adjournment of Congress before making provision for Puerto Rico. The open question was: what powers might a military government exert without authorization of Congress?[2]

The first expression of the military authorities on civil rights was made by General Miles in his proclamation to the people of Puerto Rico on July 28, 1898. It reads in part:

> As a consequence of the war which necessitated action by the United States against Spain, in defense of Liberty, Justice, and Humanity, her military forces have come to occupy the Island of Puerto Rico. . . . They bring you the armed support

of a free nation, whose great power rests in her justice and humanity for all who live under her protection. . . . The primary effect of this occupation will be the immediate transition from your former system of government, desiring that you accept with joy the system of the Government of the United States.

The principal aim of the American forces will be to abolish the armed authority of Spain and to give to this beautiful Island the greatest degree of liberty compatible with military occupation. We have not come to bring war against a people which has been oppressed for centuries; but . . . to bring protection, not only to you, but also to your property, promoting your prosperity and bestowing upon you the guarantees and the blessings of the liberal institutions of our Government.[3]

General Miles, appointed military governor in command of the Army of Occupation and administrator of civil affairs, was empowered to issue orders that had the force of law, in accord with General Orders 101, Series 1898. This power he used when instructing Major General J. H. Wilson that "it becomes their [Puerto Rico's] duty to yield obedience to the authority of the United States, the power of the military occupant being absolute and supreme and immediately operating upon the political conditions of the inhabitants."[4]

General Miles, while allowing the usual courts and town councils to continue functioning, was preoccupied with the absolute power of the military. Municipal laws affecting persons and property and punishment for crime, along with the constituted judges, were continued in force as long as they were submissive to the United States military commander. Where there was need for the maintenance of law and order, he empowered his subordinates to abolish or change tribunals and to replace or expel officials. In this, the officer was to be guided by his own "judgment and a high sense of justice." The native police force was to be continued "so far as may be practicable." And lastly, the personnel of the United States Army was not subject to the criminal courts of the island. In respect to trade, ports were to be opened to all neutral nations as long as it was noncontraband and upon the payment of the prescribed duties.

Consequent upon these instructions, custom-house, criminal, and civil courts were opened within the area of United States occupation. The official exchange rate was set at two Puerto Rican (Spanish) pesos to one United States dollar. From the date of United States occupation of the Puerto Rican ports to February 1, 1899, the tariff of duties and taxes levied and collected was fixed by the president in his executive order dated August 19, 1898; these rates differed from those of local Spanish and continental United States rates. The collection of the customs was made by United States Army officers who kept these receipts separate from the other insular revenues. After July 6, 1899, all of these revenues were paid in full to the treasurer of Puerto Rico.

During this period, there were serious violations of public order by bandits who committed violence against both Spanish and native merchants and planters. This can be explained in part by the serious poverty of the people and by the remembrance of their exploitation during the period of the wartime blockade by the United States. Though the military intervened to protect the people, it was difficult to pursue the bandits into the mountain fastnesses. It was clearly attested, however, that "the disorderly element is a very small fraction" and that "the timidity of the property owners is largely due to the paternal system to which they have become accustomed."[5]

Because the period of General Miles's control of the island ended with the peace protocol of August 14, 1898, it was so short-lived that it did not give rise to the disillusionment of the people of Puerto Rico. It did, however, contain within its military orders the plans that would burgeon into bitterness under Generals Brooke and Henry. The great majority of the people, as Tomás Blanco remarks, merely reflected the confusion of the leaders (*los estratos superiores*); as the word of liberation from Spain passed from lip to lip, they took interest and enthusiasm.[6] It was to be in the days of other governors— military and civil—that they would learn resentment.

GENERAL BROOKE: OCTOBER 18, 1898, TO DECEMBER 9, 1898

As we have already seen, the basic authority for the United States Military Government in Puerto Rico was found in General Orders, No. 101, of 1898. This authorized the military governor to change existing laws. But in changing codes not in conflict with the Constitution of the United States, some of their acts may have been in excess of their authority. Nevertheless, in the absence of instructions, it was regarded as the duty of the military governor to use the means preparatory to a territorial regime.[7]

General John R. Brooke assumed command as governor of Puerto Rico on October 18, 1898. He is described by Roberto H. Todd as "a military man who always acted in character and who was very pompous, grave, and slightly communicative." Todd describes an interview with General Brooke that was quickly terminated when he noticed that the letter of introduction from Theodore Roosevelt—then governor of New York—had misspelled his name. In praise of General Brooke, Todd quoted a cabinet member as saying that "he was always attentive and courteous with them" and that he respected the autonomous government set up by Spain under the presidency of Muñoz Rivera.[8] His determination to command, however, became obvious, as appears in a letter from Dr. Carbonell, secretary of public works, written three days before Brooke became military governor. The secretary corrected the impression that Muñoz Rivera, in asking for revolvers "to arm the American police in this city," was arrogating "the supreme authority which he in the said letter recognizes as being Your Excellency's." He attributed the error to bad faith in the interpreter and expressed his eagerness to serve the governor "in either a public or private capacity."[9]

With no directives from the Congress of the United States, General Brooke proceeded to make what he considered necessary changes. By act of October 18, 1898, he divided Puerto Rico into two civil and military jurisdictions, with Ponce placed under Brigadier General Guy V. Henry and San Juan under Brigadier General F. D. Grant. This announcement in the *Gaceta Oficial* was accompanied by a copy of the Constitution of the United States; and on October 22, extensive laws pertaining to the constitution of territories were printed. The use of English in the *Gaceta* first appeared on October 26 when General Brooke ordered the opening of the normal schools. On that same date, the spelling of the island's name was arbitrarily changed to "Porto Rico."[10]

Shortly after taking office, General Brooke reiterated many of the laws that had been issued as orders by General Miles. His first order was a clarification of the supremacy of the military, adding that "Wherever the inhabitants yield obedience to the civil representatives of law and order, it is not intended that the military shall intervene." Secondly, provincial and municipal laws, in respect to the rights of persons and property, were to be enforced, "unless they are incompatible with the changed conditions of Puerto Rico." Lastly, private property, the property of the United States, as well as that belonging to provincial government or municipalities, along with schools, churches, and religious houses, had to be protected. The "Council of Secretaries," which had been brought into existence during the Autonomous Constitution of 1897, was to continue, and all local centers of administration in the island were to maintain relations with it. This council was composed of Luis Muñoz Rivera, secretary of government; Juan Hernández López, secretary of justice; Julián E. Blanco, secretary of finance; and Dr. Salvador Carbonell, secretary of public works.

The tax system established by Spain was continued by General Brooke with a few exceptions. He especially emphasized that "the territorial tax levied on rural and town property, on cultivation and cattle growing, and on industry and commerce, shall continue in force as heretofore." He was insistent that taxpayers and officials "hasten to perform their duties," since this would prevent him from having to resort to extreme measures.[11] He did, however, abolish all taxes on contracts and on property in its transfer of title.

The first month of General Brooke's work was highly approved at Washington as is evidenced by a letter of November 16, 1898, from the adjutant general's office: "The President no less than the Secretary of War feels that you should remain in Porto Rico at least until Congress provides for a form of government and it is put under way. If, however, at any time you feel you should come back, don't hesitate to say so and I will take pleasure in seeing that this . . . has careful and if possible, favorable consideration."[12]

General Brooke abolished the Provincial Assembly (Diputación Provincial) on November 29, 1898, since he regarded it as "wholly unnecessary and incompatible with the present administration of public affairs." The duties assigned it under the Autonomous Constitution of 1897 were reassigned to the Insular Council. The secretary of government was to take charge of charitable institutions, public health, and the examination of accounts; the secretary of public works (*fomento*) was to have charge of public works and education; the secretary of finance (*hacienda*) was to take over the existing assets and liabilities of the defunct representative assembly, collecting its claims and liquidating its debts. In addition, he created a commission with the following members: a secretary of justice, an assistant secretary of finance, an attorney of the supreme court, and an assistant secretary of government. This commission was assigned the duty of ascertaining the assets and liabilities in the departments of government.

Since the transfer of sovereignty had left the island without a supreme court, General Brooke, on October 26, appointed the members of a new court, retaining two members of the former court. On

December 2, under General Order No. 19, the supreme commander decreed that a full bench of the Supreme Court was to "hear all the appeals pending decision." In respect to cases that were pending decision before the Supreme Court of Madrid, they were to be "claimed through diplomatic channels . . . and transferred to the hearing of the Supreme Court of Justice" in Puerto Rico.[13]

The re-establishment of an effective court system was one of the chief concerns of General Brooke, since it was in this period that the north-western section of the island—Arecibo, Lares, San Sebastián, and Las Marías—was suffering from outrages and murders. These were mostly directed against Spanish property owners, and this activity "no doubt had its origin in old grievances for fancied or actual wrongs done under a system of peonage and oppression that was little less than the worst form of slavery. . . ." The general, however, reported that the troops soon brought this situation under control. He further explained that his purpose was "to leave undisturbed existing conditions, believing it to be for the best interests of the Island that the former system of laws, though unequal and oppressive in many respects . . . rather than to run the chance of chaos and disorder by instituting changes with which the people were unfamiliar because of their language and the general lack of education which prevails." In cases where he suspended the law—"this has been seldom"—and made new appointment of officials, he required "the unanimous action of the Council of Secretaries." While he admitted not having followed their advice "in many instances," he was convinced that their recommendations were based on "patriotic and unselfish motives, and that they have at heart the best interests of the islands." The general also had the prisons investigated; and on the recommendation of the secretary of justice, released a number of prisoners who had been confined "for political or trivial offenses and had never been tried."[14]

In this long report to the adjutant general, General Brooke stated that the schools were reopened by mid-November, that English was required as an important feature of the curriculum, and that "out of a population of nearly 900,000 not more than about 30,000 can read and write." He stated that the Puerto Rican budget of 1897-98 showed a surplus of $403,157.81 that had disappeared, since he found the treasury empty. Lastly, General Brooke noticed that the courts were slow to produce convictions because of intimidation from the criminals. To remedy this difficulty, he created, on December 8,

1898, a special military commission for the trial of such cases. The effectiveness of this new instrument of justice was immediate when it became clear that trial would be brought "without partiality, favor, or affection," and conviction would produce a sentence.[15] These military commissions remind one of the courts of Star Chamber that the Tudors set up in England in order to remedy the judicial disorder consequent upon the Wars of the Roses. They likewise served an initial good purpose.

In answering the question of Puerto Rico's reaction to the Brooke regime, we have to realize that it was a short period of only two months, a time of much confusion. We do, however, have a direct statement by Luis Muñoz Rivera who, when asked by United States Commissioner Henry K. Carroll if the system of the Autonomous Charter was then in operation, replied: "I cannot consider that we are today an autonomous government, because the fact of the invasion dissolved the chambers, and the secretaries are not responsible members of the government. They have to appeal to General Brooke." His recommendation was equally direct; "Porto Ricans desire that the military occupation should be as brief as possible."[16]

The island's press is another source of interesting information on the people's reaction. As early as September 20, 1898, Herminio Díaz Navarro was writing in a dispassionate tone of the opportunities for Puerto Rico under United States' dominance.[17] In early November, 1898, *La Democracia* expressed faith in the expansive, liberal, and democratic policy of the United States in dealing with its colonies. The editorial speaks of Puerto Rico as in a transitory period, hoping to convert itself into an "autonomous people" with the dissolution of the old parties and their bitterness. Again this paper gives indirect praise to the United States by means of an article quoted from *The Ladies' Home Journal* in which the United States is shown to be superior to all European nations in size and number of houses, inventions, ships, telephones, typewriters, commerce, mines, industry, gold, railroad, schools and libraries. A little delicate criticism, however, is suggested by an editorial of Alejandro Albizu, in which he urges that instead of sending United States troops into the hill country to check bandits who are ravaging the farms, General Brooke need only issue a proclamation to the local authorities, telling the people that the United States will do justice to all. He explains these happenings as a result of "our former administration."[18]

Two further news items in *La Democracia* reveal that the press was becoming disillusioned with some Americans. On November 12, there was the description of an American missionary who preached and sang in English in the public plaza, drawing about him a hundred curious onlookers. When the preacher became well worked up, Don Eduardo Newman mounted the improvised stage and re- marked to the throng that this was a "sufficiently well civilized people; that such manifestations were ridiculous; and that each one will alone work out his welfare by his own means." Thereupon the crowd applauded Newman, who was promptly led off to the army camp by two American guards. In protest, an immense throng gathered outside the camp, and within a few minutes, "the profane orator" was released. In the "general news" of *La Democracia,* there was a report of another American who, while in the theater, La Perla, took off a shoe that annoyed him and rested his foot on the back of the seat in front of him. This act drew the laughter of the audience and the commentator's remark that "these tourists from the North are funny (*chuscos*) and above all, friends of comfort."[19]

The press also reflected the bitterness that existed between the two factions of the Autonomist Liberal party, i.e., "Liberales" (Fusionistas) and "Puros" (Ortodoxos). On the matter of friend- ship with the United States, *La Nueva Era* (Puros) charged the secretariat of the island government with being Hispanophiles and so unable to appreciate the spirit of the American Constitution. *La Democracia* (Liberales) replied that *El Autonomista* (original name of *La Nueva Era*) had been most strong in protesting loyalty to Spain and had spoken of Americans as "hucksters" (*mercachifles*), but after the invasion this language had changed to elegies and dithy- rambs. By December 5, *La Democracia* was more blunt in its criticism of the Americans who had come to the island and of their official organ, the *San Juan News.* It spoke of the Americans as "a cloud of adventurers who undoubtedly believed that Puerto Rico was open for conquest." It charged the *San Juan News* with stating that those papers that would not conform to their political ideas (*política ratonera*), could go to Spain; and it maintained that it was going to ask that the military power be kept in Puerto Rico.[20]

This paper described itself as "an American newspaper, the only one on the Island. We are supported by and owe our existence to the best people of Puerto Rico of all classes. For it is the wealthiest and best people in this island who understand the English language." This periodical obviously antagonized many Puerto Ricans; it was strongly pro-American, Republican, and Protestant. Its columns carried constant references to the arrivals and labors of Protestant ministers; its Christmas issue was filled with Anglo-Saxon joy in the form of holly, evergreen, Santa Claus, and turkey.[21]

These overtones of Yankeeland were perfectly in accord with the freedom of the press but were seriously lacking in tact when we consider the sensitivity of a Latin people who had ever resented the many implications of the "Black Legend" when expressed by Anglo-Saxons. In *La Democracia,* there is a caustic reference to a Reverend Pastor Manuel Fernando of the evangelical sect that "is devoted to the sport of pamphlets" and whose philosophico-religious tracts were resented. The editorial argued: "We do not need to be educated by any Fernando. . . . If there is any liberty of religion in this country, then let each one embrace the religion that better suits him, while respecting the rights of others."[22]

This growing resentment expressed itself in a feud between *La Correspondencia* and the *San Juan News.* The editor of the Liberal paper acknowledged with sarcasm the remark of the *News* that it did not oppose the continuance of *La Correspondencia* and the *Boletín Mercantil,* "as long as we behave like good boys. . . ." It added: "Our gratitude knows no limits. Thanks, Señor Elefante." In sharp reply to the *News's* statement that those disapproving of things on this side of the Atlantic can take a steamer to Spain, the Liberal journal remarked that "we Puerto Ricans who are respectful of the law have a better right to remain in this land that those adventurers who come here in a thirst of wealth."[23]

In this same spirit of criticism, Luis Bonafoux, correspondent of *La Correspondencia,* wrote from Paris of the approaching signing of the treaty. He described the Spaniards as a great family come to grief, who with their sad gravity and incurable melancholy come to a breakfast of chocolate and buns. On the other hand, the Americans are early to rise; and after bathing and shaving, they come in their summer suits to a breakfast of ham and eggs, sweets, tea, and milk. On the political issues, he commented that: "The Yankee commissioners will cede nothing, nothing, nothing. The American Government, aided by the English Government, will carry out their *expansionism* to the seizure of all the Philippine Archipelago. And no nation will prevent it, certainly not our fallen Spain. It doesn't seem possible that anyone will intervene, not even Germany, because of the influence of England.''[24] This alertness of Puerto Rico to the action of the United States in other sections of the world became more noticeable when she saw the growing hopelessness of achieving from the United States something similar to the Autonomous Constitution of 1897. Her press was closely following the revolt of the Philippine patriots against the United States, and her sympathies were with the Filipinos and General Aguinaldo, their leader.

Another area of grievance was the result of the drunken brawls of some soldiers and sailors. Because of their abuses, an editorial urged that they be prohibited from wandering through the streets at all hours of night and that they should be prevented from carrying fire-arms except when on active duty. A representative expression is found in Jesús María Amadeo who found his country chilling towards United States occupation because of constant incidents between troops and civilians. While noting that the goddess of liberty was suffering in this emancipated land, he added: ''We who know the North American nation do not lose faith in its future.''[25] By the end of General Brooke's regime, the story of disenchantment was well under way. In an undated letter (probably early 1899), a certain ''Wright'' reported a conversation with General Brooke. It reflects the General's analysis of his success in Puerto Rico and in Cuba:

> While stationed on the western frontier [of the United States] my attention was drawn to the subject of the Latin American races and I spent several years in the study of the subject. I find the information then obtained very valuable now, but military men are not experienced in affairs of civil government and there are many perplexing questions which we find ourselves unprepared for.
>
> Here for instance, is a remonstrance against the free importation of Porto Rican coffee into Cuba. An intelligent decision requires hours of study in tariffs, crop reports, markets, etc. . . . Military rule, at best, is only a temporary expedient, and I suppose, in due time, a civil government with sufficient military force to preserve order will follow.[26]

In reviewing the action of General Brooke in Puerto Rico, it seems clear that he was a sincere, honest, and efficient military governor— a man who fulfilled his duty as he understood it and with no little ability.

GENERAL HENRY: DECEMBER 9, 1898, TO MAY 9, 1899

While resentment against the United States' occupation was growing daily, General Brooke was replaced by Brigadier General Guy
V. Henry on December 6, 1898. Henry has been described by Roberto
Todd as "thin and boney," with a type of character that changed
quickly from an affable tone to one of annoyance. He "admitted no
discussion, nor that anyone contradict him; he commanded and
wished to be obeyed." Todd also noted in the new general an ability
for good friendship; "he has the goodness to treat us with kindness,
and even consulted us on some very delicate matters."[27] Before
taking up the position of governor, General Henry had formed some
definite opinions of Puerto Rico, as is evidenced by his letter written
to the adjutant general from Ponce on December 3, 1898. He saw the
need of two regiments of United States Cavalry to preserve law and
order. This force he was determined to use in the pursuit of justice:
"The indifference to bringing men to trial or punishment which we
have not yet been able to do in the civil courts, seems to encourage
these men in their depredations. . . . It is almost impossible to get any
of these men to give evidence as to who are the guilty parties . . . due
to this indifference or fear on the part of the inhabitants."[28]

Within a few hours after the general took office, the members of
the Insular Cabinet that had been formed under the Autonomous
Constitution resigned. General Henry refused to accept their resignations and so won the praise of *La Democracia*.[29] This initial good impression was brief, for the General was bluntly determined to do an
efficient job. While honest and hard-working, he was not patient or
tactful. This is evident in one of his first letters to the adjutant
general in Washington:

> I am getting in touch with the people and trying to educate
> them to the idea that they must help govern themselves, giving
> them kindergarten instruction in controlling themselves with-
> out allowing them too much liberty, and in this way satisfy
> their . . . pride that they have some interest in their own gov-
> ernment. . . .
> Allowance must be made for reports received from here
> as the people, notwithstanding their gentle and peaceful
> nature, have acquired very liberally the Spanish habit of lying
> and cannot be trusted. Lying seems to be one of their virtues
> . . . to each other as well as to outsiders. This may have resulted
> from dishonest administration. . . . It is hard for them to
> realize that an official can be in power without making money,

so they naturally accuse everyone in office of making all they can out of it, they taking advantage of the same opportunity when placed in a similar position.[30]

With such a generalization in mind, General Henry was doomed to some tactless dealings with the people of Puerto Rico. Though, on retiring from his position in early May, he expressed his sincere liking for the people, he had by then elicited much enmity from the leaders, especially Muñoz Rivera.

One of the first acts of the general was to arrange for a meeting of the delegates from the principal towns of the island, along with the Cabinet of the Insular Council. The purpose of this meeting was to discuss the wishes of the people; but the general made it quite clear that he would conduct the meeting. His program included the following: improved sanitation methods; revised election standards, since only 14 per cent of the people were said to be literate; education in English, with women school teachers brought from the United States at $50.00 per month; the United States police system; and a check on the freedom of the press. In the meeting, he also made a strong point of union of effort between the two political parties. This meeting was said to have been marked by a friendly spirit.[31]

During the last days of the year 1898, General Henry issued some important decrees. One of the first of these was an order from President McKinley which forbade the granting of public franchises in Puerto Rico for the construction of public works, "except upon the approval of the major-general commanding the military forces of the United States in Puerto Rico, who shall before approving any such grant or concession be so especially authorized by the Secretary of War."[32] This act of the president appears to be in accord with what he described as his desire "to put the conscience of the American people into the islands of the sea."[33] In late December, Henry ordered strict enforcement of sanitary regulations and forbade—in the interest of the poor—the taxing of bread and fresh meat. In the order he imposed a heavy tax on alcohol and tobacco, hoping that it would close a number of saloons and so remove the temptation of drink. He spoke of it as a vice that "tends to demoralize its people, cause misery and suffering to the innocent, and interfere materially with moral progress, upon which depends the success of any nation."[34]

The year ended in a full-scale conflict between the military government and the local press. The issue got under way when *La Democra-cia* editorialized on its belief that, in time, the military government would be removed. On the next day, the military government made it very clear that "This General Government does not allow the publica-tion of writings in which reference is made to the Army of the United States or to the Military Government, lest the extreme case of such publicity can be justified with conclusive proof." This issue brought charges and countercharges within the press of the island. *El Imparcial* and *La Nueva Era* made the charge that *La Democracia* was censuring the United States government. This organ of the Liberal Autonomist party replied that it was friendly to the United States government but had no intention of abdicating its right to criticism; it believed in a free press. Another editorial spoke of the great United States tradition of the freedom of the press. With implied criticism of the United States, it then attacked by looking forward to a new year that might bring liberty and progress, not dictatorship and injustice.[35]

The same spirit of criticism appeared in the columns of *La Cor-respondencia* which, while praising General Henry for his desire to prefer native Puerto Ricans for government posts, noted that the chief of the American police deemed it his task alone to select his subordinates. This meant the rejection of the selections made by the town council of San Juan. And so, the paper concluded: "Such an attitude in conflict with the autonomy of the councils [*ayuntami-entos*] . . . has profoundly disgusted the councillors [*concejales*] and public opinion."[36]

The vigorous editor of *La Democracia,* Mariano Abril, carried his battle over into the new year when he charged the opposition party, Republicans (Puros), with making trouble by their attacks on Muñoz Rivera. He characterized Muñoz as a man who was sacrificing his personal life for the benefit of the Insular Cabinet. He asked: "What would happen to the political and juridical personality of Puerto Rico, if the council were to disappear and if the island were left absolutely in the hands of the military government, a government that doesn't understand our way of life?" After this bit of innuendo, he sought to lighten the blow by quoting Henry's statement that he desired to govern with the representatives of the people and even preferred them to Americans for governmental posts. Abril again returned to the attack by citing Senator Teller to the effect that though the United States had taken possession of Cuba, Puerto Rico, and the Philippines, they were not under such colonial control as India was under Britain. Abril's acid comment was that this expression of Teller's was a bit of rhetoric for the benefit of the press and the public and that it would have more meaning when it was given definite resolution.

Mariano Abril maintained the necessity of a government of Puerto Rico by Puerto Ricans when he urged that Puerto Rico become American—not by waves of Americans "coming here to absorb us" but by Puerto Ricans going to the United States to learn new ways and ideas and then bringing them back to the island. He believed that his country was in a paradoxical situation: "We are and we are not Americans. . . . The flag . . . flies over the capital . . . but the territory . . . has no prerogatives, because it has no personality. And where there are no personal rights [*fueros*], there can be no right [*derecho*]; and without right, all responsibilities cease."[37] The editor of *La Democracia*—considering the short patience and military mind of General Henry—was quite daring; and for his direct editorials, he was going to find it convenient within two months to leave Puerto Rico.

While the island's press was growing more critical of the military government, General Henry issued many orders for the solution of pressing problems: tax assessments were imposed in proportion to the value of land and the success of cultivation; the holdings of absentee landlords were heavily taxed; United States regulations on immigration were imposed on Puerto Rico; Catholic cemeteries were to be used "only for the burial of those of that faith"; exhumation and the stacking of bones in the corners of cemeteries became prohibited practices; and the police force of the island was taken away from the control of the Puerto Rican State Department and put directly under the governor general. Frank Techter, an American, was put in charge. Another American, General John Eaton, was appointed superintendent of public instruction for Puerto Rico, and all teachers and school officers were ordered to report to him.[38]

These last appointments came as a result of ever-increasing friction between the governor general and the Insular Council. On February 6, 1899, the first break came with the resignation of Dr. Carbonell, secretary of interior. His tasks were turned over to the military with, as we have seen, General Eaton taking over education and Commander Josiah Pierse given charge of public works and agriculture. On this same day, General Henry dissolved the Insular

Cabinet as "not compatible with American methods and progress." From a council, the posts were converted into independent departments—state, justice, finance, and interior—with the chief of each department under direct control of the governor general. In protest, the secretaries, Luis Muñoz Rivera, Juan Hernández López, and Cayetano Coll y Toste resigned; they demanded a legislative body that would truly represent the people. General Henry rejected their petition as premature and a matter for the legislation of the United States Congress.[39]

A new government was set up on February 12 with Francisco de Paula Acuña as secretary of state, Herminio Díaz Navarro as secretary of justice, Cayetano Coll y Toste as secretary of finance, and Federico Degetau y González as secretary of the interior. It was clear that these "secretaries" of the government were to be mere instruments of the governor general. They had lost the autonomous powers that had been given the Insular Council by the Constitution of 1897; democracy in the island had taken a step backward. These officials were subjected to another change on March 23 when Degetau resigned, and the post of secretary of interior was taken over by Francisco del Valle Atilés.[40]

It is necessary to recall here that the ousting of the Liberal party under the leadership of Muñoz Rivera was not universally reproved. At this time, three members of the opposition party (former Separatists) were in Washington; they were Eugenio M. de Hostos, Manuel Zeno Gandía, and José Julio Henna; their actions may have helped in causing the suppression of the Insular Council. The charge was made that the commissioners had informed the president of the United States that "There are at present practically two governments upon the island: the American military government which is rigid and exacting, and the insular government which is pernicious, insufficient, and altogether without merit, a mere relic of Spanish sovereignty." The truth of this statement was denied by De Hostos in the pages of the *Correo de Puerto Rico*. In answer to the implied charges, Muñoz Rivera stated to a reporter of *La Democracia*:

> Now that the only organism which gave reality to the personality of the country is dissolved, it was impossible for us to continue in the post of the Secretariat. These had lost their character, on being converted into mere offices [*jefaturas*] of the administrative departments, under the inspection of American officials. . . .

We fell from power because we refused to accept the wiping out of the shadow of *self-government* that still existed. . . . We seek to serve the United States; but in serving her, we will never abdicate our ideals. . . . I believe that, before giving us the American laws, they should not take away from us our autonomous law. In Cuba, President McKinley sustains the civil rulers in the full exercise of their former authority.[41]

The final charge of Muñoz Rivera was that General Henry was trying to convert the secretariat into some form similar to the Cabinet of the United States and so was destroying all form of representative government in the island.

One of the most bitterly debated actions of General Henry was his suspension of the law of foreclosure. It was issued on February 12, 1899, and reads: "It is hereby directed in the interest of equity and to save the agricultural industry from loss and ruin that the said law of foreclosure and all legal or judicial proceedings thereunder with reference to agricultural property and machinery be . . . suspended for the period of one year . . . provided that the interest of such debts is paid when due at a rate of not exceeding 12 per cent per annum."[42] The opposition came in part from John G. Meyers who, representing Spanish business interests, found that it "paralyzed the credit system on the whole island." Unemployment became widespread because there was no capital with which to pay the workingmen. Meyers' clients charged that Henry did this with intent to ruin Spanish enterprises.[43] Another objection was raised by W. S. H. Lathrop of Boston, Massachusetts, who described himself as having lived in Puerto Rico almost since the beginning of United States occupation. He charged that the order was a serious mistake, for in Puerto Rico "the basis of all credit is the mortgages on land." The general's order made it impossible to raise money for improvements.[44] In favor of the suspension was Henry K. Carroll, who admitted having urged General Henry to issue the foreclosure order. He found it an emergency measure in a country where money was scarce because of poor banking facilities and retiring Spaniards who took large amounts of cash with them. He maintained that bankers and merchants were holding money and granting no credit or, if they were granting credit it was at rates of interest up to 24 per cent. He believed that it had brought relief to the planters and added that the hurricane of August, 1899, had been responsible for the extensive hardship in the island.[45]

While the foreclosure law was under debate, the issue of the freedom of the press became more pointed. For its direct criticism, *La Democracia* was brought to court; it exulted in being "the first periodical to suffer a civil process under the new American system. Until the present, all the papers that had been fined or suppressed were so treated by the military authority; *La Democracia* was under "direct denunciation of the court."[46] By order of February 24, 1899, *La Metralla* of Ponce was suspended from publication, and its editor was brought to trial "for publishing an article derogatory to a public official."[47] In the battle that ensued, *La Democracia* strongly criticized the injustice of the courts. On February 28, it published a letter from Charles M. Boerman, a member of the New York bar and a resident of Puerto Rico. He said: "You very rightly say that Puerto Rico should be governed by Puerto Ricans. Home-rule is the true American and democratic doctrine. It is that of the party that follows the path [*derrotero*] marked out by the great democrat Thomas Jefferson."[48] On the same day, Dr. Rodríguez Castro of San Juan had a letter in *El Territorio* stating that the small-pox vaccinations were expensive and harmful. He ended his letter: "I am not a Tagalo, nor from Hawaii, nor a redskin." Within a week, an order from General Henry's headquarters was addressed to the editor stating that "any similar articles appearing in his newspaper will at once result in the suspension of that paper. . . . The Secretary of State will at once notify Dr. Castro to discontinue his articles criticizing the Government, or to suffer such penalty as the case merits."[49]

By this time, *La Democracia* realized that its only hope must be in Washington. And so, the editor, Mariano Abril, left Puerto Rico for the United States. His interim editors, Gumersindo Rivas and Rosendo Rivera Colón, praised him as "one of the most intimate friends of Muñoz; together they had carried the burdens of the political campaign." The party of Muñoz was not in favor in Washington, and *La Democracia* cited an article in *The Independent* (Washington) which reflected the American attitude toward the Liberal party of Puerto Rico:

> He [Muñoz Rivera] is a man of great natural ability, born to be a leader, though fulfilling it wrongly. He is an egoist and of slight scruple.
>
> When an autonomist, he was accused by his former party fellows of having sold out to Sagasta, and that by the favor

of the last Governor General—though he then had no official position—he took charge of the elections for the first autonomist legislature in a manner that was both violent and unscrupulous [*engañosa*]. . . .

It is said that this autocratic politician will soon come to Washington to exert his influence for the removal of General Henry. We believe that his mission will fail.

At the same time, General Henry was having his problems with the press of the United States. Rumors had been spread that there would be an armed revolt in the island. This false report was quickly answered by General Henry who cabled the War Department and informed the *San Juan News* that the reports "are absolutely false. . . . There have always been political agitations here, but they are now less than before. The truth ought to be known in the United States, and no injury should be done to the island by false reports."[50] On April 14, General Henry decreed that all periodicals were to come under the direct control of the military government.[51]

There are many instances of the strong-arm methods of General Henry. Early in his regime, it was reported to him that the military was interfering with the proceedings of the town councils. He immediately instructed Secretary of State Muñoz Rivera that "There is no authority for officers or soldiers to interfere with the proceedings of the town councils, or even to enter therein." He took instant action against an officer who was charged with interfering with the civil court's proceedings in Toa-baja. On the other hand, where he believed that disorder and corruption existed among the councilmen, he suspended civil authority; such use of power was made in Aguadilla and Moca.[52] One of the most typical examples of General Henry's use of power is found in an order of February 20, 1899: "Alcaldes and councilmen are reminded that orders are issued to be obeyed. . . . It can not be too strongly impressed upon municipal councils that the interests of the municipalities depend upon their honesty, zeal, and attention to duty."[53]

While a triangular friction among the party of Muñoz Rivera, the "Puros," and the military government was growing in the island, General Henry was kept busy at work. With his approval, Secretary of Justice Herminio Díaz Navarro established a new code of marriage regulations. The following are some of the interesting provisions: first, marriage is prohibited to priests or members of religious groups that are prohibited by vow; second, both civil and religious marriages are allowed; third, marriage of those in the direct line of descent or in the collateral line to the third degree is forbidden; fourth, accomplices in the murder of a spouse are forbidden to marry; fifth, divorce is allowed on the grounds of adultery, violence, corruption of children, the permanent confinement of a party, and absolute impotence. This divorce was to be absolute, that is, it allowed civil remarriage. Additional legislation provided that Puerto Ricans were allowed to enlist in the United States Army; state and church buildings were exempted from taxation; children were subjected to a curfew on the streets at night, and the police were ordered to work for their good morals; regulations were drawn up for the public schools, normal schools, and for the organization of a university; qualifications for teachers were set down, and an eight-hour day was decreed; and extensive rules were offered in the establishing of a branch of the SPCA. A last attempt was made by General Henry to gain good will when he exhorted the Puerto Rican people to regard with favor the generous efforts of the United States government. He also issued a judicial order of amnesty for all those arrested by Spain in the exercise of their individual rights, and he stopped all legal proceedings against those charged with abuse of a free press during the rule of the United States.[54]

By the end of May, 1899, General Henry was recalled from Puerto Rico at his own request and replaced by Brigadier General George W. Davis. Returning to New York City, Henry died there on November 4, 1899. In attempting to evaluate his five months of administration, one must recognize the complexity of the problems that faced him and his own rigid temperament. Roberto Todd in recalling those first days of the military government relates an incident in which Federico Degetau y González, the secretary of interior, met him outside the governor's office. Degetau was presenting to the governor a petition of some ladies of Caguas in behalf of an American soldier who had been court-martialed for a horrible crime. Todd was asked to join them as interpreter and, in the interview, quickly noticed that the general became impatient as Degetau protracted the introduction. In reply to the petition, General Henry said that he would give it due consideration, and then, bowing to the ladies, he hurried out of the room. During the interview he never addressed the ladies, but the next day the soldier's sentence was commuted from death to life imprisonment.[55]

As we have seen, the friction that developed between Muñoz Rivera and General Henry was sharp. In a letter to *La Democracia* on May 13, 1899, Muñoz Rivera attributed the removal of "that [person of] neurotic temperament" from Puerto Rico to his errors and to the energy of the secretariat. Muñoz maintained that he had given information to the Kennedy Commission, to General Brooke, and to the minister of war. Though he desired no evil for Henry, he believed that "he was transforming my country into a madhouse." Within three days, *La Democracia* published a letter from Robert Graham, a British subject, who denied that the action of General Henry had made Puerto Rico a madhouse. He found that the general had increased order within the island; he charged that the real evil could be attributed to the political system of Puerto Rico. In rebutting this, the newspaper listed arguments against General Henry as follows: first, he suppressed and threatened the press; second, he resisted and threatened the authority of the City Council (Ayuntamiento) of San Juan; third, the president of the Court of Justice in Ponce was forced, while the court was in full session, to go before General Henry in order to assist him as a notary; fourth, he freed from jail in Guayama certain criminals without consulting the mayor or the judge.[56]

In evaluating the work of General Henry, one must remember that his position had been a difficult one and that, though he often failed in tact, he was honest, well-intentioned, and effected much good. He came as a military commander to a people who had regarded the United States as the great democratic power of the world and who believed that they would receive from the North Americans even more than had been granted under the Autonomous Charter of 1897. Their disappointment in failing to achieve this brought bitterness. The party conflicts within the island only succeeded in confusing Washington, which believed that a military government would for a time be the most effective instrument of United States sovereignty. It was also quite normal that the occupying power would look with greater favor on the newly formed Republican (Puros) party that showed greater friendship to the United States. It is also true that the policy of the United States government was not very subtle; it had failed to make overtures to the Muñoz party that had won autonomy from Spain and had a large backing in the island.

GENERAL DAVIS : MAY 9, 1899, TO MAY 1, 1900

When the first civil governor, Charles H. Allen, submitted his report to the president of the United States, he acknowledged "the valuable assistance rendered him by General Davis."[57] That the general was both a capable and tactful man seems to be confirmed by all. *La Democracia* printed a letter from Mariano Abril—written on May 11, 1899—in which he expressed confidence in President McKinley and General Davis. This is significant because this Liberal paper found that the labors of Muñoz Rivera were under attack at that time by the opposition party and by Dr. Henry K. Carroll.[58] The record of General Davis in the island is a testimonial to his level-headedness, integrity, and deep sympathy with the people. He dealt tactfully with Puerto Rico but did not compromise principle for popularity. A decade after his governorship, he expressed his personal reactions in a conference at Lake Mohonk:

> Among the native inhabitants of this beautiful and rich island I have many acquaintances I prize and whose friendship I would be pained to lose. It is possible and I also fear probable, that some of my friends still hold views at wide variance with those here expressed, but whatever may be the merits of their position . . . all Porto Ricans have learned that not by means of an attempted paralysis of their government are they likely to succeed in its reform. *I was glad to see ended the military rule that I once exercised and to see launched nearly ten years ago a civil regime that should not require for its maintenance the intervention of superior power.*[59]

In his thorough reports, directed to the adjutant general of the army, he spoke sympathetically but honestly of the island. Though he attested "the universal kindness and deference that has been extended to me by the native Porto Ricans," he found it necessary "to advert in strong terms to the general unfitness of the great mass of the people for self-government."[60]

One of the most pressing problems that presented itself to General Davis was the existing law in Puerto Rico and the operation of the courts. Though both General Brooke and General Henry had proclaimed the continuance of Spanish law in the island, they had also seen the conflict of some parts with the law of the United States; and in the absence of Congress' provision of an organic act for the island, they abolished some Spanish laws and set up American law by decree. This was not done arbitrarily, but wherever they believed that it served the common good. General Davis was presented with petitions that the delays in the courts be remedied, that much of the Spanish law be abolished, and that conflicts with United States law be removed. At the same time, he was quite aware that the Spanish system of law had evolved over the centuries, that it was customary with the people, and that some aspects of United States law were inapplicable to Puerto Rico. For this reason, he changed only what he believed to be urgent.

In speaking of the courts of Puerto Rico, he guardedly remarked that "they are probably the same as are the Spanish courts everywhere, more or less corrupt and inefficient. . . ." This idea he received from various petitions. One group of twenty-four, describing itself as businessmen who had already petitioned Dr. Carroll, President McKinley, the Insular Commission, and General Henry, complained that "the offense of the official class against the person and property of the people is proverbial." They stated that "judges here, as in Spain, allowed their decisions to be influenced by the political leaders and Caciques, and when a fault is in the habit of a people it survives for generations." Their solution was "to wipe out Spanish law and Spanish politics; and to set up the American system."[61]

General Davis' reform of the courts began on May 24, 1899, when he ordered that the judges of instruction and courts of justice in the island take over from the military commissions the trial of criminal cases still pending. It will be remembered that General Brooke had set up these courts a half year before, with the intent of giving prompt justice to brigands that had intimidated the regular courts. By the end of May, Davis again ruled that the writ of *habeas corpus* might be issued by justices of the Supreme Court, by a justice of the *audiencia,* or by a judge of instruction. It was made clear, however, that such issuance would not prevail in favor of a prisoner subject to United States authority. In fuller explanation of this writ, General Davis issued an instruction on July 3 which was a full and new legal device for Puerto Rico.

In order to handle the increasing legal business of the island, General Davis, on the authority of the president of the United States, set up a "United States provisional court." The court consisted of three judges; the law judge was to preside and to decide all technical questions of law, and the associate judge with the trial judge were by a majority vote to determine all matters of fact. The jury system was allowed at the discretion of the court. The court's jurisdiction was to extend to all cases cognizable by the circuit or district courts of the United States; the decisions of the court were to follow the principles of common law and equity. Within a period of ninety days, an appeal for a writ of certiorari to the Supreme Court of the United States was allowed.

Another significant change in the courts was their removal from the control of the Department of Justice, which made the courts free from this secretary's influence. It also discontinued the office of the secretary of justice, replacing it with a department that was under the control of a judicial board of five members who were all to be lawyers and to serve without salary. The administrative control of this new office was put into the hands of a solicitor general. This and other changes in the law of the land were made slowly in order to allow for adaptation. General Davis, in referring to the completed code of the Insular Commission, suggested that "the arbitrary installation at this time of any system, no matter how perfect, would be most unfortunate. . . ." He adverted to California which still "preserves in its laws some features of the old Spanish-Mexican code in force there at the time of its conquest." He hoped that "the same practice will follow here, should an autonomical government be finally established for this island." In late July, General Davis facilitated the operations of the "provisional court" by empowering military commanders as court commissioners with the right to administer oaths, issue warrants of arrest, and hold preliminary hearings. He further ordered that two statutes dealing with conspiracy to overthrow the government of the United States and with the fitting out of filibustering expeditions were to be under the enforcement of the military department of Puerto Rico. He maintained that it was a "well-established principle of American law that if a publication be calculated to alienate the affection of the people by bringing the Government into disesteem . . . the writer and publisher are punishable." In respect to filibustering, he found that no one had a right "to hazard the peace of the country or to violate its laws upon vague notions of altering or reforming governments in other States."[62]

On August 7, General Davis was called upon to handle a novelty in election procedures. The election for municipal officers was held at Adjuntas on July 25, and during the noon hour, the election supervisors left for lunch, taking with them the ballot box. The commanding general was satisfied that "no corrupt practices were resorted to"

but regarded the action "technically as a vitiation of the election."
And so another voting was ordered for August 22. On the same day,
August 7, he ordered the reorganization of the judicial system of
Puerto Rico. The island was divided into five judicial districts, with
capitals at San Juan, Ponce, Mayagüez, Arecibo, and Humacao. The
court was to consist of one chief justice, José Severo Quiñones, and
four associate justices.[63]

In the summer of 1899, the War Department began the translation and publication of the Spanish statutes in force in the islands
ceded by Spain. The intention was to make them available to those
who understood only English. Under Section 40 of the First Organic
Act of Puerto Rico (the Foraker Act), provision was made for a
commission of three members to compile and revise the laws of
Puerto Rico. The codification was intended to contain: first, the laws
of Spanish origin that were applicable to Puerto Rico, along with
those statutes and decrees that were applied to the island; second,
the statutory laws of the United States that were locally applicable;
and third, the military orders promulgated by the commanding
generals of the United States in Puerto Rico. The general was convinced that this was only a stop-gap bit of legal labor; he explained
his idea clearly in a circular. The American Constitution was based
on the "principle that the people themselves are to make and enforce
their own laws." He maintained that he used every means possible
to determine the views of the people, in order that he might adapt the
system of laws to that which Congress may be expected to enact. He
believed that his major task was to adapt the laws and administration
"to suit the change that may soon come and which all desire, that
is, *complete territorial autonomy.*"[64] This is an amazing document
when we consider how advanced the views of General Davis were in
contrast to the Organic Act of 1900.

Another legal problem that General Davis had to handle was
that of the Spaniards who had elected to remain on the island. In
accord with Article IX of the Treaty of 1898, Spaniards who chose to
remain in Puerto Rico were allowed a year in which to determine
whether they desired to retain allegiance to Spain. If such declaration was not made before a court of record within a year from the
time of the exchange of treaty ratifications, these individuals would
be considered to have adopted the nationality of the Puerto Ricans.
The difficult position of these Spaniards was brought out by General
Davis in his testimony before the Senate Committee on Pacific Islands

and Puerto Rico; this committee was discussing the Foraker Act. Davis pointed out that "A large part of the mercantile and exporting houses are owned and conducted by Spaniards, men who under the treaty preserve their Spanish nationality. A great many of the natives who are in debt—and almost every one who could secure credit is in debt—are at the mercy, so to speak, of these creditors. The seizure of these farms by the money lenders, who are often hated only because they are Spaniards, will in the minds of some be regarded as confiscations." He further added that the robbery, pillage, and arson that accompanied and followed the military operations "were largely based on this hatred, I am told."[65] He hoped that the foreclosures that would follow upon the revival of the law of foreclosures would not cause a recurrence of the former lawlessness.

A glaring instance of discrimination against Spaniards is found in the treatment of Spanish lawyers by the secretary of justice, Herminio Díaz Navarro. Under Article IX of the Treaty of Peace, Spaniards were allowed to retain property and to carry on their professions. The secretary of justice, however, by judicial order, limited the right of Spanish lawyers to but one year of practice. General Davis quickly rescinded this unjust decree by the order of May 24, 1899. He argued, first, that the War Department allows them to practice because such is the provision of the Treaty of 1898. Under the term "property" is to be understood the right to practice law, as the Supreme Court states in "Ex parte Garland, 4 Wall. 333"; besides, the treaty mentions the practice of a "profession," and law is a profession. He also argued that the Executive Order of July 13, 1898, which was pertinent to Cuba was also effective in Puerto Rico in its general principles; it stated that under the new political power "the inhabitants . . . are entitled to security in their persons and property and in all their private rights and relations. . . ." Finally, General Davis stated, that there was no instance of a Spanish resident in Puerto Rico who had failed in loyalty to the United States; rather they have "looked upon the American Administration as the emblem of justice and equity toward all." He found no instances of intentional injustice to Spaniards by American officers; but there were instances of gross injustice against Spaniards by American officers who were "artfully deceived by native professional politicians in office, [who were] without public faith or patriotism." A strong charge is made against Herminio Díaz: that he induced Governor Henry "to put his signature under such falsified order (Spanish lawyers)''; such procedure ''is the rule with the Secretary of Justice and with the majority of his professional fellow politicians.''[66]

In turning from a consideration of the legal condition of Puerto Rico to that of the economy during the Davis administration, one sees some very serious problems. Before American occupation, General Davis says, ''there is no conflict of opinion as to the condition in which we found Porto Rico.'' He quoted extensively from Cayetano Coll y Toste whose article in 1897 won the award of the ''Economic Society of Friends of the Country.'' Dr. Coll y Toste wrote:

> If it be true that our population has increased so much that from a census of 138,758 people it has mounted . . . to 802,439 inhabitants, unfortunately, at the heart of such a state of enlightenment a black stain is projected. . . .
>
> Only the laborer, the son of our fields, one of the most unfortunate beings in the world, with a pale face, bare feet, lean body, ragged clothing, and feverish look, walks indifferently, with the shadows of ignorance in his eyes, dreaming of the cockfights, the shuffle of the cards, or the prize in the provincial lottery. . . .
>
> In the miserable cabin, hung on a peak like a swallow's nest, this unhappy little creature comes into the world; when it opens its eyes to the light of reason, it does not hear the village bell reminding him to lift his soul to the Divine One and render homage to the Creator of worlds; he hears only the hoarse cry of the cock crowing in the early morning, and then he longs for the coming of Sunday to witness the strife and knavery of the cockfights. When a man, he takes up with the first woman to be found   and makes her his mistress. . . .
> In the wretched tavern the food he finds is only the putrid salt meat, cod fish filled with rotten red spots, and Indian rice.[67]

The extensive poverty of the people is attested to by General Roy Stone, in a letter of April 10, 1899, to the American Red Cross. He found the hunger of the coffee-workers so terrible that it should arouse the sympathy and prudence of the American nation. ''To allow this friendly and loyal people to suffer and die while we live in the midst of prosperity constitutes not only a scandal for us before the world, but also a danger for our peaceful occupation.''[68]

To add to this already serious situation came the terrible hurricane of August 8, 1899—popularly called San Ciriaco. The immediate result of this hurricane was the death of nearly 3,000 people, and the destruction of millions of dollars worth of property.

Most of the food supply was destroyed, and starvation threatened. Since about 250,000 of the poor depended on coffee for jobs, and since the maturing crop of 1899 was valued at $7 million, it is obvious what the sudden wiping out of 80 per cent of this crop meant for the island. Banana, corn, and potato crops were also ruined. Roads were rendered impassable and business was paralyzed. There was no money available. Thousands were homeless, and anemia and dysentery were spreading.

On August 12, 1899, General Davis directed a note to the mayors of the island expressing his deep sympathy and informing them that he had petitioned the aid of Washington. He set up a Board of Charity on the island "to take charge of all matters respecting charitable institutions, including homes and asylums for succor of the poor, sick, and incurable . . . together with matters relating to assistance for the suffering by the recent hurricane."[69] Dr. Cayetano Coll y Toste, civil secretary to the governor—a new office created on August 12—made a series of suggestions to the military governor. First, he suggested that a loan of $10 million be made and that the insular treasury be empowered to issue notes of from $1.00 to $100, up to the amount of $10 million. Second, to the landholders in need, 20 per cent of the real value of their arable land was to be facilitated to them in these notes. The loan was to be at 5 per cent yearly interest and payable in ten years by tenth parts. Third, these notes were to be admitted in the payment of municipal taxes and internal revenues up to 50 per cent of taxpayer's due. Lastly, commercial interests, banking houses, and chambers of commerce were to be bound by their own agreement to accept these notes without depreciation.[70]

The civil secretary's plan was not adopted, but United States aid came quickly. By order of the secretary of war, supplies began to arrive; between August, 1899, and May 31, 1900—the last date of arrival of foodstuffs—about 32,445,00 pounds of food came, in addition to considerable quantities of clothing and medicine. The distribution of food was made by ration-cards that stated the indigence of the person and his family, but difficulty arose in determining the degree of indigence, because a large proportion of the population was chronically on the verge of starvation. Another problem was the difficulty of getting vessels to carry food to the coastal towns, because sailors feared a return of hurricanes in the stormy August weather. Mountain roads were impassable, and access to many towns became impossible. As the coastal areas began to recover, the mountain towns suffered terrible poverty because of the time that it took to rebuild roads and bridges. In aid to Puerto Rico, close to $1 million was expended. Needless to say, during this period the island suffered from an unfavorable balance of trade.[71]

At this time of disaster, General Davis divided the island into twelve military districts in order to determine the extent of damage and to aid in the rendering of relief. He also instituted an "advisory board" for the consideration of questions on insular policy, for devising measures in industrial and economic improvements, and for quick relief for sufferers from the storm, especially in the restoration of their homes, fields, and shops.[72] The impact of the continuing poverty of the island appeared in a letter from General Davis to the secretary of war, dated February 26, 1900. In discussing the lack of schools, he admitted that even with increased schools "the attendance would be meager and the result unsatisfactory. The anemic, half-starved and often naked children would not or could not attend." What advantage, he asks, would come to society and to the pupils from schooling if they would then "return to their homes of squalor and filth . . . their parents indifferent or unable to satisfy the natural cravings of hunger and what the children had learned would but make them unhappy and discontented. . . ." He found that the visitor to Puerto Rico from a temperate zone "was shocked at the evidence of the ravages of smallpox and anemia, and was in constant dread of yellow fever."[73]

After seeing the disastrous economic situation of the island during the military governorships, we must consider the political problems that affected Governor General Davis. First of all, the general was strongly convinced that the island was not prepared for self-government: "If universal or manhood suffrage be given to the Porto Ricans bad results are almost certain to follow. . . . The ignorant masses will be manipulated and controlled and corrupted by the political bosses, just as they were accustomed to be by their former masters."[74] Another letter to the adjutant general asserted that there is one class on the island that has held office so long that "they have grown to feel that they have an inherent right to office," and they resent change. A second class works "entirely for their own interest and that of their particular party, under cover of seeking liberty and freedom for Puerto Rico." He concluded his sharp criticism with the statement that "the absence of a middle class is the great drawback to reform and change"; an honest election "would be an impossibility without the closest supervision of American officials."[75]

Since the military governments had little confidence in the municipal elections, a long list of election regulations was promulgated. According to this, an officer of the army was to have charge of the elections in each town. The political parties were to submit their lists of candidates who were to be selected by convention twenty days before the date of the election. Those eligible for office were limited to the upper two-thirds of literate taxpayers. Boards of registration were set up for every ten thousand inhabitants; the president of the board was to be an army officer, and one representative of each party was to be on the board. Lists of registered voters were to be posted two days before the elections. The Australian ballot was required; and each voting place was limited to three hundred voters. Voters had to be twenty-one years of age, male residents for two years in Puerto Rico, and be a resident for six months in the municipality before the election. A taxpaying record of $1.00 was required. Many penalties were provided for fraud; and on the closing of the polls, the ballots were counted, and the results sent to Army Headquarters in San Juan.

With the intent of simplifying administration and reducing expenses, General Davis completely remodeled the government. He abolished the departments of state, treasury, and interior. In their place, he set up a bureau of state and municipal affairs, a bureau of internal revenue, and a bureau of agriculture. These three bureaus were placed under the newly created office of civil secretary, to the extent that he was to completely reorganize them and to hire and fire as he believed was demanded by efficiency. The bureau of education was continued, but under the Board of Education whose president became directly responsible to the military governor. The former bureau of public works was placed under the control of the board of public works. In making these appointments, Davis touched upon a sensitive point that "there may seem to one of the political parties a preponderance of numbers of officers of another political party." He answered this quickly with the assertion that he selected his men by merit and that "he has in no case been actuated by a thought of promoting the ambitions of any party, and should it be found that any public officer uses his position . . . in promoting any personal or partisan purpose, he will be immediately removed."[76]

In summarizing the attitude of the United States toward Puerto

Rican self-government, we find that Elihu Root, the adroit secretary of war, was in favor of giving peoples under our sovereignty ''individual freedom, self-government in accordance with their capacity, just and equal law, and opportunity for education, for profitable industry, and for development in civilization.'' He noted a difference of opinion among ''those who had to do with the actual operation of a government with Porto Rican assistants'' and those ''who were impressed by the broad culture and personal intelligence of a great many Porto Ricans with whom they had been in contact professionally, socially, or in a business way. . . .'' The former group believed Puerto Rico to be unprepared for self-government; the latter group favored autonomous government.[77] The opinion of those conducting the government of the island prevailed, and autonomy was to be deferred until the middle of the twentieth century.

One of the most vital problems that had to be faced by General Davis was that of the church. The occupation of the island by the United States meant the immediate cessation of financial aid to the church. In a financial statement, Davis remarked that, under Spain's rule, the clergy had been allowed a yearly budget of about 190,000 pesos. This payment was promptly terminated on October 18, 1898, and thereafter no money was advanced to bishops or to priests or for religious purposes. The remaining legal problem was difficult; by a Concordat in 1857, the church had agreed to the state's legal ownership of the property on the condition that the state would care for the expenses of the church and its ministers. With the title to church property in the name of the state and the revenues from the state terminated by American occupation, the church was liable to cessation of operation. The poverty of the people left little room for freewill offerings to support the church. One example was the case of the school conducted by the Escolapios (Piarist Fathers) who were supported by the Provincial Assembly. The immediate cessation of this aid caused the Fathers to abandon the school and return to Spain. Because of this type of difficulty, General Davis informed Washington, ''It is very important that this question be speedily resolved.'' Since this became a serious and long-debated issue in the courts, it will be dealt with in a later chapter on the church.

Other religious issues were handled by the Davis administration, such as chaplaincy in a jail. By order of the general, all chaplaincies of jails were to cease on June 10, 1899. The order, however, allowed the conducting of any religious service and the visits of ministers

upon the application of the same to the warden. Soon thereafter, a
strong order was issued against duelling; this provided severe
penalties not only against the principals but also against any physical
or moral co-operators.[78] The fact that the continentals were conscious
of the morals of the island is apparent in a letter from the WCTU of
Aumsville, Oregon. This group requested the president to prevent
"as far as possible in the Island . . . bigamy, fornication, divorce,
bull fights, prize fights and the circulation of obscene and gambling
matter by mail and commerce. . . ." In this reference to Cuba,
Puerto Rico, and the Philippines, they urged the allowance of "civil-
magistrates and Protestant ministers as well as priests to officiate at
marriages, to promote temperance, and to make regulations for the
proper observance of Sunday."[79]

An interesting insight into the powers of General Davis appears
at this time in an opinion of Judge Charles E. Magoon who was the
law officer of the Division of Customs and Insular Affairs. Judge
Magoon, in reply to the secretary of war who had asked about the
legality of General Davis' issuance of an order to regulate marriage
and divorce of civilians, stated:

> I am of the opinion that the officer in command . . . is with-
> out the authority to legislate for the civilian inhabitants of
> Porto Rico, that authority being vested in Congress alone. . . .
> When the war ended, the civilians were relegated to the
> civil code. The commanding general in time of peace cannot
> exercise the right and powers of a commander of a belligerent
> force. . . . The President is the Commander-in-Chief of the
> Army of the United States. He has called upon Congress to
> legislate for Porto Rico. . . . Therefore, the General in command
> . . . is now prevented from exercising such authority by the
> action of his superior officer, the President of the United
> States.[80]

Despite the opinion of the legal officer, General Davis proceeded to
make necessary provisions for public education and health. In education, under orders of General Henry, a code of school laws was
compiled and promulgated. This authorized coeducation and separated the schoolhouse from the residence of the teacher or any other
family. It abolished the fee system, eliminated religion from the
public school classroom, and limited the school year to nine months.
Under General Davis, the degree of bachelor was abolished in Puerto
Rico's educational system; in place of this, the Insular Board of

Education issued a certificate of the courses passed by the student. This board of education had been set up by the governor's order on July 8, 1899. It consisted of five men who received complaints and petitions, approved warrants for appropriations, and approved the appointment of administrative officers and teachers in the secondary and higher schools. In comparing the statistics of the last days of Spain with those of the United States control in education, we find that under Spain there were 22,265 boys and girls taking public instruction; in the year 1899 to 1900, there were 24,392. The increase was significant when we consider that schools were separated from private homes, that the economic condition of the island following the hurricane was tragic, and that new standards of education needed newly trained teachers.[81]

To handle the complex health problems, the military governor set up a "superior board of health" composed of six members. The problems that faced them were manifold. One of the most pressing was that of vaccination, since many of the mayors (*alcaldes*) neglected it and the people either resisted it or regarded it with indifference. Strong penalties insured the enforcement of this law. The board of health was assigned many duties; among these were the supervision of public health, the study of its vital statistics, the making of sanitary investigations, and the dissemination of information among the people. New laws were to be recommended for the improvement of conditions in the island.[82]

In closing, it can be summarily stated that the military governments that controlled administration until the inauguration of the first civil governor, Charles H. Allen, on May 1, 1900, were preparatory instruments. Despite their errors, the military made a serious and honest effort to better the conditions of the people of Puerto Rico. Their greatest failings were in the lack of understanding of a people with different traditions and in the rather blunt expression of chauvinism. If blame is to be laid for the failure to initiate an autonomous government in Puerto Rico during this early period, it is not the fault of the military governors. It rather belongs in Washington where policies were made, and from whence orders were issued to the local authorities; in Puerto Rico they were fulfilled in the way that is normal for the military. A portion of the blame can be rightfully laid to the local conditions in Puerto Rico: the political strife, the countercharges of corruption and bad faith, and the economic and social weakness of the country. Despite the "superiority complex" that characterized the American administration in this period, even the impartial observer must conclude that the ground was not adequately prepared in Puerto Rico for independence nor for wide autonomy under United States sovereignty.

IV

How the Foraker Act
Came into Being,
1898-1900

In the previous chapter, the reader has seen the immediate action of the military governments that—in the absence of a congressional organic act—ruled Puerto Rico. It was a government of military orders moderated by intelligence and honesty of purpose. It is now appropriate to investigate the many factors that influenced the Washington Congress in the writing of a special constitution for United States civil governance of Puerto Rico. In addition to the official reports of the military governors and the private letters and magazine articles of interested parties, there were official commissions. All of these had their weight in influencing a Congress that was composing the Foraker Act of 1900.

Among the specially commissioned agents of information, we find a first survey of the conditions in the island made by the Reverend Thomas E. Sherman, S.J., who was chaplain of the Fourth Missouri Division of the United States Volunteers. His trip around the island was ordered by General Brooke and began on October 19, 1898. Under the date of December 30, 1898, he incorporated his report into a letter; an edited account of this report was given to the public by order of Assistant Secretary of War Meiklejohn on January 10, 1899. This report delineates in a rather incisive way the social, economic, educational, political, and religious problems of the island. Its presentation gives the impression of an unbiased account that seeks to inform the military authorities of the real conditions of the people, while holding strong sympathy with the inhabitants.

While Father Sherman traveled about the island, word came to Puerto Rico that President McKinley had appointed the Reverend Henry K. Carroll to head a commission to study the civil government of Puerto Rico under the Spanish regime and report on conditions. The commission was to make recommendations on urgent matters. Dr. Carroll was a distinguished member of the Methodist Episcopal church and was accompanied by his secretary, Charles E. Buell; Alfred Salomon, a Puerto Rican; and five interpreters. In the spring of 1899, another group called the Insular Commission was ordered to the island in order to make a survey and report with recommendations to R. A. Alger, the secretary of war. The members of this commission were General Robert P. Kennedy, Major C. W. Watkins, and Judge H. G. Curtis. About the same time, Washington received information from Philip C. Hanna, United States consul in San Juan.

Along with these official reports were the military reports that the commanding officers—who filled both military and civil functions—sent to Washington. Both groups also expressed their opinions in magazine articles. A valuable source of information is to be found in the letters of prominent persons who visited the island, either in a public or a private capacity. Their correspondence of an official nature can be found in the Bureau of Insular Affairs Archives, in the National Archives at Washington. Another source of information is the Census Report of 1899 that was directed by the Census Office of the War Department.

Representing the different interests of Puerto Rico are such groups as that of Luis Muñoz Rivera who came to the United States in the interest of the Federal party (former Liberal-Autonomist or Pactistas), and the Puerto Rican commissioners who represented one of the opposition interests. The latter group was composed of Eugenio M. De Hostos, M. Zeno Gandía, and J. J. Henna. In the same year, 1899, the civil secretary of Puerto Rico, Dr. Cayetano Coll y Toste, published an outline of conditions at the time of the change of sovereignty; it is called *Reseña del Estado Social, Econó-*

mico, y Industrial and constitutes more of a compilation of statistics than an analysis of conditions.

In dealing with these many and often conflicting reports on conditions, an attempt will be made to show the similarities and divergences of viewpoint and to gather together the recommendations. For greater unity, these views will be incorporated under topical headings such as politics, law, economic life, religion, education, and public works.

POLITICS

In beginning his survey of the island, Father Sherman started out from San Juan, proceeded along the northern coast toward the west, and then turned down along the southern shore. He also went into the central section of the island, in the area of Aibonito, and from there he moved to the east coast of Fajardo and Carolina, as well as to the Island of Vieques. He found much peace and close contact between the military and municipal authorities. Yet the removal of the troops, he believed, "would in all probability be attended by disastrous consequences at any time in the near future; and [such removal should wait] until the strong passions aroused by the political revolution here shall have died away." He found timidity in the property owners and in the civil authorities, and he attributed this to the newness of the relations with the United States. This priest emphasized the needs of an island that was mountainous, with poor transportation, and centers of population that provided inadequate employment. To meet the dangers of banditry that might grow, he urged that "the strong hand of the military arm, aided and abetted by a system of civil police and rural guard [be] composed where possible of some of the better class of Porto Ricans," and he recommended holding all civil authorities beginning with the commissaries of the barrios personally responsible for the good order of their districts." His last remark is to note the welcome extended by the people "by reason of political sympathy and a sentiment of confidence in our desire to govern for their good." He believed that Americans were bound to "show them the largest measure of confidence, furnish them promptly with a civil territorial form of government using the military arm as a protection, but not as a source of authority and holding out the promise of statehood speedily under definite conditions."[1] Father Sherman recognized factional differences existing in the island but remarked that the same thing existed in the United States. His report was both optimistic and constructive; it favored an autonomous Puerto Rico.

In his extensive report on Puerto Rico, Dr. Henry K. Carroll was also sympathetic with the people. He pointed to a bitter class struggle that had developed between the insular and peninsular Spaniard, remarking that their former system of government was "not the most suitable for developing efficient, independent, impartial, and honest public servants." Nevertheless, he had "no hesitation in affirming that the people have good claims to be considered capable of self-government." Dr. Carroll's recommendations were very specific and, though in conflict with the later provisions of the Foraker Act and some Supreme Court decisions, were quite in conformity with the United States tradition. He first suggested that "the Constitution and laws of the United States be extended to Porto Rico." Secondly, he urged that "a Territorial form of government, similar to that established in Oklahoma, be provided for Porto Rico," with executive, legislative, and judicial branches. In his plan, the governor general was to be appointed by the president and was to have the power of veto over the elected legislature's bills. The bill, however, could be passed over the governor's veto by a two-thirds vote of each house. The island voters were to be permitted to elect a delegate to Congress. Though Dr. Carroll recommended the county unit as the form of local government, he would leave this to the determination of the governor general and the legislature of Puerto Rico. In the municipalities, the councilmen were to be elected by the people, and they in turn were to elect the mayor.[2]

While Commissioner Carroll was in favor of autonomous government, he was well aware of the strong political factions that might make for anarchy. He discovered the quick adjustment that was made by the two parties to survive the war. The Historical Autonomists (Puros) were reorganized into the Republican party during March of 1899. They stood for American institutions, autonomous government in the island, retirement of the provincial currency, protection of the island's industries, and free trade with the United States. The Liberal Fusionist party (Pactistas) was re-formed under the name of the Federal party. It identified its interest with that of the United States, and sought a territorial form of government and the extension of the suffrage to all resident citizens. It urged free trade between Puerto Rico and the mainland, greater freedom for banking institutions, municipal autonomy, and an American system of education. The differences between these two parties, Dr. Carroll believed, were not essential, but strongly personal. The existence of extreme bitterness was admitted by the leaders of both parties in their hearing before Commissioner Carroll. Whereas the Liberals (Pactistas) believed that the Historical Autonomists (Puros) had unfairly refused to co-operate in the Autonomous Charter of 1897, the Puros charged the Pactistas with submerging insular interests into Spanish politics. This rancor appeared in the conflict between Luis Muñoz Rivera and Dr. José C. Barbosa. Muñoz charged the Historical Autonomists (Puros) with being embittered by their losses in the election and with resorting to violent struggles that led to personal insults. Barbosa, on the other hand, charged the Liberals with illicit election practices.[3]

A point of view on self-government similar to that of Dr. Carroll appeared in the correspondence of United States Consul Philip C. Hanna. Writing to the assistant secretary of state, John Bassett Moore, at the end of 1898, he suggested that "the ordinary territorial form of government is . . . very well adapted to the needs of this island and the situation here demands that some such form of government be provided for Puerto Rico at this winter's session of Congress." He saw the people as desiring the change of Spanish institutions but opposed to a long military rule by the United States. He urged that in case Congress should not at once offer a territorial government, "the urgent demands of the situation be remedied . . . by applying such United States laws to this island [as] are in effect in the District of Columbia." His immediate recommendation was that a commission be appointed to handle the governance of the island.[4]

Such a commission, called the Insular Commission, was appointed by the president of the United States and came to the island in March, 1899. The members—General Robert P. Kennedy, Major C. W. Watkins, and Judge H. G. Curtis—were introduced to the public of Puerto Rico by General Henry who stated: "I shall be only too glad and feel my hard work well rewarded if this Commission finds that the island is capable of self-government and not in need of military control."[5] The commissioners set up offices in San Juan where they invited all classes of Puerto Ricans to come and make their representations; they then visited all of the important towns and cities. This commission found the people "abundantly satisfied with the transfer to the care of the United States, and upon every opportunity give expression to their loyalty and devotion to the Government which relieved them from Spain's oppression.'' In relation to the political order, they recommended that ''the Constitution and laws of the United States locally applicable shall have the same force and effect in the island of Porto Rico as elsewhere in the United States.''[6] In the files of the Bureau of Insular Affairs, however, there is a letter signed by C. H. Watkins—under date of June, 1899—which commends the military governorship of General Davis but adds that the people bridle at the idea of a military rule. Watkins was of the conviction that ''after mingling with the people for several weeks,'' Puerto Rico was not yet ready for self-government. He favored a ''colonial form of government'' as meeting the conditions existing in the island.[7] This Insular Commission was rather crude in its recommendations. On discussing the economic and religious questions, the strong opposition that the commission aroused will be brought to light.

As has already been noted, one of the keenest insights into the problems of Puerto Rico was that of General George W. Davis. In his testimony before the House Insular Affairs Committee on January 8 and 10, 1900, he asserted that the Puerto Ricans expected with the coming of the American flag ''all rights and privileges which Americans everywhere else enjoy respecting trade.'' In respect to their form of government, he recommended that they be given opportunity to show their capacity ''for an exercise of political privileges and responsibility.'' And so the island should be given representation in a legislative council, with a majority of the persons appointed by the president under statutes drafted by Congress.[8] Within the same week, Davis was writing in *The Independent* of the necessity of a civil government in Puerto Rico. Though he regarded the transitional period from Spanish rule to that of the United States as necessarily military, he found American army officers opposed to the continuance of any purely military rule; ''all steps thus far taken in Porto Rico have been in the direction of ultimate self-government.'' He was convinced that ''The people are entitled now to a limited share in the government of the island; in due time they may exercise a still larger share, and ultimately be trusted, I believe, to complete control of their own affairs under the general laws of the United States.'' For the present, he was, however, convinced that government ''should be centered . . . in a body appointed by the President made up of natives and Americans.''[9] The general's realism was never handicapped by unbalanced idealism. This appeared in his message to the secretary of war shortly after being relieved

by Governor Allen, when he spoke of his duties as a "great burden."
He prophesied that the House of Delegates would form "a cantanker-
ous body" and that its deferred meeting would be a help to the new
governor.[10]

A very significant report on the conditions in Puerto Rico is
found in a letter of Brigadier General F. W. Grant who, writing to
the adjutant general on March 19, 1899, found the social and political
conditions of the island to be serious. The people, he said, were in a
desperate state of poverty and were being led by petty leaders into all
sorts of political agitations. He found, however, no organization
"looking towards rebellion against the United States authorities,
though I am convinced that most of the people are disappointed with
the conditions they find . . . by the change of government."[11]

In Washington and New York, Muñoz Rivera and Mariano Abril
were lobbying for the interests of Puerto Rico. Abril described an
April, 1899, meeting with Republican Senator Platt who was regarded
as a typical Yankee politician—dedicating all his attention to the
matters of his respective states "without bothering himself with
the future of the new colonies." He said that Muñoz Rivera was
spending most of his time "breaking the wall of ice formed by the
indifference with which these politicians look upon our affairs." He
spoke of American congressmen as ignorant of the problems of Puerto
Rico and "preoccupied with our personal differences which is the
only thing that the press considers." Through the press, Muñoz
Rivera expressed himself bluntly: first, Puerto Rico needs its own
government with a minimal control from the United States; second,
since the arrival of the United States, Puerto Ricans have been peaceful, and so the military government should be removed; third,
General Henry has committed many errors in policy through his
ignorance of the new environment; fourth, the Liberal party represents four-fifths of the population, is in sympathy with American
sovereignty, and desires American citizenship; fifth, Puerto Rico does
not favor independence but union with the American people under a
territorial form of government. As a result of an interview with
General Davis in Washington, Muñoz was much impressed with the
newly appointed military governor. He quoted Davis as saying that
he proposed to govern with the widest civil powers that a military
government allowed him.[12]

The former group of "Separatists" was also represented in Washington during the first six months of 1899, petitioning reform of

government in Puerto Rico. This party sent what was called the Puerto Rican Commission, composed of Don Eugenio M. Hostos, Dr. Manuel Zeno Gandía, and Dr. J. Julio Henna. They opened their campaign of propaganda with a letter to President McKinley on January 20, 1899, urging the appointment of a civil secretary, the election of an Insular Council with power to legislate on local affairs, the absolute autonomy of municipal bodies, and the application to Puerto Rico of the personal and civil rights that are contained in Article 1, Section 9, of the United States Constitution. In a second letter to the president, on April 19, 1899, the commissioners stressed the lack of self-determination in Puerto Rico. They made reference to the first section of the Congressional Act of April 20, 1898 (Teller Amendment) in which the independence of Cuba was assured, pointing out that the exclusion of Puerto Rico "could not go as far as to declare that the Puerto Rican people are and ought of right to be deprived of the inalienable rights, including liberty, life and the pursuit of happiness, with which the Creator endowed all men." Other matters of petition were the reduction of the army, the setting up of a civil government, and the extending of all rights of United States citizens to Puerto Ricans on the basis of Article 11 of the Treaty of Peace. Lastly, an autonomous government under the legislative council was sought.

In a third letter of May 5, 1899, the commissioners reiterated their former petitions with increased emphasis. Military rule was castigated for its effects upon "the noble people they have the honor to represent." Former Chief Justice John Marshall was cited as describing the government of the United States as a government of laws and not of men. Jefferson was recalled as having sought the incorporation of Latin American countries into the American Union "not to subjugate them, but to give them a place in the empire of liberty." Paternalism should be abolished, citizenship granted, political status and civil rights conceded. In a final appeal on June 15, 1899, they referred the president to their previous communications, and while awaiting the action of Congress, they urged the ideal of Christian civilization.[13]

Before concluding this section on the political ideas of Puerto Rico that were brought to the attention of Congress, consideration must be given the recommendations made in respect to universal manhood suffrage. In his report, Dr. Carroll recommended that the vote be granted to all male citizens above the age of twenty-one years and residents of the province at the time of the occupation by the United States. He argued that "educational and property qualifications may be considered requisite by those who are distrustful of the masses, but republics are founded on trust of the body of the people, learned and unlearned." This position was in contrast to that of Muñoz Rivera who favored keeping the voting age at twenty-five years, since "the Latin race is excitable and undeliberative, and at the age of 21 years a man of the latter race has not formed character." The leader of the Liberals further cautioned Dr. Carroll that "it would be extremely dangerous to hand over our future to the masses, who are entirely without civic education and who might be wrongly directed by the audacity of agitators who would make them their tools."[14]

In his testimony before the House Committee on Insular Affairs, General Davis commented on elections in Puerto Rico during the Spanish regime as lacking freedom: "the natives tell me that they were farces; that no election was ever ordered until it was decided what the result should be and who should be elected, and those in power took care that the desired result should never fail." He opposed, therefore, manhood suffrage because of these abuses, and because "the Spanish census showed that 87% of the population can not read and write."[15] In similar manner, General Henry was of the opinion that the suffrage should be given "only to those who are males, of legal age, inhabitants of the island, or who have declared their intention of becoming such, and who possess certain property qualifications to be determined upon."[16]

In concluding the evidence presented on political ideals, it becomes apparent that though there was much sympathy with the desire for self-determination among the Puerto Ricans, the weight of opinion was in favor of a slow movement toward autonomy. The early disorders that followed upon the war, the internecine conflicts of the two principal political parties, the ineffectual municipal government, the alleged corruption of elections, and the traditional Anglo-Saxon suspicion of things Latin prompted the United States to retard its concession of self-government. That there were selfish commercial interests that colored this picture is a matter of later study.

LAW

Closely akin to the political ideals of a people is the body of laws that regulate their civil and criminal life. The Anglo-Saxon who

came from the great Republic of North America brought to Puerto
Rico a pride in his legal heritage. From a recognition of the abuses
of power that existed in some periods under Spanish governors, he
tended to generalize concerning the inferiority of Spanish law. The
terminology, the different court procedures, the detailed codes of
Spanish law, and the tradition in Spanish jurisprudence were new
to him; and in his impatience, he would seek to abolish it without
investigation. While General Henry, for instance, was most careful
not to permit lawyers from the United States—who had no knowledge
of Spanish law—to practice in Puerto Rican courts, he was most
prompt to abolish any law that he believed to be in conflict with the
American tradition or his military government. The law in Puerto
Rico was submitted to some drastic changes.

The earliest sources of information on the legal system of Puerto
Rico, as presented to the United States after military occupation, are
to be found in the report of Dr. Carroll and of the Insular Commission of 1899. The latter group made some drastic suggestions that
earned much criticism. The presentation of the situation and the
recommendations made by Carroll, however, were thorough and well-
weighed. His hearings incorporate the testimony of such distinguished figures as Herminio Díaz, the secretary of justice; José
Severo Quiñones, the chief justice; and other Puerto Rican and
American lawyers.

The legal system operative in Puerto Rico under Spain comprised
three codes: penal, civil, and commercial; in addition, there was
legislation on mortgages, education, legal procedure, and judicial
power. The penal code covered criminal acts; the civil code handled
matters of marriage, property, inheritance, and contracts; and the
commercial code dealt with mercantile life and business contracts.
These codes, according to Puerto Rican lawyers, were equitable, suitable, and effective; and were well adjusted to the needs of Latin
peoples. The strength of criticism was levelled against the organization of the courts and the methods of judicial procedure.

The judicial system in Puerto Rico had its lowest tribunal in the
municipality, where the judge was empowered to hear cases of a civil
nature up to the sum of $200; criminal cases were prepared in state-
ment by the municipal judge and then submitted to the judge of first
instance (termed "judge of instruction"). To this court of first
instance, appeals in civil cases might be made. The nature of this
court's work was an evaluation of evidence presented and a sum-

mation of the case as evaluated. This summation was presentable to the supreme court in San Juan and from here by appeal to the court of appeal in Madrid. Criminal cases were handed over by the judge of first instance to the criminal *audiencia,* of which there were two in Puerto Rico: one in Ponce, the other at Mayagüez; they were courts of exclusively criminal jurisdiction. The territorial *audiencia* was at San Juan and was empowered to handle both civil and criminal cases. The island was divided into eleven judicial districts, each having a judge of first instance and instruction. The criminal *audiencia* consisted of a president, two justices, a supplementary justice, a prosecuting attorney (*fiscal*), and other court officers. The territorial *audiencia* consisted of a president, a presiding officer of the hall of justice, five justices, a prosecuting attorney, and numerous other court officers.

One of the most serious criticisms raised against the law in Puerto Rico was that the accused were regarded as guilty until proven innocent. In the order of arrest, the charge was not included; after arrest, the accused was questioned privately by the judge and held incomunicado. After the judge had examined the witnesses, he summarized the case, and passed it on to the *audiencia* for trial. Here the prosecuting attorney examined it and passed it on to the counsel for the defense. The witnesses of the plaintiff spoke first and were followed by the defense. The written arguments of both sides concluded the case, and then the judge (or judges) gave the verdict on the facts and imposed the penalty of the law. In contrast to Spanish practice, jury trial was not allowed in Puerto Rico.

The abuses charged against the judicial procedure were manifold. First of all, the summation of the case prepared by the judge of first instance might often come to a thousand sheets of paper, and this paper was stamped with a tax. Though the judge of first instance might regard a case as of improbable conviction, the case would have to go to court, and trial might be delayed six months. In the meantime, the prisoner might be set at liberty on the chance that he was innocent. The secrecy of the proceeding injected fear into the people, who were reluctant to become involved in such action. And the low salaries of the judges made for much venality. It was further charged that this system opened the way for men of malicious purpose to have innocent men jailed for a period, while escaping prosecution for false charges. The high costs of judicial proceedings also prevented the reporting and punishing of crimes. Another abuse was noted by a property owner and former notary of Utuado, José L. Casalduc, who in reply to Dr. Carroll's question—whether the criminal pays for his defense—answered: "The rich ones do; but you don't see the rich ones up for trial, because they buy themselves off before the case comes up for trial. A popular saying here is that 'The prison was not built for people with black coats.'" It will be remembered that because of this tardy and defective operation of the courts, General Henry constituted a military commission. This brought more speedy justice and stimulated the civil courts to action.[17]

Another topic that came up for much discussion was that of jury trial. In his hearings, Dr. Carroll was constantly asking for an expression of opinion on this judicial procedure. This appeared most clearly in his questioning of the Puerto Rican Chief Justice, Don José Severo Quiñones. In response to the question of the practicality of adopting the jury system in a territorial form of government, the chief justice replied: "I think not for the present, as I do not consider the people in general sufficiently well educated to pass on questions of that sort, and because just now political feeling runs very high." When Dr. Carroll suggested that there might be a difficulty in adopting a system of government under the United States Constitution without including the jury system, Mr. Quiñones replied: "If the adoption of the jury system is a constitutional right of citizens of the United States, no matter what the result might be in this country, we would be bound to accept it and would be glad to accept it. Yet, as a lawyer and a man of conscience I prefer judges by prevention rather than judges by adoption."

Another expression of doubt about the application of jury trial appeared in the testimony of Judge Joaquín Servero Silva of the court of Mayagüez. Judge Servero Silva said: "The jury system is a great system, but if it is going to be given to the people, it requires that the people who are going to dispense justice thereby should have a considerable degree of culture and education." On the other hand, Alfredo Arnaldo, judge of the court of first instance in Arecibo, believed that the "introduction of the jury system here is an indispensable improvement." This position was controverted by a lawyer, Francisco de Paula Acuña, who said: "I do not consider the status of this population sufficiently high to give this method of justice good results. It is preferable to leave the system of criminal justice as it exists today."

Secretary of Justice Herminio Díaz did not explicitly express

himself on this matter in the hearings of Dr. Carroll. He did, however, urge caution, since "our laws, the majority of which are
codified, are not a capricious system, but a collection of laws
which . . . lay down in their precepts the solutions which at the time
of their promulgation were accepted by the most radical and
advanced European schools of lawyers for the intricate problems of
law which juridical experience presented." He admitted the need of
reform, since the laws stem from the Spanish political principles
which "are diametrically opposed to the republican institutions of
the United States." He believed that the old laws should not be
abandoned where they have been useful in the social development of
Puerto Rico. He warned against American commissions making
modifications in the law on the basis of but a few days in the island
and with no knowledge of its legal history. Despite this recommendation, Dr. Carroll advised Washington to send a commisison to codify
the laws and to make provision for "trial of criminal cases before
juries; also, of certain classes of civil suits."[18]

In respect to the legal and juridical system of Puerto Rico, United
States consul Philip C. Hanna was one of the first to express his
opinion. He advised Assistant Secretary of State J. B. Moore that
the president should appoint a commission of representatives from
each department of government and that, "under the direction of the
Commission of Justice, courts be established to administer United
States laws in the island." He was convinced that "This island not
only needs American officials to administer law, but it sadly needs
American law to be administered. The greatest barrier in the way
of a smooth and successful administration of affairs today is, that our
American officers here are called upon to administer a set of laws
which made Spain a failure for four hundred years."[19] Commissioner
Carroll made several suggestions in respect to the reform of the legal
and juridical system of the island. As we have seen, he favored the
immediate installation of jury trials. He further advised that a
commission of five persons, three from Puerto Rico and two from
the United States, be appointed by the president to revise and "if
necessary, recast the codes." For the present, however, "the penal,
civil, and commercial codes [were to] be continued in force, in so
far as they are consistent with the Constitution of the United
States." Another commission, he suggested, was to be appointed, to
study all claims to property, ecclesiastical and secular, arising under
the terms of the Treaty of Paris. Federal banking and patent laws

were to be extended to the island. The mortgage law was to be modified to meet present needs. Finally, all codes, the laws of the territorial legislature, and official acts of the governor generals should be published both in Spanish and English.

After summarizing the changes made in the legal system by Generals Brooke and Henry, Dr. Carroll came to the matter of recommendations. He found the people respectful of law:

> They are not turbulent or violent. Riots are almost unknown in the island; so is organized resistance to law; brigandage flourished only for a brief period after the war and its object was revenge rather than rapine.
>
> They are not a criminal people. The more violent crimes are by no means common. Burglary is almost unknown. There are many cases of homicide, but the number in proportion to population is not as large as in the United States. Thievery is the most common crime, and petty cases make up a large part of this list of offenses. The people as a whole are a moral, law-abiding class, mild in disposition, easy to govern, and possess the possibilities of developing a high type of citizenship.

Carroll favored giving Puerto Rico "local self-government after the pattern of our Territories and she will gain by her blunders, just as cities and States in our own glorious Republic are constantly learning."[20]

The Insular Commission of 1899 submitted its report to Secretary Alger on May 27. As the Carroll Report had indicated, it found the people of Puerto Rico "as law-abiding as any people of like opportunities." It promised to submit hereafter "as a part of this report a full code of laws, and recommend their promulgation by the authority of the Commander-in-Chief." While finding the Spanish system of laws "not all bad," the commission believed that "the best way to Americanize Porto Rico is to give them the benefit of our complete system." They urged that the constitution and laws of the United States which were locally applicable "shall have the same force and effect in the island of Porto Rico as elsewhere in the United States."[21] The commissioners made an even stronger statement in a letter of August 1, 1899: "So far Porto Rico has gained nothing by belonging to the United States; she is still under the old laws now made our own, with a few modifications; and under the same oppressions. She has lost the Spanish markets for her crops and has been excluded from our own. She is burdened today with oppressive taxation, and onerous, unnecessary and exorbitant salaries are paid the horde of office-holders playing at running a government American in form under Spanish laws, and with officers trained in Spanish diplomacy and intrigue.''[22]

In illustration of the defective Spanish laws and court procedures, the commission stated that two thousand prisoners were awaiting trial in the jails of the Island ''for the most trivial offenses''; another two thousand not confined were awaiting trial. It found the Supreme Court of Puerto Rico pompous and consuming the good part of a day in disposing of a case that in the United States would be handled ''by a police justice within a few minutes.'' The commission, therefore, urged that the municipal judges be given a larger jurisdiction; that the judges of first instance be given jurisdiction to hear and try cases and impose penalties; that the ''courts of *audiencia*'' be continued as courts of appeal in criminal cases and minor civil causes, as well as of original jurisdiction of civil causes and of felonies. A new Supreme Court of five members was to be constituted. In addition to these local courts, the commission recommended a system of federal courts, with like powers of those in the states and territories of the United States. These courts were to have original jurisdiction concurrent with the other courts of the island in civil, criminal, and probate matters and to have exclusive jurisdiction of federal questions. Appeals from these courts might be made to the Supreme Court where there would be jurisdiction.[23]

The recommendations of this commission were almost immediately subject to vigorous attack. One of the few who approved the report was Roberto H. Todd, who wrote to General Kennedy in favor of the ''code of laws'' and of the mixed commission of five to govern the island. He found that ''it is impossible to civily [sic] govern a country with only 12% of its inhabitants knowing [how] to read and write.'' In the code he hoped for a guide in right governance. He warned that ''those who expect to live on the country will oppose your plan, but the good men will uphold it.''[24] Differences within the commission itself were noted, as, for example, the retirement of Horatio S. Rubens. Rubens, in a confidential letter to Todd many years later, explained that he could not agree with many of the opinions and recommendations of the commission. He opposed ''the entire replacement of existing laws'' and ''the creation of an entirely new set of tribunals based actually upon the American system which could not possibly conform to the practices under the existing Spanish laws.''[25]

One of the men most intimately involved in the court system was

Secretary of Justice Herminio Díaz, who found the report "the echo of the false and calumnious imputations of the *San Juan News.*" He was especially annoyed that the commission advised the sending of judges from other territories of the union to fill the courts in Puerto Rico; this, he maintained, "would be a violation of the constitution of the United States." He also found only ten men in jail and that the length of time was not years but months without trial. General Henry, in forwarding these comments, added: "The work of the Commission does not seem to have left a pleasant impression on some, nor do I approve of any proposed radical changes. Whatever report they make should be carefully considered, if we desire to be just with these people and retain their affection, and lead them gradually in our ways which they are anxious to adopt."[26]

In reply to the remarks of Herminio Díaz, the commission answered that the secretary's criticism was in violation of a military order that forbade publication in the newspapers of criticism of the government and its officers. Besides, it argued, Díaz did not give the full report on the prisoners who were long jailed without trial, and Major Sharpe found the charge correct. The commission was further shocked at the statement of the Puerto Rican officials to the effect that the United States military government could not make necessary civil changes. It added that the commission had not criticized the judges personally but, rather the system of the courts and had recommended changes. The commission then added some documents that criticized certain judges.[27]

Further criticism of the commission's recommendations is evidenced in a letter of W. H. West who doubted "the propriety of the President's devising any system of territorial government, or promulgating a civil code therefor." The furnishing of a government for Puerto Rico should be left to Congress.[28] It was with much truth that General Henry, in a letter to Major Pershing, stated: "The report of the Insular Commission . . . would raise a racket in Porto Rico. . . . It is a good thing that this Commission has been *useless*[?] and all educated people feel that way." The advice of the general was: "Apply our laws . . . make the Porto Ricans carry them out . . . and go poco [a] poco."[29]

ECONOMIC LIFE

Political idealism divorced from economic stability provides a very unreal world. It is good for pure speculation and bad for statesmen who have the obligation of building a country in both its moral and material needs. It was therefore the serious concern of the investigating commissions and of the military governors to analyze conditions and make recommendations for economic improvement. A summary of the facts and suggestions can be made under the following headings: the physical condition of the people, systems of taxation, private industries and investments, island tariffs, and financial problems.

In studying the condition of the people of Puerto Rico during this time of transition, the Insular Commission concluded that "after a complete survey of the island, we can state, unhesitatingly, that no such starvation exists, nor is it at all likely to exist in Porto Rico." The report makes a distinction between starvation and "great poverty"; it believes that the frugality of the people and the productivity of the soil supply the necessary foods.[30] It is to be remembered that this report was written about two months before the terrible hurricane of August, 1899. Father Sherman saw the conditions with a great deal more realism: "There is a great deal of poverty on the island. The malformation of so many of the children is due to imperfect nourishment. The great excess of infant mortality is probably due in part to the same cause, and some stringent public measures should be inaugurated to ameliorate the condition of the lower classes."[31] General Davis, before the House Committee in early 1900, found that "There are . . . certainly more than 100,000 families whose entire worldly goods, of a family consisting of father, mother, and from three up to twelve children, are not of the intrinsic value of five dollars. An iron pot and a palm-leaf thatch with a dirt floor, without a bench or a table or a chair or a bed, or knife or fork or spoon."[32] Governor Davis, in writing to the secretary of war a little later, found the situation the most difficult that he had ever encountered. A series of inconsistencies appears in this letter. First, no issues of food relief are necessary; but if they are not freely made, thousands will starve. Second, nearly all the planters who have been assisted misapply the issues and convert them to their own uses; yet these same planters observe their promises to give useful employment to their peons, to the benefit of their plantations and hands. Third, the issue of rations is pauperizing the people and corrupting the communities; yet such issues are indispensable. Fourth, a good many rations are stolen; a very few are. Fifth, all the money should be

given in aid directly to agriculture; at the same time, road work
is the best relief.

To add to his problems, General Davis had a visit from Creelman
of the *New York Journal,* who "came here specially, I think, to
develop frauds, abuses, and all sorts of wrongdoing by the military,
hoping to connect the administrations with them. . . . His effort
failed, if one can depend on his statements at sailing to return."[33]
The general's real problem, however, was severe poverty, malnutrition, and a high death rate: "I find that the deaths from September
1st [1899] to January 31st [1900] have reached 53 per thousand. . . .
That is to say, since September 1st, over 9,000 persons have died
who would have been alive had the health and food conditions
continued normal. This takes no account of the 2,700 people more or
less who were killed by the cyclone." The general attributed the
deaths to exposure, change from accustomed to unaccustomed food
which resulted in dysentery and anemia, inability to secure medicine
and medical treatment, and general inanition and discouragement.[34]

Charles E. Buell, a member of the Carroll Commission, saw the
great mass of the population as exceedingly poor. They lived in rude
abodes without funiture; the occupants used piles of leaves for beds
and ate a scanty meal from the ground. He wrote:

> These people earn from 20 to 30 cents a day . . . when they
> can get work. . . . The payments for their labor are not usually
> in cash, but in brass checks that must be traded out at the
> planters store where they can purchase, at high rates, rice,
> beans, and cod-fish, upon which they subsist chiefly, seldom,
> or never, tasting meat.
>
> Men testified before the Special Commission that they were
> selected by their comrades to make the statement in behalf of
> farm laborers, because they were provided with clothing
> which would permit of their appearance before the Com-
> mission, and these were very poorly dressed.[35]

In the Carroll Report, extensive information on the condition of the
laboring classes may be found. The daily wages of the common field
laborer ranged from 35 to 50 cents in "native money"; the more
skilled might get from 60 to 75 cents a day in the mills. One instance
is given of female coffee-sorters who made from 12 to 18 cents a day.
The labor in the mills was from sunrise to sunset; in the cane fields,
from 7:00 A.M. or earlier to 3:00 P.M., working steadily. Some of the
most poignant testimony was given by Severo Tulier of Vega Baja,
who represented a group of peons. He stated that: "They have meat

only on Sundays, and only in those cases where wages are paid in money, because otherwise they can only take what is kept at the proprietor's store; and that never has meat.'' It was the conclusion of Dr. Carroll that the condition of the working classes could not be improved unless agriculture prospered and minor industries were developed. He advised ''a revolution in the methods of raising and marketing crops, and it can not be accomplished without the influx of new capital.'' He would raise the working classes ''to a higher level of intelligence, of efficiency as laborers, of power and influence as citizens, and of comfort and enjoyment as social creatures. Give them remunerative work, and all the rest is possible.''[36]

While there was terrible poverty among the masses and great indebtedness among the planters, the island was without debt. General Davis was convinced that if it had the authority to make the obligation, it could obtain credit; and ''unless it has financial assistance from some source, continual industrial paralysis must characterize the future.'' He further saw that trade conditions must be improved and that taxation, in the prostrated condition of the island, could supply adequate revenue.[37]

With its usual exaggeration, the Insular Commission stated that ''the system of taxation which has prevailed in Porto Rico was, briefly, to collect all that was possible from the people and to expend all that could be collected. The tax-gatherer was the ever-present evil, and his shadow was always present over the poorest and humblest home.'' The incomes and profits derived from property were assessed for taxation; where there was no income, no tax was imposed. The tax-gatherer favored the richer classes at the consideration of a price.[38] The Carroll Report also found evils in the system of taxation: tax reduction by bribery of officials, favoritism toward Spaniards, and the concealment of one's true income. The tax burden fluctuated from 12.5 per cent upward, in accord with the financial exigencies of the provincial and municipal treasuries. The custom was for the government to set the total budget-need to be carried by taxation. The *gremios*—groups of professional and industrial enterprises, of which there were about forty in the island—then apportioned the tax burden to be handled by each of its members. Municipal taxes were the following: the *consumo,* which was on food, drink, and fuel coming into the town; the tax on territorial, industrial, and commercial wealth, to the extent of about 7.5 per cent of value; and revenues raised from fines, leases, licenses, and rents. The chief source of insular revenue was from customs duties on imports and exports, special taxes on loading and unloading freight, and taxes on passenger travel. In the testimony given before the Carroll Commission, it was maintained that the taxation would not have been oppressive if it had been honestly administered.

As we have already seen, General Henry initiated a new system of taxation, assessing valley-lands at $1.00 per acre, middle lands at 50 cents, and highland areas at 25 cents. For nonresidents, the tax was doubled, by the decree of January 19, 1899.[39] It was shortly after this that the Puerto Rican commissioners were writing to the secretary of war urging that the ''territorial tax''—levied on income, not on value of property—be abolished, since it had reduced production to one-twentieth of the arable zone. It urged that taxes be levied on the value of property.[40] This suggestion would have had the effect of stimulating cultivation of land with the result of increasing the food and income of the island while giving greater employment. It avoided the oversimplification of General Henry's plan that had categorized land by such generic terms as upland, middle land, and lowland. Uplands, for instance, had to be used as woodlands, ''in order to attract the rain, as we have no rivers here [Vieques].'' A property-owner in Guayama found that the Henry tax on cane land was just, but too high on pasture lands. The consensus of opinion among many Puerto Ricans was that a tax should be imposed on the valuation of property.[41] With this opinion, General Henry was not in accord: ''The land tax is all right. The 25 cents on poor land is to make them cultivate it . . . which they can do.''[42]

In the reduction of taxation, the military governments abolished the position of many officials whose posts were regarded as a sinecure and whose salaries were considered too high. The Insular Commission was direct in its criticism of the ''horde of office-holders.'' It will be remembered that General Henry economized by abolishing many of the offices of the Secretariat; it was noted that the salaries of these secretaries exceeded those of senators and representatives in the United States Congress. The commission charged that ''many of the offices were regarded as personal property, to be transmitted or assigned for a consideration . . . the continuance of the present civil government, which is substantially that under which the island was formerly governed by Spain and which has been largely experimental by the present government, has proven absolutely that radical changes are necessary to give to the Porto Ricans opportunity for advancement under our systems and laws."[43] This same criticism was raised by General Davis who reported that "a number of persons were dispensed with and salaries were very much reduced."[44]

As the Spanish governmental policy was hard on taxpayers and as the regulations of General Henry wrought inequities, so the private investments of the island suffered damage. In the postwar period, industries that had been handicapped by Spanish regulations now lost the free markets that Spain had allowed in Cuba and in the peninsula. Whereas, in 1897, the balance of trade was valued at well over a half-million dollars in favor of Puerto Rico, under American sovereignty the island was deprived of many markets and thus of much income. The major industries of the island were coffee (which found its market chiefly in Europe and Cuba) and sugar (which was shipped to the United States and Spain). Though there were such small industries as salt, hats, rum, soap, and chocolate, Spain did much to discourage industries that might compete with her home production. Flour-milling, for instance, was restricted by Spain's putting the same rate of duty on grain-wheat as on ground flour; in this way, Spanish merchants could take wheat from the United States, grind it in Spain, and then send it to Puerto Rico. The soup-paste and soap industries were killed in the same way.[45] Many of these regulations remained on the books under the American military government. Besides, with Puerto Rico subject to American tariffs, the cost of living grew alarmingly. In the absence of capital and technical knowledge, it was unlikely that industries would be developed. Dr. Carroll was convinced that "the starting of new industries is an economical necessity, and it should be the policy of the United States to encourage it." The same lack of balance was found in the agricultural industry. Since the tariff policy of the United States affected the sugar industry adversely, and since tobacco and coffee were affected by the tariff and the hurricane, and since most of the foodstuffs of the island were imported, it became clear that the economy would have to be reshaped. Dr. Carroll advised improved culture of crops, with increased attention to vegetables and fruits. The greater production of rice, potatoes, and fruits for its own consumption became urgent in the interim needed for developing non-agricultural industries.[46]

Another grievance was the exorbitance of the fees that were charged for the transfer of real estate. The notaries and recorders who were necessary officials in the transactions charged usurious fees.

In the borrowing of money and in the mortgaging of property, the rates of interest averaged about 10 or 11 per cent. Some mortgages were placed at rates that ranged from 15 to 24 per cent. It was because of such abuses and the serious economic decline that General Henry temporarily suspended the Spanish law of foreclosure.[47] At the same time, it was advised that public franchises be granted to industrialists for the building and operating of railroads and that, though no lands nor bounties be given, the capitalist be granted a favorable charter. The sale of public lands was also urged as a means of getting income for the benefit of public schools.[48]

Of all the complaints raised by the people of Puerto Rico against United States policy, the most forceful was that of tariff barriers between Puerto Rico and the mainland. In a series of letters directed to President McKinley, to the secretaries of war and the treasury, to the New York City Chamber of Commerce, and to the press—extending from January to June, 1899—the Puerto Rican commissioners argued an extremely cogent case for free trade between Puerto Rico and the United States. First, the United States Constitution required free trade in interstate commerce, and that of Puerto Rico was coastwise trade, since the island became a part of the United States by the Treaty of Paris. Second, the working classes of Puerto Rico were impoverished because of the cessation of the free prewar markets in Spain and Cuba. The commission noted that they had been far better off under Spanish rule in the days of President Harrison than under the "Amended Customs Tariff and Regulations for Ports in Puerto Rico" that was promulgated by the War Department on January 20, 1899. For under the Harrison administration, Secretary Blaine had arranged reciprocal commercial agreements in the benefit of Cuba and Puerto Rico. At the time of the Cuban insurrection of 1895, Puerto Rico's trade with the United States increased greatly. Today, however, the commission added, foodstuffs that were of immediate need were burdened with customs. Third, better trade relations would make for better political relations. Fourth, the president was not authorized to enact and enforce the tariff arrangement of August 19, 1898, since at that time Puerto Rico had not yet become a part of the United States; and the tariff of January 20, 1899, was imposed when Puerto Rico became a part of the United States and should have been exempted from tariff.[49]

About the same time that the Puerto Rican commissioners were pressing their case in Washington, *La Democracia* was publishing an interview with Muñoz Rivera of the opposition party. The leader of the Federalists saw that ''The future of the island . . . is truly critical. We have no markets for tobacco and sugar, and business is paralyzed. . . . During the Spanish domination, we always had a market for the tobacco and sugar that we produced. . . . Today the sugar is resting in the warehouses . . . and the tobacco is thrown away at the depots.''[50] This opinion was also held by General F. W. Grant, who made it clear that ''unless the laws are changed, so that the planters can market their sugar at a fair price, there will be as great distresses in the sugar districts of Puerto Rico, as there is now in the coffee districts.'' He realized that the United States was bound to enact free trade for Puerto Rico if she would prevent the destruction of the agricultural industries.[51]

The Insular Commission also regarded the position of Puerto Rico in its trade with the United States as anomalous. In addition to the loss of many advantages possessed under Spain, the island now suffered prohibitive duties in its trade with the new mother country. These duties were imposed as though Puerto Rico were a foreign country. Besides, the island could not avail itself of the advantages of the United States reciprocity laws that allowed the making of agreements with foreign countries since it was not a foreign country. The commission recognized the seriousness of the situation but was unwilling to make any strong recommendations: ''It would seem that the relations between the island and the General Government would emphasize the need and utility of such reciprocity and of some means through which the President would be authorized to give relief to the island and some advantage for marketing our surplus of agricultural products and manufactured goods.'' While the commission was willing to recommend that Congress be asked to legislate ''modifications in the tariff schedules between the United States and Porto Rico,'' it did not consider it right to offer opinions ''on the general questions of trade, the status as it now exists under the law and the laws to be enacted by Congress, as to the right to maintain duties.'' The best that it could recommend was that ''some measure of relief be afforded the people there.''[52] An insight into the thinking of this commission is given by Horatio S. Rubens who retired in disagreement from the commission: ''I . . . advocated the immediate free trade between the United States and Puerto Rico, while the others who were high tariff advocates could not see the necessity for this.''[53]

General Henry, in an interview on May 17, 1899, remarked that "the Puerto Ricans are anxious for a territorial form of government; but the question is how are they going to get money if the customs duties are wiped out." The Puerto Rican commissioners opposed this opinion of the general by insisting that the people had submitted a full plan of revenue to Spain on asking for the abolition of the custom houses.[54] That this opinion was temporary becomes clear from an article of General Henry written in November of the same year: ". . . the tariff now levied in Porto Rico on imports from the United States, and in our own ports on goods coming from the island, will surely be abolished under the conditions now governing interstate commerce."[55]

In a preliminary report of December, 1898, Dr. Carroll asserted that "the question of absolute free trade between the United States and Porto Rico suggests a point which can not be fully settled just now." He believed that it was a question that would have to be discussed in connection with the form of government to be given to the island. He therefore recommended that "it would seem to be prudent not to revise the Porto Rican tariff so as very greatly to reduce the customs revenue, at least for the period ad interim." He urged the abolition of export duties on coffee, wood, and tobacco, and the revision of the Puerto Rican tariff following that of Cuba, with some exceptions. These recommendations by Dr. Carroll were approved by Robert P. Porter, special commissioner to Cuba and Puerto Rico, and incorporated in an executive order of January 20, 1899. The new rates were framed on a revenue-yielding basis of 15 per cent ad valorem. On October 6, 1899, Henry K. Carroll suggested that Puerto Rico be given a form of government modeled after that of our territories. He admitted that this meant "the abolition of customs duties between our ports and those of our new possession." He also saw that the Puerto Rican was more concerned with "free access to our markets . . . than the possibility of statehood."[56]

On this complex subject of tariffs, General Davis gave some practical but no constitutional advice. He believed that "If Porto Rico could have the same trade privileges that Hawaii enjoys, I believe the lands could all be brought under profitable cultivation and remunerative wages paid . . . and by that word I mean wages about one third or one fourth those paid in the United States."[57] He was convinced that free trade with the United States was essential to Puerto Rico; that it would not be detrimental to us, since both the sugar and coffee crops are small.[58] Lastly, he asserted that "If Congress should grant free trade to Puerto Rico, or permit her exports to be marketed in the United States for some small percentage of the home rates, then all the sugar lands in the Island will soon come into cultivation and production."[59]

In this difference of opinion on how constitutional provisions should be applied to such a "territory" as Puerto Rico, a new doctrine in United States constitutional history was to be evolved, that of "the non-incorporated territory." The discussion of this matter will be left to a later chapter in which the pertinent decisions of the Supreme Court of the United States will be explored.

Before concluding this section on the economic life of the island in the years preceding the Foraker Act, we must briefly indicate certain pressing financial problems. In the first days of the United States' administration, there was a Spanish bank—authorized under Spanish law to issue bank notes—that was redeeming this money and asking the permission of the United States to issue more notes. The Insular Commission believed that this bank had no such "vested right as would necessarily have to be recognized by this Government" and so recommended that it not be allowed to issue further notes.[60] The Puerto Rican commissioners were concerned with the banking situation and, after requesting the extension of federal banking laws to the island, made some comments on the banking situation. First, they attributed the decline in Puerto Rico to its present system of onerous loans. Abuses by loaning concerns (*refaccionistas*), they charged, ruined the farmers by interest rates of from 12 to 30 per cent, by short-term loans, and by cruel contracts and foreclosure proceedings. They recommended the establishment of agricultural banks that would lend money on easy terms and at fair rates of interest, and they expressed the hope that the national banks function "for the promotion of business and industrial enterprises, and at a fixed rate of interest."[61]

In his analysis of the situation of the banks, Dr. Carroll saw the need of banks in the chief centers of the island. He realized that United States national banks could not meet the need of agriculturists for long-term mortgages on real estate but that they would aid merchants and business men. Without offering any further recommendations, the commissioner cited the agriculturists who asked for an agricultural bank with many branches, a large increase in its capital, the guarantee of its securities by the government, and its recognition in the stock market of the United States.[62]

The currency also came up for consideration, since in Puerto Rico during the early days of the American military government there was a double currency—that of the United States dollar and the Puerto Rican peso. The managers of the Spanish Bank of Puerto Rico and the Territorial and Agricultural Bank of Puerto Rico both favored the valuation of the peso at 75 cents. The bankers, merchants, and agriculturists of Ponce and Mayagüez proposed that the peso be retired at 66⅔ cents American. The borrowers—chiefly the agriculturists—asked for a low valuation of the peso, as low as 50 cents.[63] The Puerto Rican commission entered into this problem with much the same realism. It found the intrinsic value of the peso to be from 41 to 42 cents; but the conventional value was set at 66⅔ cents. They therefore suggested that the just valuation should be an average between the intrinsic and the conventional value.[64] By direction of the president on January 20, 1899, the value was set at 60 cents, and business was carried on under the double standard. General Henry required that official salaries that were formerly paid in Puerto Rican money now be paid in gold. This, according to the Insular Commission, increased prices by 40 per cent and so produced confusion, so the commission recommended the retiring of Puerto Rican currency through the customs houses or the banks. The loss suffered by this conversion was to be made up by the Puerto Rican customs.[65] In his testimony, Nicolas Oyanguren, a merchant of San Juan and a director of the Banco Territorial y Agrícola, recommended the retiring from circulation of the Puerto Rican money at the established rate of 60 cents for $1.00. He found that there was little protest to this exchange rate.[66]

A critique of the budget in the island revealed many items that the Insular Commission had "ordered" to be stricken from the budget. Among these, the commission singled out certain pensions; amounts for the celebration of patron saints, the king's birthday, and for Holy Week; and amusingly a pension for the royal mace bearer of the Municipality of San Juan.[67] From over-all policy to the most minute detail, the United States found that in the acquiring of the beautiful Caribbean island, it had added a complex economic problem to its continental one.

RELIGION

The matter of religion had never been a dormant issue in Puerto Rico, and it acquired a new look with the coming of the Anglo-

American and Protestant government. Since a later chapter will be devoted to the religious problem from 1898 to 1904, this section is intended merely to outline the issues that had to be faced by the military governors and the reports that were influential in the congressional casting of the Foraker Act.

The handling of the available material on the religious practices of the people, the position of the church as a social agent, and its rights in transition from Spanish sovereignty to that of the United States are problems that are open to prejudice. At one extreme, the existent abuses were glossed over; at the other, generalizations were made from particulars and the testimony of biased witnesses was preferred. The problems that arose concerned the religious practices of the people, the marriage mores, church property, and military orders in the solution of church problems.

In his rather direct manner, Father Sherman labeled the condition of religion in Puerto Rico as "very unsatisfactory." Though all the inhabitants were Catholic, most of the men were merely Catholic in name. Sunday was not observed, since the "stores are open, the country people gather into the villages, traffic is far more active on that day than on any other." He found concubinage widespread and that the number of illegitimate children exceeded that of the legitimate.[68] The Insular Commission found the same condition reported earlier by Father Sherman, but it went on rashly in the attributing of blame: "This condition has risen from the fact that the charges of the officers granting marriage permits, and of the priests for performing marriage ceremonies, were so exorbitant that the poorer people were unable to pay them." The commission suggested that such cohabitation "in good faith be declared binding as a common-law (or civil law) marriage and the children legitimate" and that divorces be decreed by the courts for good cause, as allowable in the United States.[69] Father Sherman had answered the criticism of the clergy: "It is often asserted that the Catholic clergy are partly to blame for this deplorable state of affairs because marriage is said to be expensive. This is a calumny. No charge has been imposed for ordinary marriage ceremonies and no obstacle thrown in the way of legitimate unions save the ordinary ecclesiastical impediments recognized by Catholics all over the world." In further discussion with the priests of the island, he found that because of the union of church and state some priests became too interested in political matters; but he added: "there are many excellent priests in Porto Rico."[70]

Dr. Carroll, writing in a Protestant missionary journal some time after his official report, summarized his impressions. He found the peasant superstitious and prone to mixing religion with gambling, such as the promising of a Mass to the Virgin if she would help with the selection of the right lottery ticket. Though this may very well have been true, the commissioner, who was usually rather moderate in his judgment, described the devotions of the people: "Superstition is general. After the Sunday morning Mass I have seen, particularly in country churches, devout colored women going from shrine to shrine, from statue to statue, bowing and worshipping, telling their beads, kissing the feet of the tawdry representations of the Virgin, and showing the utmost religious fervor." That these actions need necessarily have been superstitious is a rather gratuitous assertion, since the motivation of a person's use of sacramentals is something that is better left unjudged on such slight knowledge. This is mentioned only as an example of the almost unconscious prejudice that could crop up in the mind of a person as intelligent and usually fair as Dr. Carroll. In discussing the clergy of the island, he cited Salvador Brau to the effect that there were "many priests who do not lead very moral lives, and who frequent gambling houses." Referring to Brau as a Catholic and therefore an authority hardly provides adequate proof of the assertion, and moreover, Brau's degree of Catholicism is subject to some suspicion. The commissioner does give us some insight into the people when he says that they "seem to have little or no prejudice against Protestantism. . . . No instances of religious hatred came under my notice. Nobody asked me whether I was a Catholic, or what my faith was, although I talked to scores of people on the subject of religion." He was convinced, finally, that "Protestant worship, in neat, attractive churches, with plenty of good singing . . . with Sunday school, young people's societies, etc., each church becoming a social center, would command many worshippers."[71]

In his official hearings, Dr. Carroll tried hard to get to the bottom of the charge that exorbitant fees were charged by the church for marriage. To a direct question, Father Juan Perpiñá e Pibernat, the capitular vicar of Puerto Rico, replied: "They [the clergy] are not allowed to receive any [fees for the sacraments] by law, but there have been abuses. Where these abuses have become known the clergy have been punished." He explained further that "when people have come to ask the sacrament of marriage or baptism and said they were unable to pay for it, the same has been performed gratuitously, at

least in my time, and as far as I know.'' After introducing much
testimony to the effect that marriage had a fee attached to it, Dr.
Carroll asked Father Baldomero Montañez, parish priest of Guayama,
about this. The answer was to the point: ''It costs them now because
we have no other means of living; but before we charged them
nothing for any of the sacraments. Now that our salaries have been
taken away, we have to have some means of livelihood. . . . In
Guayama you can ask the people, one by one, and you will not find
one who has been charged. I have been here fourteen years and have
never charged a marriage fee, and I am not the only one.'' More light
was shed on the subject by the parish priest of Arroyo, who stated
that fees were charged for marriages in the evening. The same practice was employed by the priest at Aibonito, who further stated in
respect to the poor, ''I will marry them for nothing. I have always
been disposed to do so and will do so now; but they prefer to live in a
state of concubinage.'' Mayor Muñoz of Cayey confirmed the statement that those who marry in the morning are not charged, whereas
marriage at other times bears a fee. This, as in other group testi-
monies, produced a difference of opinion and often some bitterness.
A Mr. Mejía of Yauco volunteered the information that ''If people
got married in the daytime the priest did not charge for the
ceremony, but he collected for the bans and for the dispensation to
marry.''

The change of sovereignty of Puerto Rico on October 18, 1898,
produced the abrupt separation of church and state and the ending of
state support of the church. By royal decree of 1858, the Spanish
government assumed the entire pay of the clergy: with the advent
of intervention by the United States, all income was taken away from
the church. Capitular Vicar Father Perpiñá said that he ''would
have advised the United States to establish a separation between the
church and state, because that is its Constitution, but not immediately
and suddenly as it was done.'' He was willing to accept gratuities,
but not a salary, from the municipalities; this was an expression of
the desire to be independent of the municipalities and a hint at the
coolness that existed. This flared up in the vicar's testimony on
February 10, 1899, when he charged: ''At present the *ayuntamientos*
(town councils) are bad ones, put in by Muñoz Rivera. They are bad,
very bad, and they are working against the church.''[72]

Father Sherman fully appreciated the situation and remarked
that the priests, deprived of governmental aid, were leaving the

country but that those of native origin would remain. He found it desirable that "a Bishop be appointed who is thoroughly conversant with both English and Spanish and who is young enough to endure long and fatiguing journeys on horseback." He further believed that "the change in the ecclesiastical system was too sudden, causing a kind of paralysis and consternation among a body of men accustomed to lean on the government."[73] With a great deal less understanding the Insular Commission made its recommendations that: first, a complete separation of church and state be made; second, all property, including cemeteries purchased with the public money, be declared government property, "except that churches used for religious worship exclusively be allowed to remain in the *possession* of the congregation"; third, priests and others with the vow of celibacy be permitted to renounce said vows and enter into marriage relations; fourth, divorce be allowed; fifth, cohabitation apart from marriage, after issuance of this order on making cohabitation legal marriage, be severely punished; sixth, feast days, Holy Week, etc., no longer be given official recognition, nor be supported at public expense.[74]

This blunt statement by the commission elicited some sharp reactions. General Henry commented: "They had better let Church matters alone, for the good of all concerned."[75] The Fifteenth Grand Council of the Young Men's Commission criticized the commission's recommendations as "an impudent and insulting assumption of power . . . an interference of the civil power with religious matters . . . and a gratuitous and uncalled for insult to the members of the Catholic Church."[76] Needless to say, there was a strong reaction in the Catholic press of the United States.

The two most serious problems in the status of the church became that of consecrated ground in the cemeteries and the possession of church property. General Henry handled the first by ordering that cemeteries that had been held for Catholic burial should continue so, even though the municipalities had paid the expenses of acquiring them. Dr. Carroll believed that the church's argument from traditional usage made a strong case; yet he doubted the right of General Henry to order "the municipalities to allow the priest to indicate those entitled to burial in consecrated ground." On the subject of church property, the commissioner favored the position of the church:

The Church was debarred by the Hypothecary, or Mortgage Law, from registering its houses of worship. This is one reason why it cannot today appeal to the books of the registrars to prove titles. . . .

The churches were built in almost every instance by public money . . . for Catholic worship and for no other. . . . To deprive the Church of this property now that the relations of Church and State are dissolved . . . would be . . . a virtual act of confiscation.

In most if not all the municipalities a feeling that justice would not be done unless the Churches are reserved for Catholics seems to prevail; and *alcaldes* who were strenuous in asserting the rights of the municipalities admitted that those rights might be waived at the request of the majority of the people, or might be surrendered on the payment of a small sum of money.[77]

In this same article, Dr. Carroll stated that "the common impression in the United States that the Catholic Church is rolling in wealth and has accumulated vast properties in Porto Rico is at fault." He found little ecclesiastical property, a small endowment by the state, and few inheritance gifts from the wealthy.

EDUCATION

The matter of education had a position of equal delicacy with religion in a Puerto Rico that was under revision by the United States. The official census of 1899—prepared and published at the end of 1900—revealed that the number of children between five and seventeen years of age was 322,393, with 8.1 per cent attending school. Of these the highest attendance percentage was in the cities, in the following order: Mayagüez, 27.7 per cent; Ponce, 24.0 per cent; and San Juan, 22.4 per cent. In reference to illiteracy, the census showed that of the 659,294 persons over ten years of age, 77.3 per cent were unable to read. This represents an improvement, since the 1860 census showed only 8.8 per cent able to read, and the 1887 census showed only 13.8 per cent. The comment on this low literacy rate by the census officials was as follows: "The proportion of illiterates in Porto Rico was higher than in any of the States of this Union or any of the other West Indian Islands. Guatemala is the only country in the region where the proportion of illiterates is higher than in Porto Rico." The improvement that came in the reduction of illiteracy can be found in later census reports. The census of 1910 showed that illiteracy had been reduced to 66.5 per cent; in 1920, it was further reduced to 55 per cent.[78]

In respect to the ability of the Puerto Rican child, there is great unanimity among the investigators of conditions. Father Sherman stated that "the children are bright and quick; they develop earlier than ours and many are capable of learning to read and write much sooner than American children."[79] The Insular Commission, after finding a "dense cloud of ignorance" over the island, remarked that "these people are bright, and with the same opportunities afforded the children of the United States, the children of Porto Rico would quickly become as intelligent as any others."[80] Dr. Carroll visited many schools and "found the children wonderfully bright and quick."[81] General Henry paid tribute to the people by saying that "the better element of the population . . . is as refined and educated as its corresponding class in the United States, and that is the class upon which the political and commercial redemption of Porto Rico must mainly depend."[82]

The evils that existed in the educational system of Puerto Rico are most extensively summarized in the reports of the Insular Commission and the Carroll Commission. With great consistency the Insular Commission found conditions very bad. Nine-tenths of the island was illiterate, and this was because the Spanish government believed an ignorant people to be more governable. No building had been erected specifically for educational purposes, and the existing quarters were hovels without desks; the schools were crowded and the environment unwholesome and unhealthy. "The books most generally found in these schools are a primer, a catechism and a mental philosophy, and the system of education consists almost entirely of memorizing alone." The commission did admit good conditions in the Beneficencia, which cared for 450 poor children, under the charge of the nuns of the Catholic church, but it spoiled its effect by adding that "the education is limited to that usually received in Catholic institutions." It also mentioned a school run for two hundred or more students by the Religious of the Sacred Heart in Santurce. These students, the commission added, "were placed upon inspection before Secretary Alger upon his recent visit to San Juan, in the plaza of the capital, and presented a neat and pleasing appearance."

Other observations of this commission revealed the Institute and Normal School of San Juan as pretentious, peopled by children of public-school age, and with no distinguished professors. The commission believed that this institution should no longer be maintained at public expense. Another abuse was noted in the merging of the taxes collected for school purposes into the general fund and their expenditure at the will of the officials.[83]

Dr. Carroll, in reviewing the education, mentioned the historical background. Public schools were under the direction of the Provincial Assembly; under the Autonomous Constitution, public education became a bureau within the Department of Public Works. Expenses in rent, instruction, and supplies depended on the municipalities that had their school boards, which were composed of the most intelligent men of the township. The classrooms were rented rooms that were ill-lighted and poorly ventilated, as well as crowded. He found one-fifth of the student population registered, but only one-seventh in actual attendance. The system of instruction was ''generally superficial and not solid, and theoretical rather than practical.'' He found the following general educational institutions: a conciliar seminary for the education of priests, the Provincial Institute (which had been recently suppressed), the high school of the Piarist Fathers, a girl's high school run by the Religious of the Sacred Heart, the Colegio de San Ildefonso, and the School of Arts and Industries. To the commissioner, the list of needs was obvious: first, suitable, sanitary buildings; second, a more efficient corps of teachers; third, more schools in the rural districts; fourth, larger provincial appropriations, until the municipalities would be in a condition to support their own schools; fifth, reorganization of the studies and better textbooks; sixth, effective provincial supervision; and seventh, better normal schools.

Incorporated into his general recommendations, Dr. Carroll asked that ''the governor-general and legislature of Porto Rico be required to make provision for universal and obligatory education in a system of free public schools, in which the English language shall be taught.''[84] In his nonofficial capacity, Dr. Carroll had other ideas. He believed that ''the churches [Protestant] might do a vast amount of good by opening both primary and secondary schools in certain localities.'' He noted that the high schools already opened under missionary auspices were crowded, that parents were ''very anxious for their children to learn English, and there are many who can afford to pay for advanced instruction for boys and girls who have already a fair primary education.''[85] When one reads through the commissioner's appendix to his Report on Education, the impression is that the selection of witnesses and the direction of questioning was not too favorable to the Catholic system of education. In his questioning of Dr. Carbonell, the seceretary of interior under whose charge the Bureau of Education came, one sees that religious instruction and prayer were under inspection. In fact, Dr. Carbonell had already suppressed a course in religion and morals taught by a priest. A more vigorous attitude appeared in the testimony of a teacher in Naguabo, Pedro C. Timothee. This teacher favored "progress" and considered it of "urgent importance that the intervention of priests and Sisters of Charity should cease in the schools, as they do not benefit." It was the opinion of Timothee that "religion should be removed from the schools altogether, and lessons of pure morals instituted." He further recommended the establishment of gymnasiums, coeducation, salary graduated to teacher-load, establishment of public libraries and adult schools, teacher organization, and a school for the blind and deaf.

Another spokesman for the avant-garde was Eduardo Neumann of Ponce, who favored night school for adults, kindergartens, the use of American textbooks, and the teaching of exclusively practical subjects in the elementary schools. This last idea he found in accord with "what Mr. Spencer, the great sociologist, has written." Antonio Sánchez Ruiz of Aguada recommended that "the system of education should be absolutely nonclerical and obligatory. Morality and good habits should be exacted from teachers." And finally, Dr. Carroll gave the opinion of "many citizens" of Isabela: "Education in Porto Rico is still submitted to the slavery of religious fanaticism, which makes it necessary to forbid religious teaching, substituting for it moral teaching and physical development—in a word, all the reforms called for by modern progress." They allegedly favored schools "on the basis of the American system, which has produced such beneficial, moral, and material results."[86] In this appendix on education, one looks in vain for any expression of opinion that might have favored religious education. The impression is conveyed to the reader that either those so thinking failed to testify before the commissioner or that he did not regard their opinions—if they did testify—as matter for citation.

The recommendations made by the Insular Commission were succinctly these: the building of more schools, the expenditure of taxes as budgeted for schools, and that the majority of teachers be American and teach in English. The full spirit of the commission appears in the following lines: "Put an American schoolhouse in every valley and upon every hilltop in Porto Rico, and in these places the well-fitted and accomplished American school-teachers, and the cloud of ignorance will disappear as the fog flies before the morning sun.''[87] This bit of amusing chauvinism must have been rather trying to the Puerto Ricans who found defects in the American teachers who did come. It is unfortunate that so many of the BIA files, concerning those teachers who came to the island during the early years of American dominance, were destroyed because they were thought to be of little worth. They might tell an interesting story in accomplishment.

Other recommendations on public instruction are found in the Puerto Rican commissioners who submitted a plan to the secretary of war on February 10, 1899. They suggested that at each of the seven departments of Puerto Rico there be established a kindergarten; that seventy-three public schools be added, four normal schools, one school of medicine, one law school, two schools of agriculture, and one manual training school. In addition, attendance *at the public schools* was to be made compulsory between the ages of five and fourteen years; and the month of August was to be vacation time.[88] Before the House Committee on Insular Affairs, General Davis made a succinct statement on education in the island: ''The Insular budget this year allots for schools over $300,000. . . . That suffices to give limited instruction to about 30,000 children. . . . There are 300,000 children of school age in Puerto Rico.''[89] Late in 1900, Victor S. Clark, former president of the Insular Board of Education, wrote an article for *The Forum* on education in the island. He attributed the initiative in school reform to a popular representative assembly that met in San Juan, on October 30, 1898. This assembly passed the following resolution:

> . . . the best means of advancing our people would be through kindergartens and normal schools as established in the United States. Our elementary and superior schools should be re-modelled and graded according to modern pedagogic methods. Secondary instructions should be a continuation of the primary and a preparation for superior and collegiate [*sic*]. Universal education should be introduced. There should be established schools for adults, Sunday schools, schools of Arts and trade, libraries, museums, academies of fine arts, and literary clubs.
>
> Education must be obligatory and gratuitous, and it must be compulsory upon every municipality to sustain its own schools, the number being fixed by law with reference to the population. If the municipality is unable to sustain all the

schools, the State should establish the additional ones that are necessary.

Mr. Clark in this article gives us an insight into the first days of American control of education. General Henry found confusion, schools closed, and salaries in arrears in the postwar period. The law of March, 1899, placed the control of schools in the town. But the hurricane of August 8 destroyed school buildings, and having devastated the plantations, it ended local taxes destined for the support of the school. Moreover, of the eight hundred towns and barrios, fewer than a score organized a school board; buildings and furniture were not provided; and personal interests clashed over the election of teachers to work under such conditions. Yet it was General Davis who doubled the proportion of the "public revenues devoted to education, raising it from 6 to 12 per cent."[90]

PUBLIC WORKS

One of the greatest shortcomings noticed by the Americans in Puerto Rico was a limited system of communication and transportation. Father Sherman described the condition of the island's roads as "wretched"; he reported the municipalities as pleading inability to make improvements owing to a lack of means. He advised that "a liberal public outlay on the roads would add immensely to the commerce and security of the island."[91] The Insular Commission found them "in the worst possible condition." The exceptions were the military road from San Juan to Ponce and the roads from Cayey to Guayama, from Toa Alta to Bayamón, from Bayamón to Río Piedras and from Bayamón to Cataño, and from Ponce to Guayama. They found the other roads "in bad condition and . . . greatly in need of repair. Substantially no work has been done upon them for many years, and in many places they are almost impassable." They advised that this condition be speedily improved, so that the products of the country could reach the markets without too great an expense in transportation. The mountain areas that were described as rich and productive "should be at once opened up." The major provincial roads, they believed, should be provided for by the general government, while intersecting and local roads should be a matter for municipal care.[92] The roads became one of the biggest projects of the United States in its attempts to put men to work and to improve transportation, especially after the hurricane of midsummer, 1899. General

Davis reported to the secretary of war on April 19, 1900, that "I have received authority to expend $660,000 on roads, $25,000 on hospital help, and the remainder of one million on relief for the destitute. It will be for the new government to decide on applying relief in other directions."[93]

Another matter for development, according to the Carroll Report, was that of railroads. A plan had been projected of skirting the island with a railroad, but the gaps were longer than the lines. From San Juan to Camuy, there was a line of sixty-one miles; from Aguadilla to Hormigueros, a line of twenty-four miles; from Yauco to Ponce, a line of twenty-two miles. There was another short spur from San Juan to Carolina; three more lines extended from Cataño to Bayamón, from San Juan to Río Piedras, and from Añasco to Alto Sano. The total for all lines was 154 miles, and all lines were of narrow gauge. Dr. Carroll's conclusion was that "quick and cheap rail communication between the various points and ports on the entire coast of Porto Rico must be provided at an early day if the resources of the island are to be properly developed." A related matter was that of wharves. The situation was described as primitive, since there was no wharf even for small boats at most of the ports. A lighter—in the form of a flatboat—was brought as close to the shore as possible, in order to roll hogsheads into it. He found that planters and merchants in Humacao, for example, were not raising more rice, pineapples, oranges, and coconuts, "because of lack of facilities of transportation."

Another matter of most serious concern in this period was that of public health and sanitation. The prevalent diseases were malaria, tuberculosis, typhoid, small-pox, and venereal diseases. Extensive malnutrition and high infant mortality, because of midwife deliveries, were also a serious cause of concern to the new government. It was for this reason that General Henry was very forceful in imposing the law of vaccination. The inefficient disposal of garbage and excreta caused serious parasitic diseases of the intestines, and the coming of the American army added to the prevalent venereal diseases. Army officers and Puerto Rican physicians did an effective job in cleansing markets and streets and in the purification of the water supply. A virus farm was set up for the producing of vaccine, and the distributing station was arranged at Coama Baths. In the towns, the leaders of the precincts summoned the people, and it was customary for a vaccinator to care for 225 in a day. Before long, the island was completely vaccinated. The significance of this is clearer if one recalls that small-pox had been for years one of the serious scourges of the island.[94]

Before closing this discussion of public works, we must note that the Insular Commission found this section of the Department of Interior still following the old Spanish methods, by which they meant a department riden with sinecures, and they immediately recommended firing many of the hangers-on. In the name of economy, it was suggested that simpler methods and practical road builders replace the highly detailed plans and the long list of scientific engineers.[95]

The various commissions, along with official army reports and the testimony of private individuals, were the sources of information on Puerto Rico that helped form the minds of the executive and legislative branches of government. This material, along with the congressional hearings, helped the United States Congress to formulate the first Organic Act of Puerto Rico. This act became known as the "Foraker Act" and was in force from May 1, 1900, to March 2, 1917. As we recall, it was on this date in 1900 that Charles H. Allen became the first civil governor of Puerto Rico under the sovereignty of the United States.

V

The Foraker Act and the
Beginnings of Civil
Government, 1900

The issue of autonomous government was the most sensitive point in relations between the United States and Puerto Rico at the turn of the century. The military governments had been honest but lacking in an adequate form of local representation. The tariff laws of Spain and the United States were operating to the detriment of the Puerto Rican economy, for, while Puerto Rico lost its privileges in the Spanish system, it gained none in the American. A serious hurricane had destroyed the major sources of income from sugar and coffee. The government had no hope of raising sufficient revenue through direct taxation of property. It had been no easy matter to draft the Foraker Act. The islanders were dissatisfied with this form of government with its system of "temporary tariffs." Within the United States, the legislation for Puerto Rico became a political football. The Democrats charged unconstitutionality and sugar lobbying. The Republicans believed that United States interests should be protected and denied any unconstitutionality, maintaining that the Supreme Court would sustain their position.

With no little insight into the situation, Worthington C. Ford

wrote, in midsummer of 1899, that "what Cuba and Puerto Rico were
to Spain they are to continue to the United States." He regarded the
reciprocity treaty with Hawaii as making trade "practically free,
only eight-hundredths of one per cent of the imports into the United
States paying any duties." Navigation laws limiting the carriage of
products to American vessels were extended to Hawaii and Puerto
Rico. He saw, however, that the Puerto Rican trade would be more
seriously affected for "of imports into the United States from that
Island less than 16 percent were brought in American vessels, and
about one-fifth (22 percent) of the exports were taken to the island
under the American flag." Of the exports from Puerto Rico in 1896,
the United States took less than one-tenth. Now the United States
had decreed the application of the minimum tariff of Spain to the
island; this was becoming onerous because it applied generally to
articles of necessary consumption. Besides, the "consumer of Cuba
was paying lower rates of duty than the same in Puerto Rico." Ford
believed that the island would become another sugar plantation and
that our export trade would not profit "unless some means is hit upon
to give the island a commercial crop, and in such a way as to make it
more profitable than it has been." He advised that in Puerto Rico
there should be "a tariff for revenue only and the free entry of its
products into American markets."[1]

This idea of the admission of Puerto Rican products into a free
market in the United States was not granted under the Foraker Act,
but the revenue received from such exports to the United States did
accrue to the benefit of the island. Congress passed, on March 24,
1900, an act "Refunding Customs Revenue Collected from Porto Rico
for the Relief of its Government and People." It read in part.

> Be it enacted by the Senate and House of Representatives
> of the United States of America in Congress assembled, that
> the sum of $2,095,455.88, being the amount of customs revenue
> received on importations by the United States from Porto Rico
> since the evacuation of Porto Rico by the Spanish forces on
> the 18th of October, 1898, to the first of January, 1900,
> together with any further customs revenue collected on im-
> portation from Porto Rico since the first of January, 1900,
> or that shall hereafter be collected . . . shall be placed at the
> disposal of the President, to be used for the government now
> existing and which may hereafter be established in Porto
> Rico.[2]

At the time of the act of Congress, the total amount available for expenditure under the direction of the War Department was $2,118,826.97. This "gift" of revenues collected to the island was regarded by some as a policy of largesse; by others, the mere existence of a customs barrier between the United States and its territories was regarded as a violation of the constitution. In the forging of the Foraker Act, then, two dominant issues were vigorously discussed on the floor of Congress and in committee: first, the right of Congress to impose a tariff barrier between the United States and Puerto Rico; and second, the political and legal status of Puerto Rico in relation to the Constitution of the United States.

THE FORAKER ACT IN COMMITTEE

It is maintained by Pedro Capó-Rodríguez that the authorship of the original draft of the Foraker Act belongs to Elihu Root.[3] Whatever truth may attach to this statement, it is undeniable that Senator Foraker of Ohio fought vigorously to establish in committee and in Congress the idea of Puerto Rico as a "nonincorporated" territory to which the constitution did not extend and consequently could be subjected by Congress to a tariff in its commerce with the United States.

Two bills on Puerto Rico were introduced almost simultaneously during the first session of the 56th Congress. Senate bill No. S.2264, described as "to provide civil government for Puerto Rico," was sponsored by Senator Foraker on January 9, 1900. He had it referred to the Senate Committee on Pacific Islands and Puerto Rico, of which he was chairman. On January 19, 1900, Congressman Payne introduced into the House No. H.6883, a bill "to extend the laws relating to customs and internal revenue in Puerto Rico." It was duly referred to the House Ways and Means Committee.[4]

During January of 1900, there was much discussion of the form of government proposed for Puerto Rico. The House Committee on Insular Affairs was conducting its hearings on the island, and the first to appear was General Davis. In respect to civil government, he maintained that, despite the clamor of political leaders in the island, a territorial form of government should not be granted and that universal manhood suffrage should not be allowed because of the lack of education. In economic affairs, he criticized the United States for taking away Puerto Rican markets and not replacing them with some other outlet. He was followed by General Stone who believed that the Puerto Ricans might be given "full territorial government" in five years. He favored an appointed rather than an elected legislature.[5]

Again on January 17, the House Committee on Insular Affairs met to hear William R. Corwine of the Merchants Association of New York. He stated that depressed trade conditions had prevailed in the island since American occupation, that foreign markets had been cut off, and that the production of tobacco had been curtailed about 60 per cent and sugar about 30 per cent. He found the chief imports from the United States to be flour, linoleum, cotton goods, hardware, paints, and leather goods. He gave an illustration of a triple-imposed tariff on paint: on the paint itself, on the can containing the paint, and on the wooden case carrying the cans. Corwine's recommendation was in favor of free trade as it existed between the states of the Union.[6] Two days later, Dr. J. J. Henna presented himself to the committee as a member of the former Puerto Rican Commission and as an elected representative of the Chamber of Commerce of Puerto Rico. Though he had lived in the United States for thirty years, he was well informed on the conditions of the island. He was convinced that the Puerto Ricans were fitted for self-government and suggested the application of the United States Constitution to the island as it was applied to the territories. He further advised that the upper house of the legislature be a mixed chamber, with half of the members elected by the Assembly and the other half appointed by the president. A governor general was to have a veto that could be overridden by a two-thirds vote. Dr. Henna contested the statements of both General Davis and the Insular Commission in relation to ability for self-government and literacy. He found that 695,328 could neither read nor write; that 96,867 could read and write; and that 14,513 could only read. The doctor became highly indignant at the end of his testimony: "The occupation has been a perfect failure. We have suffered everything. No liberty, no rights, absolutely no protection; not even the right to travel. We cannot travel today because we can not get passports. We are Mr. Nobody from Nowhere. We have no political status, no civil rights."[7]

Some very significant suggestions to the House Committee came from George I. Finlay who had been a resident of Puerto Rico for thirty-five years and was the British consul there. He found the people in favor of a territorial form of government and favored Congressman Henry's idea of a governor with a veto on the local legislative body. He asked for the free introduction of sugar into the United States, believing that "when we have free trade between Puerto Rico and the United States, that all, or a great part of the imported dry goods from Europe will then be imported into Puerto Rico from the United States." He then raised the issue of the change of currency, maintaining that it should only be changed after the extending of the American tariff to the island. Otherwise, he argued, they would be ruined:

> We should be paying everything in gold, and we would have nothing back for it. Produce would tumble down, because today sugar and coffee and all those things that are exported have a little fictitious value; a little value over the gold value on account of the exchange. We sell sugar to the United States and we are getting 66% on the dollar, and we are paying the labor there with the provincial money. If you were to pay that provincial money in gold the labor would benefit by it, but the exports could not stand it with your heavy duties on this side. Therefore if we get the tariff and you change the money everybody will prosper there, because what they are getting today on a 60 cent dollar they would get in a 100 cent gold dollar.

Finlay saw the peso as intrinsically worth 40 cents but believed that it should be redeemed at 75 cents. He lastly foretold that sugar would become the best industry of the island.

Dr. Azel Ames, who described himself as a native of Massachusetts who lived in Puerto Rico without any party affiliation, suggested good laws, free trade, exchange of money, and territorial loans. For revenue he would allow a small customs duty and a modified internal tax. The territorial loans, he believed, should be extended through the island by means of the Agricultural Bank. On political and legal matters, he stated that the islanders were well prepared for self-government and that there should be no appointed delegates in the legislature, but rather representatives elected by universal suffrage. He did not see why the constitution should not be extended to the island. He favored a code of law as simplifying practices and able to give satisfaction, while stating that "the common law is too involved, too broad, for ready adaptation to the conditions which exist there." Ames favored "a few Americans to lead and guide things into our methods." But he believed that the island must "be allowed to make its own laws" and have a governor's veto, an appointed judiciary, and a final check from the United States Congress.

He indicated, finally, that both Spanish rule and United States military government had brought suffering to the Puerto Ricans. He added that they were still suffering from ''an autocracy at the palace of a few secretaries—a little official circle of bureaucracy.''

Immediately following Dr. Ames before the House Committee and praising his statement was Tulio Larrinaga, an official representative of the Federal party of Puerto Rico. Larrinaga, gave a brief summation of the occasions in Puerto Rican history—in 1812, 1873, 1876, and 1898—when the people had been granted autonomy. He stated that the people of the island expected this from the Congress of the United States, that is, ''a territorial form of government, with representation in the United States Congress.'' Carlos Armstrong of Ponce advised that free trade should be granted first and then civil government. He noted that 90 per cent of the coffee crop had been destroyed and that it would take five years for replacement. Arturo Bravo testified that the planters were hoping for the highest return yet on their sugar crop as a result of the duty's being remitted. He urged free trade.[8]

While these appeals for free trade and autonomous government were being made, the opposition was presenting its viewpoint. Henry C. Curtis, a former member of the Insular Commission, strongly opposed free trade between the United States and the island. He also opposed any form of self-government for the present, on the argument that ''they are not fit for legislation by themselves, and it will be unsafe from sanitary conditions and legal conditions and tax conditions . . . until they have had lessons from us.'' He suggested a temporary military government, operating under the code of laws that was prepared by the Insular Commission members and the Code Commission. He opposed a territorial form of government on the principle that the constitution would have to be extended to the island along with it, and with the constitution would come the common law and all its consequences such as jury trial. For these, he believed, the people were not adequately prepared. For present conditions, the president's war power was better fitted than an organic act of Congress. He noted that the final report of the Insular Commission incorporated a full code of laws and that it was in the office of the secretary of war but not yet printed. A lack of funds was the alleged reason for nonpublication, but Senator Foraker was said to have stated that publication was stopped by the secretary of war who disapproved of the commission's recommendation that the common law be substituted for the Spanish law.

With even stronger convictions, Henry G. Oxnard, who represented the American Beet Sugar Association, expressed himself before the committee. He had just given testimony before the Senate committee on Pacific Islands and Puerto Rico, and he requested a voice before the House Ways and Means Committee. His statement was exclusively directed to the tariff question: "While we are perfectly willing to let them come in, we think they will very largely increase their production of sugar, and probably be a reproduction of what Hawaii did, and we claim they are taking, and will take in time, a larger proportion of our market from us, and we would like to have some tariff put up against them." In the course of the questioning by Congressmen Payne and Clayton, it was revealed that the Oxnard Sugar interests had enjoyed a greatly growing beet-sugar industry, in the face of free trade with Hawaiian sugar, for ten or fifteen years. Oxnard found damage in the increasing Hawaiian sugar and his fear was that "large investments will go into Puerto Rico . . . as soon as it is found that this immense profit can be made." He did not believe that the admission of the present sugar crop would injure his interests. What he opposed was "expansion in the beginning."

Southern interests in the United States of a different type were represented by Dr. S. Nathaniel Knapp of Lake Charles, Louisiana. This rice-producer stated that Puerto Rico imported about four million pounds of rice in 1895 and that ten million pounds of rice were waiting in the United States market for outside consumption. He saw no danger in "free trade," adding that the only product to influence our markets would be sugar, but it would be so insignificant as to have "no weight whatsoever." The month's hearing before the House Committee on Insular Affairs ended on January 29, when Nicolás Oyanguren of San Juan testified. This witness was a Spaniard, a merchant, and one of the directors of the Banco Territorial y Agrícola. He remarked that the island was in wretched condition. He urged:

> Give Puerto Rico a free interchange of products with its metropolis and a retirement of our provincial money. . . . Put them in a position so as to enable the island to raise a loan wherewith to build roads, public schools, and reconstruct the farming interests of the island. In framing commercial treaties with other countries protect in them Puerto Rico coffee as you would protect wheat, corn, or other staples from your States.

See that our coffee be admitted free or at a low duty in Cuba,
our sister-island, with whom Puerto Rico used to have a free
intercourse of products.

Oyanguren recommended a loan of $10 to $15 million for the
advance of public works, believing that it could be made at from 6 to
7 per cent interest rates. When Congressman Payne suggested that
they could get from $4 to $5 million from island revenues, Oyanguren
replied that the high tariff would defeat this.[9]

At the same time that the House Committee on Island Affairs was
conducting its hearings, the Senate Committee on Pacific Islands
and Puerto Rico was taking testimony. As we have seen in a previous
chapter, General Davis, H. G. Curtis, and Dr. J. Julio Henna
presented their ideas on January 17, 1900. On January 20, Lucas
Amadeo of Barros, Puerto Rico, and president of the Agricultural
Society of Puerto Rico, represented two thousand planters before this
Senate Committee. His stated purpose was to get free trade between
the United States and Puerto Rico and to arrange a loan to aid
agricultural interests and public works of the island. On civil matters
he found the Puerto Ricans well satisfied with General Davis,
"because he is a very cautious governor, and the country esteems
him at his worth." But they were dissatisfied with the form of
government. "We aspire," he said, "to a territorial form of government as it is applied here to the Territories." He requested a "joint
government in which the Puerto Ricans should have a majority."
Admitting the inexperience of the Puerto Ricans in American legislative systems, he found them capable of self-government.

On the same day, Enrique González of Río Grande, Puerto Rico,
secretary of the same Agricultural Society, reiterated the viewpoint: "In Puerto Rico we tried universal suffrage previous to the
American occupation, and we have seen that our uneducated classes
knew how to use this privilege. . . . I am in favor of unrestricted
suffrage." When asked by Senator Pettigrew if the people would be
satisfied with the form of government that Spain gave them, he
answered quickly: "Yes, sir. The last government it gave them they
were pretty well satisfied with that, as it approximates very closely
to the American form of territorial government." On the subject of
free trade he recalled that the island had enjoyed it with Spain, "and,
in spite of being burdened with taxation, enjoyed general welfare,
because at least they had one market, where today all of them are
closed."[10] George I. Finlay, representing the San Juan Chamber of

Commerce, gave his testimony to the Senate three days after his appearance before the House Committee. His statement was so valuable that it seems appropriate to quote extensively from it:

> It will soon be two years since Puerto Rico lost its markets with Spain and Cuba, with which it had free trade relations and which consumed and purchased coffee, sugar and tobacco to the amount of $10,000,000 annually; that is, $5.5 million for Spain and $3.5 for Cuba. This enormous loss has not as yet been compensated, and has brought about a tremendous crisis in all the producing centers of the Island.
>
> Merchants have therefore been compelled to limit their operations, banks have suspended making advances, agricultural properties are heavily mortgaged, and in many ways the work has been suspended, laborers are out of employment, whole families are in misery, and hunger threatens everywhere, the poor farm laborers being in such a state of destitution as they never have been before in the history of the island.
>
> The United States Government . . . is sending rations and supplies to relieve the poor, but this is insufficient. A more heroic remedy becomes imperative, and this can only be found in justly applying and with all urgency, *free trade with the United States, thus giving the country the benefits of the interchange of commerce with the North American Republic, of which Puerto Rico is an integral part.*

He concluded his testimony with an appeal for "cheap and substantial food from the United States" in abundant supply. He asserted that free trade with the United States would in no way injure the producer of sugar or of any other product.[11]

While these island interests sought free trade from congressional legislation, the sugar and tobacco lobbies were pressing for protection. Henry G. Oxnard of Oxnard, California, who was a manufacturer of about 400,000 tons of beet sugar and had two factories in southern California, two in Nebraska, and one in Colorado, criticized the Foraker Bill as a "great injustice to our competing 'home industries.'" He found it a danger to the labor market of the United States, a violation of "protection," and a bad precedent. This manufacturer sturdily lectured the senators on the principle of "protection" in the Republican party. He also went a little afield when he described the school system in Puerto Rico as worthless, with "the Roman Catholic catechism as the principal textbook." He found that "the Latin race, after years of the rule of despotism, suddenly given power, is a troublesome if not a dangerous factor with which to deal.''

Another disciple of protection was Herbert Myrick, President of the Orange Judd Company, a company that published many farm magazines. He was also chairman of the League of Domestic Producers, which had representatives from such associations as beet sugar, cane sugar, tobacco, wool, cotton, fruits, vegetables, rice, and nuts. He stated that his purpose was ''to put into the pockets of the farmers, capitalists and laborers of these United States the $100 million now exported annually to pay for imported sugar.'' The demands of his league were: first, the denial of duty-free admission of Cuban and Puerto Rican sugar and tobacco; second, the defeat in the Senate of pending treaties of reciprocity with the British West Indies which would reduce the tariff rates on sugar and other products; and third, the opposing of a reduction in duties on sugar, wool, and hides from Argentina. He regarded Puerto Rico as ''the first step in the free-trade policy foreshadowed by the pending reciprocity treaties with the West Indies, British Guiana, Argentina, and France.'' After teaching the committee the meaning of ''protection,'' he hammered home his point: ''Don't deceive yourself into thinking that you can take away the farmers' protection while leaving it upon the manufacturer. Our farmers haven't the money to maintain talented lobbyists at Washington, but they have the votes with which to maintain their interests. . . . Treat our farmers just as fairly and honestly as you treat the manufacturer, or we will elect a Congress that will.'' In a hassle with Senators Nelson and Fairbanks, Myrick was willing to have the Puerto Ricans ''put a tariff on all exports they can not produce as cheaply as they can import from the Northwest.'' He was convinced that ''we are bringing Puerto Rico vast blessings by our policies'' and that Dingley shared ''our views.'' In full agreement with Myrick was H. S. Frye, who for the past ten years was president of the New England Tobacco Growers' Association. This organization regarded free trade with the insular possessions as abandonment of protection and the destruction of the American system of political economy. Frye had no fear of the present competition of Puerto Rican tobacco but ''of the precedent it might set.''[12]

By early February, the House Committee on Insular Affairs was still hearing testimony. Lucas Amadeo and Enrique González were urging immediate free trade and a loan of not less than $16 million to be expended on public works. They pointed to the daily fact of "an enormous number of deaths from starvation, and the rest of the people are becoming pauperized." To inspire confidence in United States capital, an absolute and stable civil government must be established. Under a territorial form of government, the island could handle its own internal affairs. The voting of the illiterate populace he regarded as a lesser evil than leaving the government to the "parasites," a term he applied to the office-holders. Louis Sánchez Morales, the San Juan representative of the Republican party, asked for United States citizenship, territorial rights, and the selection of the members of the lower house by universal suffrage. Though he was willing to accept as a temporary provision the educational and property qualifications for the vote, his party stood in principle for the general suffrage. Lastly, he stated that only by free trade could the people return to prosperity.[13]

On the same day, February 5, Senate Bill No. S.2264 was reported back from committee favorably, but with an amendment. This report (S.R.249) gives us an insight into what the committee had in mind. The government of the Foraker Act was to be temporary until the laws could be revised and codified and a more permanent form of government be formulated. Its principal purposes were the setting up of a civil government in which the Puerto Ricans would be given a significant role, the extension of United States navigation laws to the island, the enacting of tariff and internal revenue measures for insular expenses, and the retirement of the Puerto Rican currency. Senator Foraker remarked that the most thorny questions in committee were: first, whether the constitution should be extended to Puerto Rico; and second, what provisions should be made with respect to tariff duties and internal revenue taxes. On the first question, the chairman stated, "Congress did not extend the Constitution of the United States to the Territories in any case prior to the act of September 9, 1850." His conclusion was that "there is abundant precedent for not extending the provisions of the Constitution to territories of the United States for which Congress may be called upon to legislate." At the same time, the bill made provision for the conferral of citizenship on the Puerto Ricans. On the second question, the majority opinion of the committee was that if the new territory did not come under the constitution, Congress was free to impose tariffs or allow free trade between the island and the United States. The minority report of the committees was in strong opposition to any free trade provision, arguing that it would injure "the successful cultivation of tobacco, sugar, and citrous fruits in the United States." They urged a considerably higher rate of duty than 25 per cent be imposed on Puerto Rican products.[14]

In the House Ways and Means Committee the original bill (H.R.6883) had gone through a change; and the bill was reported to the House in a new form (H.R.8245). The report, in discussing Section 8, Article I, of the United States Constitution that provides for uniform duties among the several states, insisted that the term "the United States" has a wider comprehension than the term "the several States"; under the term "the several States," the territories are not included. It maintained that "the power of Congress with respect to legislation for the territories is plenary"; under that power "Congress may prescribe different rates of duty for Puerto Rico than those prescribed for the United States."[15]

Now that the committees of both houses had reported their bills to the floor, a vigorous battle ensued. Representative Robert L. Henry of Texas took a strong position, that Puerto Rico be received as "an integral part" of the United States, promising the people all the rights of United States citizens. He found the House Bill (H.R. 8245) in contradiction to our tradition; he believed that we must "abolish all customs tariffs between the United States and Porto Rico, and give her products free access to our markets." He stressed the serious poverty of the island, the injustice of the United States in not letting them legislate for themselves, and he attributed the change of mind away from free trade to the machinations of the sugar interests. He found Congress bound by the same constitutional limitations in legislating for the territories as for the states, and he cited Taney's reasoning in the Dred Scott case as the prevailing rule.[16] In opposition to this position stood Representative Richard Wayne Parker of New Jersey, who found the bill granting much largesse:

> This bill says that Puerto Rico shall have what no State in the Union has ever had. It says, first that these poor people shall have absolute freedom from the excise taxes of the United States, so far as paying a single dollar into our Treasury. . . .
>
> We reduce the Dingley tariff as against them by three-quarters. We ask them only to do the same to us, and then we declare that the payments under the tariff shall not go into the Treasury of the United States, but go to the President for the benefit of the people of that island.[17]

PUERTO RICO AND THE FEDERAL CONSTITUTION

At the same time, on the floor of the Senate, the constitutional issues were hotly debated. As early as January 11, Senator Foraker was contesting two resolutions. The first, offered by Senator Vest of Missouri, held that the United States has no constitutional power to acquire and govern territories permanently as colonies. Senator Mason of Illinois presented the second, which maintained that the government of the United States will not govern a people of any country without the consent of the people themselves. In his discussion, Senator Foraker stated that implied in the constitutional powers to make war and treaties was Congress' power to acquire and govern territories; to this effect he cited Chief Justice Marshall in *American Insurance Company* v. *Canter* (I Peters 511). Senators Teller and Foraker, against strong opposition, argued that "the provisions of the Constitution do not extend to territories, save by provision of law." Foraker then cited *Endelman et al.* v. *United States* (in *Federal Reporter*, 86th vol., p. 456): "Congress has full legislative power over the Territories, unrestricted by the limitations of the Constitution." In a further dispute with Senator Hoar, who held that the United States' acquiring of a territory is dependent on the consent of the inhabitants, Foraker used a bit of bombast: "Is it possible that this great and powerful nation of ours, powerful in peace and powerful in war, and to be powerful, we trust, in the commercial world, has no power to subserve its own necessary and constitutional purposes except only by the consent of the people who may for the time being be affected? I utterly repudiate any such doctrine." Foraker denied that he had any idea of permanently holding a people, if they are capable of self-government. In answer to Senator Turner, who argued that under the constitution the federal government has no power to acquire territory to be held and governed permanently as colonies, Foraker found all dependent on Congress. He said: "Until Congress shall legislate so as to set the Constitution in motion, these rights belong to the citizens in the Territories in an abstract way simply; they cannot be reduced to a practical enjoyment."[18]

In his autobiography, Senator Foraker recalled this speech of January 11, as "one of the most important I made during all my service in the Senate." He reiterated his argument that

> Congress must govern the United States according to the Constitution, which is the organic law of the Union, but it can

govern a Territory that simply belongs to the United States as
it may think best, restrained only by the positive prohibitions
of the Constitution and the general spirit of our institutions,
which is above all written law. . . .

    We have heard much in the recent discussion about the
Constitution extending, *ex proprio vigore,* to newly acquired
territory at the moment of its acquisition. This doctrine orig-
inated with John C. Calhoun and was advocated by him for
the first time in the debates preceding the legislation establishing the Territorial governments for New Mexico, Arizona, and
Utah, and he advocated it in the interest of human slavery, to
carry that institution into those territories.[19]

Foraker also noted that he had favored the conferring of United
States citizenship on the Puerto Ricans but that many senators had
believed this to be premature.

    In late February, *The Independent* carried an article by Congress-
man James D. Richardson who argued that the constitutional provision of uniform duties meant the whole of the Republic, both
states and territories. He cited as his authorities, first, John Marshall
who in *Loughborough* v. *Blake* (5 Wheaton 660) so ruled; second,
President McKinley who in his last message to Congress said that it
is "our plain duty to abolish all customs tariffs between the United
States and Porto Rico and give her products free access to our
markets"; third, United States consul Philip C. Hanna who held
that "free trade between the United States and Puerto Rico is a
moral question"; fourth, Secretary of War Root who stated: "I wish
most strongly to urge that the customs duties between Porto Rico and
the United States be removed." Others of the same opinion were
General Davis, Congressman Payne, and Dr. Henry K. Carroll.[20] In
the very next issue of *The Independent,* the editor took a strong stand
against the Foraker Bill, agreeing with the leader of the Democratic
speakers, Richardson, that "the bill was more dangerous to the
liberties of the American people than any other introduced during
his term in Congress." The editorial was forthright:

    The constitutional questions so elaborately argued have
    little interest to the pleaders save as a sort of excuse for the
    action proposed; the pleas of necessity of revenue and of pro-
    tection of the people of Porto Rico are utterly without
    weight. . . .
    What happened to change the conviction? No report,
    demand or request from Porto Rico; no new message from
    the President; no change in the island itself; no valid argu-

ment from any quarter. Simply the cry of the tobacco and cane and beet sugar producers of certain States that their craft was in danger. . . . The Foraker Bill, as originally drawn, proposed to extend the Constitution to the new as to the old territories; but when the cry of the alarmed sugar and tobacco producers reached our national halls of legislation there was a pause, a change of front and a change of program. The word "Constitution" was stricken out of the bill.[21]

With much greater dignity and reasoning, Dr. Azel Ames used the pages of *The Independent* to express his views on the proposed Puerto Rican tariff. He noted that the Republicans had gained a narrow victory in the imposition of 15 per cent duties of the Dingley tariff on merchandise in transit between island and mainland. He also brought out that the tariff was not to apply after March 1, 1902, and might be terminated before that date, but he cautioned that it would take two years to restore the devastated plantations and the neglected sugar mills. He saw that "commercial distrust" would be a bad effect of the tariff, in so far as changes could be easily brought about by powerful interests. He admitted that sugar would pay a small profit "under even the full 'Dingley' tariff" and that "every reduction in the tariff goes to enhance the profit of the producer." This profit he regarded as most necessary, since thereby the wages of the workers would be increased; "hitherto the profits on sugar have not been sufficient to afford more than the miserable wages—fifty centavos per day [30 cents in gold] and their breakfast -paid to these men." And so he hoped that a reduced tariff would mean larger crops, better machinery, and better wages for laborers.[22]

In early March, 1900, Senator Foraker contended with a strong opposition to his bill on the floor of the Senate. Senator Tillman asked him why it was that the president had changed his mind from "our bounden duty to have free trade" to the new tariff provision. He wondered if the influence had come from "Mr. Oxnard, the sugar-trust king." To this Senator Foraker replied that the president was justified in changing his mind on seeing more of the facts. Senator Tillman, who was from South Carolina, saw that Foraker was more concerned with the manufacturing interests of the country, whereas he was concerned with the agricultural interests of the South. He opposed the admission of the islands to the Union because he saw competition; he also opposed their admission as "subjects," rather than citizens, as a violation of our principles concerning "the consent

of the governed and the equality of men.'' He would not sacrifice
these ideas ''in behalf of this doctrine of destiny, duty and dollars.''
Foraker replied to a question from Senator Teller that Puerto Rico
was a dependency of the United States and not a part in any *integral*
sense and that ''he found no stipulation in the treaty that the territory and the inhabitants should be incorporated into the union.''
To this end, he cited Justice Bradley in *Snow* v. *United States* (18
Wallace 319): ''The Government of the Territories of the United
States belongs, primarily, to Congress, and, secondarily, to such
agencies as Congress may establish for that purpose. During the term
of their pupilage as Territories they are mere dependencies of the
United States.'' Here Foraker admitted that the bill contemplated
admitting the Puerto Ricans to citizenship. This raised the objection
of Senator Bacon, who found it ''impossible . . . to conceive of a
citizen of the United States who is not under the Constitution.'' The
immediate reply of Senator Foraker was that this had been done in
Louisiana and Florida: ''We never extended the Constitution to any
Territory until 1850, when it was extended to New Mexico, and yet
in all the Territories we were then governing the people were treated
and regarded as citizens of the United States.'' Bacon returned to the
battle with a long argument, favoring the position that the granting
of civil government to Puerto Rico automatically extended the constitution. Foraker refuted this, finding Puerto Rico a ''territory belonging to the United States.''[23]

Again on March 20, Senate Bill No. S.2264 was discussed in the
Senate. Senator Morgan of Alabama favored the granting of full
citizenship to Puerto Rico, and he saw no illegality in the tariff barrier between the United States and the island. He favored a territorial government for Puerto Rico on the model of the government
of the Northwest Territory, including a bill of rights, but not all the
rights secured in the constitution—such as the jury trial.[24] By
March 24, 1900, conference committees of the House and the Senate
had brought the discussion around to a study of the bill (H.8245)
that provided both revenue and civil government for Puerto Rico.
This bill was submitted to much caustic criticism. In the House of
Representatives, McRae of Arkansas opposed the $2 million charity
money collected unjustly from Puerto Rico and the tariff wall
destroying the trade between Puerto Rico and the United States.
Pierce and Cox of Tennessee, Wilson and Finley of South Carolina,
Cochran of Missouri, Williams of Illinois, and Levy of New York

strongly opposed the bill. For the most part, the Republican members of the House remained silent. The vote finally showed 135 yeas, 87 nays, 21 "present," and 107 not voting.[25]

In *Leslie's Weekly*, Senator Foraker summarized his arguments in support of the statement that "all the provisions of the Foraker Bill are more liberal and generous than any enacted for any territory since the beginning of our government." First of all, all of the internal revenue collected in the island and all customs were to go to Puerto Rico. Secondly, revenue by direct taxation was impracticable since the islanders had no money, no credit, and were incapable of meeting such a direct tax. Thirdly, we did not, as in the case of Louisiana, Florida, and others, take Puerto Rico with the pledge that they would be incorporated into the Union; but, rather, the Congress should fix the civil and political status of the inhabitants. Fourth, we were asking an "open door" in the Far East from the other powers; how could we close the door to them, if we allowed free trade to United States ships in the Philippines and Puerto Rico? Sixth, our doors should not be opened to cheap labor, as competition to the wage-workers of the United States and their products.[26] On April 12, 1900, the Foraker Act was approved by the president and became the first organic act of Puerto Rico under the United States. It went into operation on May 1 when the first civil governor, Charles H. Allen, took office. It was superseded by the Jones Act of March 2, 1917.

THE FORAKER ACT

This first organic act was intended "temporarily to provide revenues and civil government for Puerto Rico." As we have seen, the imposition of tariffs and the nonincorporation of the island under the constitution were the two most contested issues. In Section 2 it was determined that the same tariffs, customs, and duties collected on articles imported into Puerto Rico from foreign ports were to be imposed as those collected on importation into the United States. A significant exception to this was foreign coffee that was subject to 5 cents per pound duty; this was protection for a significant Puerto Rican industry. Section 3 set up a tariff wall between the United States and Puerto Rico; the duty imposed was only 15 per cent of the Dingley Tariff rates on foreign articles. Puerto Rican merchandise coming to the United States was to pay a tax equal to the United States internal revenue tax, whereas United States merchandise to the island was to pay a tax equal to that imposed in Puerto Rico on like articles of Puerto Rican manufacture. It was provided, however, that the president should proclaim all tariff duties between the United States and Puerto Rico at an end when the Puerto Rican Legislative Assembly had worked out a system of local taxation. Section 4 granted these revenues to be used in Puerto Rico. A last provision ordered that all tariff duties between Puerto Rico and the United States were to be ended on March 1, 1902, or sooner.

The other major provision of this act was a civil government. The governor was to be appointed by the President for four years and was empowered to veto legislation, commission officers, execute laws, grant pardons and reprieves, and give an annual report to the secretary of state. A bicameral legislature consisting of the Executive Council and the House of Delegates was provided. The upper house was a legislative-executive body, made up of eleven members appointed by the president with the consent of the Senate. Six of these were to hold the cabinet roles of secretary, attorney general, treasurer, auditor, commissioner of interior, and commissioner of education. Of the total eleven, at least five were to be Puerto Ricans. The House of Delegates was to consist of thirty-five members elected biennially by qualified voters. This body was to be the sole judge of elections and retain all power over its proceedings. Section 31 stated that bills may originate in either house; the passage of a bill was to be by majority vote; and a two-thirds vote of both houses would over-pass the governor's veto. All laws, however, were subject to annul-ment by the United States Congress. The matter of granting fran-chises was reserved under Section 32 to the action of the Executive Council with the governor's approval and was subject to check by the Congress in Washington.

In addition to the established municipal and police courts, there was set up a chief justice and associate justices of the Supreme Court whose members were to be appointed by the president. The judges of the district courts were to be appointed by the governor, with the consent of the Executive Council, while the other judicial posts were by selection of the legislative assembly. This Supreme Court of the island supplanted the United States Provisional Court that had been set up by General Davis. Section 34 provided a United States District Court for Puerto Rico. In its adjudication it was to handle the laws of the United States in relation to appeals, writs of error and certiorari, removal of causes, and so on; it was to govern in a fashion somewhat between a district court of the United States and courts of Puerto Rico. Section 35 stated that appeals from the Supreme Court of Puerto Rico and the District Court of the United States in Puerto Rico were to be taken to the United States Supreme Court in accord with the regulations for territories.

In the matter of law, it was provided under Section 8 that the laws and ordinances of Puerto Rico then in force were to continue, except as amended by the military orders when the act would take effect and in so far as there was no inconsistency with United States statutes. Three special provisions were added: first, the law forbidding the marriage of priests was repealed and annulled; second, both civil and religious marriages were made valid; and third, divorce on the basis of adultery was made legal. Statutory laws of the United States, locally applicable and not otherwise provided for in the act, were to have the same force in Puerto Rico as in the United States. An exception was made for internal revenue laws that were determined in Section 3 of the act. The legislative authority was empowered to amend or alter any law or ordinance—civil or criminal— continued in force by the act. Section 40 arranged for a commission of three—at least one of whom was to be a Puerto Rican—to be appointed by the president; they were to compile and revise the laws of Puerto Rico, the codes of procedure, and the systems of municipal government. Section 16 required that all judicial process was to be performed in the name of the United States, whereas all criminal or penal prosecutions in the local courts were to be carried out in the name of "The People of Puerto Rico," since the islanders were defined as "citizens of Puerto Rico."

Section 39 provided a "resident commissioner" who was to be elected by the people of Puerto Rico to sit in the United States Congress with voice, but without vote. Under Section 11, the Puerto Rican peso was to be redeemed at 60 cents in United States coins. The property acquired by the United States in Puerto Rico (bridges, roads, water power, streams and their beds, sub-soil of private lands, harbor works, etc.) was put under the control of the government of Puerto Rico and was to be administered for the benefit of the islanders. Legislation on such matters was up to the Assembly, "subject to the limitations imposed upon all its acts." A significant provision in Section 38 forbad export duties and refused any public indebtedness of Puerto Rico or any municipality in the excess of 7 per cent of the aggregate tax valuation of its property.[27]

As can be expected, this legislation met with some strong opposition. In the United States, it was regarded by the Democratic party as an unconstitutional use of power. In the island, it was considered as unconstitutional and a failure in a trust. That the islanders had expected more autonomy than Congress granted was a sign of ignorance of American political ideals (or prejudices) and behavior. Too much testimony in opposition to insular self-government had been given. The tariff imposed can be regarded as legislation in the interest of "protection" and the United States sugar lobbyists, or as a means of raising the revenue necessary for the operation of the island in the face of inadequate internal revenue. The constitutional arguments for "nonincorporation" seem a possible, though not generous, interpretation of the constitution, of judicial precedents, and of the Treaty of Paris.

The constitutionality came up for testing and was approved as Senator Foraker predicted in the case of *Downes* v. *Bidwell* (182 U.S. 244 [1901]). Five of the nine Supreme Court justices agreed that the island came under United States sovereignty by the terms of the Treaty of Paris but that this did not automatically make it a part of the United States in a constitutional sense. Four of the justices made the distinction between incorporated and unincorporated territory, an idea that had been already expressed by Senator Foraker on the floor of the Senate. The action of incorporation must derive from the expressed will of Congress, and Congress had not seen fit to do so. Lastly, when Congress has not incorporated a territory, she is not bound to deal with it in the same constitutional way as when dealing with states or incorporated territory. The court further held that imports from Puerto Rico could be subjected to tariffs.

A strong dissent to this decision of the majority was raised by Chief Justice Fuller who saw unequal treatment: "The logical result is that Congress may prohibit commerce altogether between the States and the territories, and may prescribe one rule of taxation in one territory, and a different rule in another." It may well be argued in contradiction of Fuller and legal commentators on the Downes case that differing rules of taxation in different territories can be equitable, if conditions require it. In reply to the assertion that the constitution must apply equally to all, it must be noted that, as Senator Foraker asserted, it was not the American tradition to extend *ipso facto* the constitution to new territories. This, rather, came as a new doctrine under John C. Calhoun in 1850 when he sought to see the constitution automatically operating in all new territories, in the interest of projecting slavery therein. The idea of a colonial status within the American system, though it had its injustices, seems to have been a clear historical fact. On this basis, the Downes case seems to have much to say for its decision.[28]

The successful outcome of the decision in the Supreme Court brought congratulatory letters to Senator Foraker from John Hay, Nicholas Murray Butler, and Governor Taft. Writing from the Philippines, on July 22, 1901, Taft said "I congratulate you on the result of the Supreme Court decision sustaining your view originally expressed on the constitutional question of so much importance to the welfare of these islands. A decision that the Dingley Tariff necessarily extends to the collection of imports in these islands would have produced a chaos, and a difficulty in government here that I dislike to contemplate."[29] On the other hand, the opposition is well expressed in a scholarly article by Pedro Capó-Rodríguez some years after the decision. This attorney found that the Downes case was the first expression in United States constitutional history of newly acquired territories as "possessions or dependencies of the United States, subject to future disposition by Congress." He carried his argument further, stating that "The inhabitants of both the Philippines and Porto Rico were deprived of the benefits of the Constitution and time-honored traditions of the Republic . . . inherent rights of the inhabitants of the former territories of the United States . . . such fundamental rights of American liberty as the writ of *habeas corpus* and public trial by jury were absolutely denied to them."[30] Capó-Rodríguez resented the system of having only one resident commissioner from Puerto Rico sitting in the United States Congress, and without vote. He pointed to Spain which, despite the "disastrous blunders of her colonial system," gave representation to Cuba and Puerto Rico in the parliament of the kingdom. Under the autonomous government, Spain gave Puerto Rico representation in the Cortes to the extent of "16 representatives and 3 Senators." The system of the United States will "subject the colonies and their people to a system of congressional dictation and imposition which . . . may be a cause of future disagreement and embarrassment." He urged a farsighted colonial policy aimed at closer union, "appealing to the natural aspirations of the people for their ultimate admission into the Union as a state thereof, on an equal footing with the other States." To this end the "American colonies and dependencies should be given an adequate representation with voice and vote in both Houses of Congress.[31]

General Davis, speaking before the Lake Mohonk Conference in 1909, stood in favor of the Foraker Act as a temporary governing constitution. He regarded the Puerto Ricans as "all of a foreign race and tongue, largely illiterate and without experience in conducting a government in accordance with Anglo-Saxon practice." He saw the intent of Congress as a desire "to observe the use they would make of qualified citizenship." In respect to revenues collected by United States officials in Puerto Rico on imports, the amount from May 1, 1900, to June 30, 1908, amounted to over $7 million. Davis saw that, in this period, the federal treasury would have gathered in from the island, in customs and excise taxes, about $25 million. He remarked: "What would be the economic condition of Porto Rico had it been deprived of this vast sum it is not difficult to imagine." He further observed that "since July 25, 1901, Porto Rico has enjoyed absolute free trade with the United States." The last observation of the general was that the population of the island would within the next forty years rise to two million, "unless there is very large emigration or pestilence." He believed that the Puerto Ricans would remain in customs and aspirations "as strictly Porto Rican as they now are." In looking into the future, he saw that "After full American citizenship must come statehood, the ultimate to which all the native inhabitants of Porto Rico who think, declare that they aspire. Porto Rico as a state would have two senators and probably a half-dozen representatives in our Congress." He then asked if this were a realizable dream. His answer was conditioned by many *ifs*. He believed that, despite the current unrest (1909) the people would merit a "larger measure of self-rule."[32] For General Davis and for many other leaders in the United States, the Foraker Act was a just and necessary step toward ultimate self-rule in Puerto Rico.

The reaction of the vigorous leader of the Federal party in Puerto Rico, Luis Muñoz Rivera, to the Foraker Act is an interesting study in evolution of thought. On returning from the United States in early September, 1899, Muñoz Rivera expressed his enthusiastic praise of the American political system, especially of the election. He saw the task of the Liberal party as the transformation of Puerto Rico into "a likeness (*spécimen*) of California or Nebraska," in that it would propose and possess its own laws and be equal in its rights and in law. He saw that to be good Puerto Ricans, "we cannot be, we ought not, nor do we wish to be—absolutely and with reservations —anything but good and loyal Americans.'' He saw, in the convening of Congress, reforms for Puerto Rico.[33] He expressed himself again in *La Democracia,* on October 5, 1899, to the effect that the Liberals were dedicated to autonomism and opposed to the tyranny that ''consists in imposing on weak peoples an authority that does not originate in the consent of the governed.'' His party, he said, called itself the Federal party because they lived by the ideal of autonomism and believed that nowhere was there such broad and indestructible autonomy as that created by the fathers of North America, both for their states and for their territories. He was convinced that, since the United States was a republic of republics, ''Puerto Rico ought to be one of those republics in the future.'' He was aware that, like other territories, Puerto Rico must go through the intermediate stage. In economic matters, he stated that the Federal party was set on free trade with the American Union.[34]

By the turn of the year, however, Muñoz Rivera had seen the Foraker Bill in formation; and, while he approved its economic provisions, he found it deficient in the political clauses. He saw that the insular legislature would be subordinate to a bureaucratic body (council) in which the Puerto Ricans would be in a minority and that all legislation would be subject to the governor's veto.[35] Three months later, Muñoz Rivera was insisting that Puerto Rico should be considered ''*an integral part* of the United States, as were Louisiana, Texas, California, and New Mexico upon being annexed to the Union.'' Yet the law would be accepted and regarded as a *modus vivendi;* for, as he believed, it would last but a year and then be replaced by a more ample and just law.[36] The ever-growing antagonism to the Republican party of the United States and their Foraker Act, however, appeared in the *Diario* of July 6, 1900, when a cablegram sent by the *New York Sun* to the *San Juan News* was reproduced. Senator Teller was quoted as saying: ''The Puerto Rican people do not please me. They, unlike the Cubans, are not fighters. They would have submitted to the Spanish tyranny for centuries without showing themselves as men by raising up opposition. Such a race is unworthy of citizenship.''[37] The smoldering dislike of the Foraker Act was well under way, for the civil government that it created had been in operation for two months. The forces of opposition to it came from the Federal party under the direction of Muñoz Rivera;

the Republican party in Puerto Rico, on the other hand, learned to walk in harmony with the new government.

BEGINNINGS OF CIVIL GOVERNMENT, 1900

When Governor Allen arrived at San Juan on April 27, 1900, no information had been received from Washington as to the civil officers who were to fill the posts under the organic act. The same act, however, allowed the military governor, General Davis, to change laws and ordinances in the interim, preceding installation of the civil government. And so General Davis, on recommendation of Governor-elect Allen published a military order "changing the existing system of government so as to make it conform to the system adopted by Congress." This Order No. 102 made the following temporary appointments: N. B. K. Pettingill, secretary; A. F. Odlin, attorney general; J. H. Hollander, treasurer; J. R. Garrison, auditor; Cayetano Coll y Toste, commissioner of the interior; and George G. Groff, commissioner of education. A realignment of duties for cabinet officers was arranged. A Judicial Advisory Board was set up with the purpose of getting recommendations on judicial matters; the members appointed were Rafael Nieto Abeille, Juan Hernández López, Manuel F. Rossy, and Herminio Díaz. Many of the former boards, such as those of prison control, public works, health, charities, and education, were transferred to the proper departments of the executive, in accord with the intent of the Organic Act of 1900.[38]

On May 1, 1900, the inaugural ceremonies took place in front of the executive mansion. General Davis presented the civil governor, taking occasion to remark that the organic act "provides a basis for industry, trade, and commerce which warrants the belief that the dark clouds of misery and want which have shadowed the past and the present will soon roll away." He advised the people that they were offered "absolutely free trade with the United States the moment ability is shown to support your government without the very moderate revenues which may still be collected on imports from the United States." Bishop Blenk, in his invocation, expressed gratitude to God for general George W. Davis and his assistants, "who, in most trying times, steadfastly, intelligently, and with genuine nobility of heart devoted themselves to the public good." A strong insight into the feeling of the people is seen in the address of Judge José Severo Quiñones, chief justice of the Supreme Court, who administered the oath of office to the new governor. He said that he could not view "with indifference the triumph of modern ideas," and he looked for the day when Puerto Ricans might become "full-fledged citizens of the great North American nation." He adverted to the grave financial crisis in the island, to the standstill in agriculture and commerce. He commended General Davis for much good done but found that much was still to be done in the alleviation of poverty. To this end, he urged a program of public works, such as highways and schoolhouses. He recalled the autonomous charter that Spain had granted and longed for "those political rights that are the most precious conquest of modern civilization." At the same time, he recognized that "during the period of their incumbency not a single case is recorded of positive abuse of power exercised against any citizen; and that if some of their decisions have given rise to heated discussions, others . . . have been hailed with general satisfaction, such as, for example, the orders relating to the organization of the courts and the reform of judicial procedure." Lastly, he looked for the time when his island "may become a free and contented State within the great federation of North America." Governor Allen spoke briefly, promising justice that "will be meted out to all" and his government "will have a sole regard for the welfare of Porto Rico and the honor of the American Government in its relation to it." He concluded with many noble sentiments: "Henceforth we are under one flag. We are under the same institutions of freedom, equality, and education. Together we move on in the great American current of advancing civilization. Loving our country, animated by a high sense of honor, devoted to a common humanity, we take our place before the world and invoke on our progress the blessing of Almighty God."[39]

With the inauguration over, the president selected from a list of candidates presented by both political parties the permanent members of the Executive Council. On June 11, 1900, he cabled the list, which retained two of the temporary appointees: Hollander as treasurer, and Garrison as auditor. William H. Elliott was appointed commissioner of interior; Martin G. Brumbaugh, commissioner of education; John A. Russell, attorney general; José Severo Quiñones, chief justice of the Supreme Court; Louis Sulzbacher, José C. Hernández, José M. Figueras, and Rafael Nieto Abeille as associate justices. William H. Holt became the United States district judge; Noah B. K. Pettingill, United States district attorney; and Edward S. Wilson, United States marshal. The five members added to the ex officio members of the Executive Council were: José C. Barbosa, Rosendo Matienzo Cintrón, José de Diego, Manuel Camuñas, and Andrés Crosas. The first two were prominent members of the Republican party; the second two were members of the Federalist party of Muñoz Rivera; and the last, Andrés Crosas, was an Independent.[40]

From the beginning of the civil government, it became apparent that Governor Allen would not have the success that attended General Davis. Roberto Todd states that, upon receiving the appointment as governor, Allen told President McKinley that he would prefer staying in Washington, as undersecretary of the navy. The president, however, was able to persuade him of his ability to fill the need in Puerto Rico. Todd further remarks that, from the beginning, Governor Allen tried to win the good will and aid of the leaders of both the Federal and Republican parties. But in this he failed because "the Federal party that was undoubtedly the majority party in the country showed hostility to him from the beginning."[41] A personal letter of Governor Allen to Secretary of War Root, on May 5, 1900, told of the beginnings of his administration: "We have started a de facto government—and it is going comfortably—thus far. But the difficulties at first seemed almost unsurmountable. No Congressional action, and we couldn't be caught unprepared. So we were ready for the worst, and when the time came we started all right. . . . Today (apart from the Customs over which I have no control) there is not a military officer on duty in any civil position in the government. . . . General Davis has been at all times as cordial and helpful as possible." A personal comment in this letter, however, reflected the growing dislike and the anoyance with the political feuding: "How I hate it! This is between ourselves."[42]

In June, 1900, the new governor in the company of General Davis made a five-day visit to some of the towns of Puerto Rico. His visit brought out some interesting personal reflections. He primarily noted a great profit potential in sugar development but criticized the lack of initiative on the part of the people. He charged that they were constantly seeking to secure government aid in every conceivable way and that they had little pride, since even wealthy planters "asked for and have received relief supplies." His solution was a strong one: "I'd tax a little life into them. Every Portorican has a right to demand that every acre of rich sugar land should be developed, and I'd tax it until they had to put up or shut up." For all of the dignity that characterized Allen, a human facet was revealed in this letter when he mentioned the Sunday habit of cock-fighting. He wished that he ''could go over there incognito, just to see if it was as bad as Gen'l Henry—poor simple soldier so innocent of civil affairs—tho't.''[43] This bit of sarcasm was undoubtedly understood by the urbane Root.

The first meeting of the Executive Council was held at the executive mansion on June 28, 1900, with William H. Hunt elected as its chairman. In accord with the Foraker Act, the Executive Council divided the island into seven districts, with the purpose that five delegates might be elected from each district. The districts were subdivided into 219 polling precincts. A serious dispute developed between the two parties over the division, and the plan of Crosas was accepted. Thereupon, the Federalist members of the Executive Council (José de Diego and Manuel Camuñas) resigned their positions, and the resignations were promptly accepted by the president. This was the first step in the ascendance to power of the Republican party, which they retained until 1904.[44]

Dissension between the two parties worsened over the matter of territorial division of the island, which was arranged according to a plan offered by Crosas. It carried nine to two in the vote, with the opposition in the Executive Council coming from De Diego and Camuñas. The *San Juan News* summarized the situation as follows:

> Mr. Crosas stated when he presented the plan that according to the returns of the recent elections [municipal] three of the districts were controlled by the *federals,* three by the *republicans,* and one so nearly even that each party had a fighting chance to carry it.
>
> The *federals,* it is said, are sure to control districts two, six and seven, while the *republicans* claim districts one, three, four and five. The federals claim five districts. No. 4 is the doubtful district.

Crosas denied interests in favor of the Republicans, stating that the plan had been suggested to him by an American, that he presented it when the Federalists and Republicans were deadlocked, and that, had the Republicans not been so precipitate in accepting it, the Federalists would not have been of the opinion that they had to oppose it.[45]

Muñoz Rivera regarded the division in a different light and accused the Executive Council of gerrymandering:

The plan adopted is unfair to the federal party (which is in the majority in this island), and is contrary to the 28th section of the Foraker Law. . . . At the general elections we had a total majority in the island of 6,500 votes. If our plan of equitable division had been adopted the federals would have won four or five districts out of the seven without campaigning. . . .

It is claimed that the republican party is American. We claim to be more American than the republicans. . . . The members of the federal party love the Americans as a nation. But we feel it our duty to protest against the present administration in this island so long as we are unjustly treated.

Muñoz cabled this message to the president and to the American press; he included information on the resignation of De Diego and Camuñas from the council.[46]

While this battle was in operation, William H. Elliott, commissioner of the interior, was receiving confidential information from Gabriel Anciaux, a special agent of Belgian origin. After an investigation of a major part of the island, he found the campaigns of both the Federal and Republican parties to be selfish. The Republicans, he charged, seek to rule the country and to obtain "all the fat berths in sight," by currying favor with the United States. The Federal party under Muñoz Rivera and Herminio Díaz seek "separation and self government under a Puerto Rican Republican Flag." He is certain that both parties "hate us equally and would unite against us, were it not that the topographical conditions of the Island are against any possibly successful uprising." He charged that, in Mayagüez and Ponce, the Republicans were using unfair means to secure victory in the coming elections and that, while all the decent Republicans had withdrawn from the Republican party in Mayagüez, the Fajardo party now ruled the town "through fear and that their so-called Republican Club is a focus of disorder, composed of Negroes and Negro-women who congregate there every night, challenging any and everybody." He further charged the Federalist Clubs with being "hotbeds of anti-Americanism." The Spanish element was alleged to be urging Puerto Rican patriotism in their anti-American program. On the other hand he found that "The mass of the People . . . are as a rule . . . in favor of the new state of things and thoroughly alive to the benefits they will derive from American institutions. . . . I have heard it expressed by people of note in both Republican and Federal parties . . . that it was deeply to be regretted that the military Government of the island should not have been carried on for some years more.'' In this despatch of the end of August, 1900, Anciaux strongly advised a military government and suggested that the polling operations should be controlled exclusively by Americans for the sake of fair play.[47]

In the meantime, election passions were rising, and the *San Juan News* reported rioting in San Juan on September 14. Judge Soto took depositions of Muñoz Rivera, proceeding to arrest the following prominent politicians: M. R. Gatell, Rosendo Infante, Juan Guzmán Benítez, Manuel H. Benítez, and Jesús Figueroa. After fifteen hours they were released without bail. On September 18 at 7 P.M., the press of *El Diario*—organ of Muñoz Rivera and the Federalist party—was destroyed by more than two hundred men and boys. The provoking cause seems to have been an attack on Mayor Egozcue by the paper on the previous day. Charges and countercharges were made as a result of this act of vandalism. Muñoz Rivera stated that he had on various occasions asked the governor for protection and that the governor had answered that he should call upon the court, since it was not a case in which the insular police should intervene. Muñoz remarked that the same police had intervened in both Arecibo and Carolina in the interest of the Republicans. Mayor Egozcue of San Juan maintained that he had never been requested, either in writing or verbally, by Muñoz Rivera for police protection and that, if he had been asked, he would have co-operated. He added, however, that the public had suffered too many insults from *El Diario;* all the disturbances had not been the work of the Republicans, but the blame fell upon Munoz himself. Dr. Barbosa, leader of the Republicans, was more direct: ''If Muñoz does not cease publishing his unjust charges (*groserías*) against the people of Puerto Rico, his life will be in constant danger. It will not be the responsibility of the Republican Party, for we can't always contain the wrath of the populace.''[48]

Further instances of political passion were reported by special agent Gabriel Anciaux. While peace reigned in Trujillo Alto and Loiza, in Carolina there were political battles and street-fights that were mostly carried on by youngsters between the ages of fifteen and twenty. They were described as anti-Republican and anti-American, and their purpose was described: ''If the American General comes with all his troops and with the Governor General . . . this people will obey no one, save the Illustrious Savior of the Puerto Rican Country, our Beloved Dictator Don Luis Muñoz Rivera.''[49] In commenting

upon this unfortunate situation that immediately preceded the
elections of the commissioner to the federal Congress and of the
representatives to the House of Delegates, José A. Gautier Dapena
states that both parties were infiltrated with force mobs (*turbas*).
Diatribes and offensive language characterized both parties in the
press and in public utterance. Apart from the differences of personality of Barbosa and Muñoz, there was a difference of outlook on
the future of Puerto Rico. Barbosa, graduate of the University of
Michigan, believed that the salvation of his land was in annexation as
a state into the United States. Muñoz Rivera, while not a separatist,
was interested in forming a civic consciousness of the people as
Puerto Ricans. Though their plans seemed often the same on paper,
in spirit there was a significant difference.[50]

In October, the Federalist party held a convention in Caguas at
which they resolved to affiliate themselves with the Democratic party
of the United States. Muñoz Rivera was to go to Washington to
establish a paper there in defense of the island. On October 18, the
Federalists selected Manuel R. Gatell as their candidate for commissioner to Congress. In the meantime, the Republicans selected
Federico Degetau as their candidate. Suddenly the Federalists
decided to withdraw from the elections of November 6. The comment
of Muñoz Rivera, as reported by the *San Juan News*, is interesting:
"My personal opinion is that the Federal Party should take part in
the elections, but for the sake of discipline, I accept the resolution of
the Executive Committee and am preparing to lend my assistance
towards carrying it out." Shortly thereafter President McKinley announced the appointment of José Guzmán Benítez and Dr. José
Gómez Brioso to the Executive Council, as replacements for the two
resigned Federalists. Both Guzmán, a Republican, and Gómez
Brioso, an independent Republican, were recommended by Governor
Allen.[51]

The results of the election of November 6 were a sweeping victory
for the Republican party in both the United States and Puerto Rico.
Federico Degetau y González was elected commissioner to Congress,
and every member of the House of Delegates was a Republican. The
Federalists had stayed away from the polls: in such strongholds of
the Federalists as Caguas, where 2,318 voters were registered, only
40 voted; at Carolina, where 1,074 had registered, only 36 voted. The
San Juan News found the election "a most significant victory" for
the Republicans and "an inglorious defeat" for the Federalists.

With no little prejudice, it concluded that "no organization can successfully live in Porto Rico which is not unqualifiedly for lasting bonds of the closest relationship with the United States."[52] In his first annual report, Governor Allen reflected that, though election passions had been high, there had been no frauds in the registrations and election, that 95 per cent of the election officers had been Puerto Ricans, and that the entire Republican ticket had been elected because of the withdrawal of the Federalists.[53] The new government got under way on December 3, 1900, when the members of the House of Delegates met in the executive mansion. The new commissioner of Puerto Rico to the United States, Federico Degetau y González, expressed his ideas of government in an interview with the *San Juan News* on December 15, 1900. He was "attracted more by the American ideals of government than by those of monarchies." Degetau expressed the hope that he would be "the last Commissioner for Porto Rico and the first Delegate for the Territory" and that the Republican program "will realize earlier than that of the Federalists the unanimous aspirations of our people to become Americans in fact."[54]

About this time, the trial of Muñoz Rivera was held for an incident connected with the election riots on the night of September 14. It was stated that about five hundred shots had been fired in front of the house of Muñoz Rivera, and the court charged Muñoz with "resistance of public authority." At the trial, the lawyer of the Federalist leader protested Judge Ramos, sitting on the case because he was a bitter personal enemy. The judge sat, but Muñoz was acquitted.[55] A deeper insight into the situation is given by Gabriel Anciaux who found that the Muñoz Rivera trial had stirred party feeling to a dangerous pitch; had the trial gone against Muñoz, "there would have been . . . an uprising among his followers in all the federal districts of this island." This special agent stated that the Muñocistas were claiming pledges from the Democratic leaders in the United States—and even from several Republican Senators—in favor of his "self-government." He found the waving of the American flag alongside the lone star Federal flag a mere "show"; in Caguas and Carolina "it was waved at the cry of 'Vivan los Federales; mueran los Americanos.' "[56]

Because of this trial of Muñoz Rivera and because of certain tactless statements of Commissioner Degetau, the *San Juan News* began to turn its sympathy to the leader of the Federalists. On January

20, 1901, the *News* criticized the commissioner for dragging politics
into the fulfillment of his office: "Whatever may have been Mr.
Degetau's politics before he was elected as Commissioner to Washington he now represents the island of Porto Rico and not any political party. This is a fact that should be impressed, not alone upon our
Commissioner, but upon the members of the House of Delegates and
the Executive Council as well." They concluded their remarks by approving Muñoz Rivera's determination to set up a newspaper in
the United States to forward the interests of the islanders. This
article strongly praised the work of the Federalists.[57]

While the sting of political recriminations was being felt on all
sides, the House of Delegates convened in joint session with the
Executive Council on December 4, 1900. It became a gala event
in the theater in the Plaza de Colón which accommodated two thousand
people. The principal address was delivered by the governor in
English and then was translated into Spanish. His message took the
form of a report and a recommendation. He reported that the
financial condition of the island showed a balance of $1,583,496.57; of
this total, $209,668.60 represented cash on hand, while $1,373,827.97
was the balance of the "two million dollars customs refunding act."
He also noted that the valuation of the island was set at $100 million
and that there was no outstanding obligation against it. He mentioned that under the Foraker Act the income from customs would
cease on March 1, 1902, if not before, and so legislation should provide
new sources of income for island expenses. He suggested a direct tax
on the assessed value "of real and personal property, an excise tax
on liquors, alcoholics, and certain other articles consumed or imported in Puerto Rico, and an inheritance tax on the devolution of
property.''[58]

Governor Allen stated that there were 800 schools in operation;
that this represented a gain of 184 over the previous year; and
that there were less than 100 American and more than 700 native
teachers. The present facilities were able to accommodate 40,000
children, whereas the census showed that there were more than
300,000 children for whom no provision could be made. On the
subject of the judiciary, the governor urged that it be kept separated
from the taint of politics; he recommended that jury trial be adopted
in criminal cases where serious penalties would result. The municipal
government was, according to Allen, both cumbersome and unneces-
sarily expensive; besides, the town mayors should be stripped of all

judicial power. He gave high praise to the insular police. He urged the continued construction of good roads and advised that nearly $1 million from the "customs-refunding act," along with $2 million of a loan-claim to Cuba, could be devoted to further road-building. He suggested that the joint session should consider whether the expenses of the island could be handled from the current revenues or if a loan should be sought. The governor strongly urged the use of military buildings as asylums for the blind, crippled, and incurable and suggested that they appeal to the president for the purpose. He closed his message by stating that, on December 15, the military department of Porto Rico would disappear; all troops, save a small force to man the fortifications, would leave the island, and "for the first time in over four hundred years the people of Porto Rico will be relieved from military rule."[59]

According to the Organic Act, the House of Delegates was to be in session not longer than "sixty days in any one year, unless called by the Governor to meet in extraordinary session." During the early days of the Assembly's meeting, bills were introduced on schools, roads, back taxes, bridges, cemeteries, mortgages, prisons, salt mines, woman suffrage, a university of Puerto Rico, duties, and judicial procedure. It must be noted that the *Journal* of the proceedings of the House of Delegates is rather uninteresting reading, since it gives a mere outline of proceedings and little of the actual debates. Of the many bills introduced, few were passed. On January 3, Representative Tous y Soto introduced a bill (H.R. No. 4), re-establishing the mortgage law. It will be recalled that the military authorities, in April of 1900, had postponed the revival of the foreclosure law until January 19, 1901. The House passed a law allowing a loan of $3 million, but this measure was defeated in the Executive Council, where five of the Americans voted against it and the five Puerto Ricans voted for it. Its purpose was agricultural relief. The more important measures that were enacted into law were trial by jury, a revenue law based on United States assessment laws, expropriation of lands to be used as cemeteries, educational acts (providing for fifty young Puerto Ricans to study in the United States), establishment of a code commission, founding of schools and charities, chartering of foreign corporations, and the reorganization of police courts, municipal taxes, and prison reform.[60] The *San Juan News*, which by now had become quite critical of the Republican party, charged the House with having introduced too many bills "that were trivial and sometimes absurd.'' They found that ''there are men in this island capable of making good laws,'' but the Republican party has proved that ''only one or two of these men are in their ranks.''[61]

Sharp criticism of the action of the House of Delegates also came from the pen of Gabriel Anciaux who saw the need of radical reform in the municipal police system. The appointments to this body were, he charged, ''left at the caprice . . . of any of the political parties that are interested in gaining or maintaining political power.'' He found the mayor's office to be the seat of ''favoritism, political bribery and intrigue with its attendant evils of undue coercion of certain citizens.'' He charged that decentralization was the ''mania of the politicians,'' that it was ''pretendedly of the People by the People and for the People, but practically of a Political Coterie for selfish political purposes.'' He suggested that a board of police commissioners be appointed by the municipal police, and that the police be appointed by the municipal council, over which the governor was to have a veto.[62]

Again in January, 1901, Anciaux criticized the municipal government in the island as utterly unfit and corrupt, in absolute subservience to party leadership, and on the border of bankruptcy. He opposed the absolute autonomy of the municipalities as fostering corruption. He would have the American heads of departments as ''organizers of this new colonial policy of the United States in all the minor branches even of public business.'' Lastly, he saw the need of a truly Republican paper in Puerto Rico to sustain the government there since the *San Juan News* had become a Federalist paper.[63] In the reading of this agent's report, Deputy United States Marshall Wilhelm Lutz commented: ''it hardly is severe enough. I have no interest whatsoever to favor either party, but consider it my duty as an Officer of the law to endorse, for the benefit of the Administration, any true statement.''

In confirmatory analysis of the situation, especially in relation to the municipalities, we have the report of the distinguished scholar William F. Willoughby who, in the fall of 1901, had become the treasurer of Puerto Rico. He says:

> Of the 36 municipal districts into which the island was divided, all but two were heavily in debt. . . . These debts consisted, in many cases, of obligations incurred years ago. . . . All, or nearly all, of the municipalities had upon their books, a large amount of unpaid taxes which, for one reason or another, had not been collected. . . .

It was open and notorious that in many of the municipalities public funds were not duly accounted for, expendi-
tures were improperly made, and money was being stolen by
municipal officials or diverted into improper channels.

Willoughby, then, stated that, under American rule, "a real civic
pride has been created . . . the municipalities . . . placed upon a firm
financial basis." Moreover, accounts are systematically and properly kept, while fraud and incapacity are reduced to a minimum.
He found the evil of "caciquism" in the mayor's office; he quoted
Dr. Hollander, his predecessor, as saying that "the most important
service rendered by his department in respect to the supervision of
municipalities was the prevention of the collection of unauthorized
or illegal taxes." Writing in 1909, Willoughby found the improvement so significant that the government of the municipalities could
be compared with those of the United States. He further justified the
intervention of the central government in local matters by citing the
conclusion of the Legal Commission: "The experience of the first year
of civil government has proved conclusively that without some form
of central control local services are neglected or inadequately performed."[64]

In March of 1901, the *San Juan News* continued to support the
Federal party on the argument of the failure of the Republican
legislature and the superior ability of the Federalist party. It
believed that the Federalists represented the majority of the voters,
the more intelligent and business elements. It advised its readers to
"rally around the Federal party." The *News* predicted that it
would win the next election and questioned why "Governor Allen
and the Administration persist in antagonizing a party and a class of
people with whom it would be easily possible to work in harmony."[65]
By June, the *News* was pleased to report that a committee of the
Federal party, consisting of Francisco de Paula Acuña, Santiago
Palmer, and Herminio Díaz Navarro, called at the executive mansion
and were politely received by the governor. They had come to offer
their co-operation to the governor in the best interest of the island;
"they felt that the time had come when small bickerings should be
overlooked." They stated that, though they could not always agree
on matters of policy, they "should agree to work for the best interests
of the Island."[66] By September the *News* was giving full favor to
the governor; Puerto Rico, they asserted, "never had a governor, like
the present Chief Executive, who has so much sympathy for the

workingmen and the poor people of the Island."[67] The paper seemed set on wedding the Federal party and the governor.

While the *San Juan News* was orienting its readers towards the Federal party, the editor and proprietor of *La Correspondencia*, Ramón B. López, was finding much fault with the government of the United States in Puerto Rico. Formerly a member of the Federalist group, he had become a political independent. Writing in *The Independent* at the end of 1900, he found the faults of the United States government in Puerto Rico to be many and most grievous. The ignorance of the American representatives of the language, laws, and customs of the people was serious. He also maintained that "they have neither desired nor . . . known how to establish harmony between the existing political parties of the island." Preference was given to Americans in the more important public offices. The press had no effect upon the government; mail service and transportation were bad; personal and property security was inadequate; and the commerce and agriculture of the island were suffering. The American government had accomplished very little in education. Lastly, he argued, a public loan should be made, in order to advance public works that will employ the laboring classes, improve the roads, build schools and a university.[68] Civil government in Puerto Rico had begun in 1900; but, though advances were made, limitations were sensed. The Puerto Rican was eager for fuller autonomy, such as he had hoped for under Spain's Autonomous Charter of 1897. The American government in the island was not so sure that the islanders could sustain greater autonomy than had been given by the Foraker Act. They pointed to the meager achievements of the first Legislative Assembly of the island and to the corruption of the municipal governments in proof of their assertion.

Ramón B. López was not alone in his opposition to the form of government set up by the United States in Puerto Rico. Muñoz Rivera, on November 15, 1900, resigned from his post on the Executive Committee of the Federal party; he was unwilling to go along with those who had visited the governor.[69] He considered that Governor Allen favored the Republicans and showed it by highly commending Dr. Barbosa in a letter of introduction to Secretary Root: "He is a man of great personal influence with his people, is a real patriot in his way of looking at things, and has been the devoted friend of Americans and of American sovereignty ever since the occupation. General Davis spoke to me of him when I first came here, and I have always found him a source of great comfort and help in many trying times.'' When Muñoz Rivera went to the United States, the attitude of the governor, however, was quite different. He told Root that: ''Muñoz Rivera is now in the United States, and I suppose will join hands with Borda in another nasty lot of false and misleading statements. But in the meantime, the island seems to be moving right along every day, and making progress.''[70] This dislike was returned by Muñoz Rivera who, in July, 1901, was publishing a letter that he had sent to President McKinley. He first charged that the Foraker Law ought never to have been passed, for it was ''unworthy of the United States,'' nor was there ''the slightest shadow of democratic thought in it.'' He recalled that in the days of Spain, ''Puerto Rico sent its deputies to the Cortes in Madrid, voted its own laws, [and] was a province of Spain equal to the European provinces under the Constitution.''

Allen, on a visit to Boston, told a reporter that Puerto Rico is an island that has no public debt and that its income covers its budget. In commenting on this statement, Muñoz Rivera made some very strong points. In Puerto Rico, he said, the people die of hunger, and in order not to die, families emigrate by the hundreds to Cuba, to Ecuador, to Santo Domingo, and to the Hawaiian Islands. Secondly, it is true that there is no public debt, but ''this is a grave evil, for shamefully it does not use its credit to strengthen its monetary circulation and to improve agriculture.'' Third, Allen counts on the Republicans who, thanks to his direct and unjust aid, have acquired a fictitious dominance that they would never have achieved by the vote of the people. Lastly, the Federal party changed its role of opposition to that of benevolence, because its leaders believe that no other conduct is possible in the avoidance of the injuries suffered by its members. Mr. Allen, he concluded, has partitioned Puerto Rico and is a poor American.[71]

ECONOMIC CONDITIONS, 1900

As we have already remarked, this period of change of sovereignty was marked by a serious poverty that affected all parts of the island. The greatest suffering was in the agricultural areas where the majority of the population lived. In late April of 1899, a meeting of farmer delegates was held to discuss their problems. This meeting brought out an interesting political overtone in a protest against Muñoz Rivera, who was representing their interests in Washington.

They charged that, since the leader of the Federalist party was representing political interests in the mainland, they wished to separate the agricultural matters from his influence. They promised a sincere support of General Henry, and their resolution was so expressed: "We seek justice, union and absolute separation from the former politics that has caused us so much harm. The interest of the country and the public prosperity [*riqueza*] demand this of every devotee of the common good."[72]

The cause of serious urban and agricultural poverty was attributed by the *San Juan News* to the island's system of landlordism. A strong editorial, on August 9, 1900, states the situation:

> When a man is enabled to demand fifty dollars a month rent for a flat in San Juan, which would be refused at ten in the heart of New York City, we must admit we are confronted with an industrial disease no less than alarming. . . . Our ailment antedates the change of the money, the mortgage law, the prohibitive tariff and the landing of General Miles. . . .
>
> Landlordism is the curse of this country. The enormous wealth of the few and the pitiable poverty of the many are chiefly due to a monopoly of the soil, maintained by its exemption from taxation, especially in our cities and particularly in the capital. . . . Not only should a tax be imposed upon all land on the island, but it should be more burdensome in the cities, and our Tax Commissioners should seriously consider this suggestion.[73]

A dramatic expression of public need occurred on August 14 when more than a hundred laboring men with their wives and children marched from San Lorenzo to the capital with the purpose of seeking work. They marched with the United States flag at their head directly to the executive mansion and asked for an audience with the acting governor. They asked the governor to open a road between Caguas and San Lorenzo, "in order that the laboring people of the district might be given an opportunity to earn a living." This was immediately granted, and orders were given to begin construction of the road.[74]

Convinced of the seriousness of the situation, Governor Allen made a week's tour of the island; on his return he made a statement to the press in which he paid high tribute to the people of Puerto Rico. His statement about Barranquitas is typical of the conditions of many towns of the island:

This community of 8,000 people is absolutely shut out from
the world, so far as roads are concerned, and every pound of
supplies is brought in over difficult mountain trails, upon the
heads of women and men or packed on the backs of ponies, and
all their produce naturally goes out in the same way. . . .

The poverty was not of the hopeless sort. The people did not
ask charity as paupers. They asked for work, and it seems to
me it would be much better for them to be paid for work in
money, even if the price is smaller than in rations.

When the governor was asked if he had found much anti-American
feeling, he replied: "None at all that I observed. The people seem
more anxious to see the prosperity of their island and their municipalities than anything else."[75]

In a study of the prosperity of the island, trade must be regarded
as most important. Before the Foraker Bill became law, the *San
Juan News* favored it, with the one exception that the editors urged
"absolute Free Trade, notwithstanding the gimlet-minded fruit and
tobacco growers." By August, however, they were publishing a
speech by General Stone that approved the trade provision: "It took
us some time to realize that it was in effect as good or better than Free
Trade while it could be turned into actual free trade at any moment
by the Island legislature." He also made clear that the tariff
revenues—15 per cent of the Dingley tariff rates—collected both in
Puerto Rico and in the United States were handed over to the island
treasury.[76] The constitutionality of this tariff came up for consideration in the "Insular Cases." In *Downes* v. *Bidwell* the court ruled
that "the Constitution does not extend *ex proprio vigore* to Porto
Rico. The mere act of cession does not incorporate acquired territory
as a part of the United States in the constitutional sense." Consequently, the court held the tariff law of the Foraker Act constitutional and found "all duties collected in Porto Rico upon goods
imported from the United States, whether under the authority of the
President of the United States, the military authorities or Congress,
are legal and valid." The same was true of importations from
Puerto Rico into the United States.[77] In July of 1901, President
McKinley decreed that free trade was to exist between the United
States and Puerto Rico. The newspapers announced that a million
dollars worth of goods were waiting on the New York docks for the
signal to rush goods to the island.[78]

In the "First Annual Report, 1901" of Governor Allen, an extensive comment is made on the trade conditions existing between the

island and the mainland. The twenty-month period of the United States military government (October 18, 1898, to April 30, 1900) reveals that the island's total imports amounted to $16,024,505; the exports, $13,895,860. The first ten months of the civil government (May 1, 1900, to February 28, 1901) which provided a tariff revenue show the following results: total imports, $8,102,460, along with $893,829 realized in duties; total exports, $5,814,083. In these statistics Governor Allen saw "great advantage accuring both to the United States and Puerto Rico from the changes made in the tariff law by the constituent act." In commenting on the fact that the balance of trade strongly favored the United States, he said that "since the days of Adam Smith no commercial fallacy has been more repeatedly or conclusively exposed than the argument that an excess of recorded imports over exports is an evidence of economic decline." He attributed the decline in exports to "a loss of accustomed markets and the destruction in part of staple crops by the hurricane of 1899." He believed that an excess of imports over exports would continue in the island, until her production would be enough to pay for her purchases. He believed that the excess of imports would be liquidated "not by an influx of currency, but by the formation of credits and the creation of investments."[79] The governor might very well have been asked who would provide the credits and make the investments, and also what advantages would be reaped and to whose benefit.

The question was quickly answered in an editorial of the *San Juan News* in midsummer of 1901: "the Sugar Trust and the Tobacco Trust will monopolize the larger share of the business of the Island." The editor was informed that "the sugar trust is increasing its capital stock $15,000,000 for the extension of its operations in Cuba and Porto Rico." The writer admitted that the tendency of such operation would be to withdraw the profits of the industries from the island. "The sugar planters, and the tobacco planters" he said, "only invest enough of their profits in the island to successfully carry on their business, and the rest is withdrawn; this is simply the existing conditions of trade and industry." He was "inclined to welcome and encourage the American trusts in Porto Rico. It means improvement, investment, development and progress."[80]

A few weeks later the same writer pictured a war of lobbyists seeking preferment in Congress. The sugar interests of the Havemeyer Sugar Trust sought to have Congress put raw sugar from the islands on the free list and to levy a high duty on refined sugar. The beet sugar growers, on the other hand, wished protection against all imported sugar whether raw or refined. The secretary of agriculture was said to have remarked that in his opinion "the country can produce all of its own sugar from beets in a few years, thereby avoiding the necessity of importing a foreign product." This idea was, of course, anathema to the Havemeyer sugar interests which, in the game of buying cheap and selling dear, had a competitive battle with the beet sugar interests.[81] The *San Juan News* imagined further evils in the new trade relations that followed the declaration of full free trade on July 25, 1901. The consumer enjoyed no benefit of reduction in price as a result of the declaration of free trade. In conjunction with an agent of a wholesale shoe house of the United States, the editor of the *News* investigated prices. The shoes were sold to the merchants by the wholesaler for 85 cents in case lots; the retail price in the San Juan market was from $2.00 to $2.50. The wholesaler said that the importing cost was about 10 per cent of the cost, making his cost in Puerto Rico 93.5 cents. The editor concluded that this was an instance of "a hundred cases which are brought to our attention."[82] To the public it was a hardship that such profits were being exacted at their expense; it was also little solace to know that progress would come with the investments of the sugar trusts when it was realized that the profits would escape from the island.

The labor conflict also came to Puerto Rico, under the leadership of a fearless and dynamic Spaniard, Santiago Iglesias Pantín, whose life is an interesting study in contrasts. For the present, he will be regarded merely as a man who split a significant segment of labor votes from the Republican party and so won the enmity of José Celso Barbosa. The *San Juan News* reported Iglesias' imprisonment as an injustice that was bent on removing him from political prominence in the Republican party. The *News* found that he had "gained the sympathy and active support of the laborers of the United States, the American administration in Washington, and the administration of the Island." The *News* editorialized: "If Iglesias does anything wrong, which is punishable under the criminal code, he should be punished. . . . We are not backing Iglesias as a man, or his ideas, or his theories, for if we were, we would have to accept many things radically wrong, but it is the principle and not the man involved in this case before the courts." The news soon reached the public that Acting Governor Hartzell had asked United States Attorney

General James S. Harlan to consider the Iglesias case, pressing it before the Supreme Court, since much "reaction in favor of Iglesias has appeared in the Island."[83]

The new civil government saw economic interests entering the island with keen investment plans. It appeared that in these first years the cost of living would be on the way up and that the wages would not ascend proportionately. Poverty was a sure prediction for the future. Social justice was a term seldom heard in those days, or if it was, it was stigmatized with the label of "socialism." Rugged individualism in business was still able to suppress labor's organization and effective bargaining. This story, however, is well beyond the scope of this paper that ends with the year 1900. These facts have been mentioned only with the intent of introducing the beginnings of civil government that would grow into future conflict.

The study of the evolution of the Foraker Act in Congress reveals a conflict of interests in the insular economy and in the application of free trade. The act attempted to protect stateside producers while giving the tariff benefits to the island government. It was sustained by the court, which interpreted the status of Puerto Rico as a "non-incorporated" territory without full constitutional protection. The degree of self-government given by the Foraker Act was very meager and earned the criticism of the islanders.

VI

Problems in Church v. State
and Education,
1898-1900

THE CATHOLIC CHURCH AND THE U.S. GOVERNMENT IN
PUERTO RICO

At the time of the occupation of Puerto Rico by the forces of the United States, there was no bishop in residence. Don Juan Perpiñá y Pibernat, the vicar capitular, was in charge of the diocese, and on September 8, 1898, he addressed the clergy of the diocese. He said that the change in government would not only affect the external aspects of life but also the moral, religious, and social interests of the Catholic church. Puerto Rico, he said, was already suffering from a decline in faith and morals because of a shortage of clergy and in some cases because of their poor formation. The tradition of recognizing priests as employees of the government, instead of ministers of God, had reduced the revenues to almost nothing. The vicar insisted that they could not admit the doctrine of separation of church and state, in the sense that the state is freed of the obligation of contributing to the material welfare of the church and the church of administering to the spiritual welfare of the state. He believed that nations holding to this doctrine of separation fail to take account of the morality and religious practice of the people.[1]

The statistics of early 1899 bear out the concern of the vicar. The number of parishioners was estimated as 921,322. The total number of priests was listed as 158, giving a ratio of one priest for each 6,000 individuals. On considering, however, that about 50 priests were either embarking for Spain or attached to special chaplaincies, we see that the ratio of priest to people was reduced to one priest for each 8,500. In the listing of priests and parishes, there are many notations of *coadjutoria vacante*—i.e., curate not supplied—or the note that a parish is dependent on another parish, as in the case of Barceloneta, which with its 7,000 persons was listed as dependent on Manatí.[2]

In the meantime, the *Boletín Eclesiástico* gave instructions on the means of supporting the church in the absence of any assistance from the new government. It read in part:

> Now that the bonds which united this bishopric with the Royal Patronage are severed by act of 1898; and now that there is a complete separation of Church and State, the Church Authorities by command and the Catholics by obedience must support their cult and ministers. For, though the Church is a Divine institution, it is made up of men and needs material means for its mission and continued existence. . . .
>
> It is clear that the Catholic Religion cannot exist without the clergy and its corresponding ecclesiastical hierarchy. And, since the ministers are men that ought to be in care of their churches without being obliged to ask alms or to sustain themselves with the labor of their hands and to the harm of their ministerial duties . . . it is most necessary to establish parochial fees. This income will in part alleviate the deplorable condition of the clergy and their parishes.

To this letter was appended a list of fees for funerals, anniversary masses, baptisms, and marriages. The fee set for baptism was one peso; of this 75 cents was allotted to the pastor, and 25 cents for the sacristan and altar boys. In the same issue of the *Boletín*, the priests were urged to preach against the evils of civil marriage among Catholics and to get those who had contracted such marriages to repent and validate the union.[3]

In order to assist in the solution of the difficult church-state problems, the Holy See appointed the archbishop of New Orleans, Most Reverend Plácido Luis Chapelle, as apostolic delegate to the Philippines, Cuba, and Puerto Rico. Archbishop Chapelle had assisted in the drafting of the religious article of the Treaty of Paris. Article VIII made special mention of ecclesiastical property: "The relinquishment or cession . . . cannot in any respect impair the property or rights which by law belong to the peaceful possession of property of all kinds, of provinces, municipalities, public or private establishments, ecclesiastical or civic bodies, or any other associations having legal capacity to acquire and possess property in the aforesaid territories renounced or ceded, or of private individuals, of whatsoever nationality such individuals may be." The apostolic delegate was in Puerto Rico from January 11 to February 9 of 1899, to study the effect of the treaty articles on the moral, social, scientific, and progressive good of the former overseas provinces of Spain.[4] Article VIII was to be the subject of much dispute during the first years of the occupation by the United States; a discussion of the legal and political issues that arose over church property will follow in this chapter.

On April 30, 1899, the *Boletín* announced the appointment of Monsignor Jaime H. Blenk as bishop-elect of Puerto Rico. The bishop was consecrated on July 2, but the date of his arrival in Puerto Rico was still indefinite since his instructions from the Holy See obliged him not to leave the United States until all arrangements had been made in regard to his diocese. In September, 1899, Bishop Blenk had a two-hour conference with President McKinley and Minister of War Elihu Root. At this conference, he and nine other Americans were appointed members of the "Central Porto Rican Relief Committee," which organized aid for the many sufferers from the recent hurricane. At the same time, the *Boletín* published a circular letter written by Bishop Blenk to the bishops of the United States, asking the aid of the Catholics under their care for the afflicted island.[5]

While Bishop Blenk was still in Washington, the Report of the Insular Commission was published; as we have already seen, it incorporated some rather intemperate remarks and recommendations. Both Archbishop Chapelle and Bishop Blenk addressed a letter to Secretary Root, on referral from President McKinley. They explained that it was a "duty for them to look after the religious interests of the people of Porto Rico who are practically all baptized Catholics, and who under the improved conditions of liberty in which the Church is placed in the island will be more loyal to their religion than ever." This letter enclosed a copy of the petition presented the previous February by Archbishop Chapelle to General Henry. In

criticism of the Report of the Insular Commission, they stated:
"From their own showing the Commissioners were not instructed to
make any report on the religious conditions of the people. It is
astonishing that the Commissioners, in their attempt to report on these
conditions, did not—so it appears—call on the proper Church
authorities for the purpose of obtaining authentic information on this
important subject." The bishops also charged the commissioners with
a "loose and misleading use of words." For instance, "very many
Porto Ricans are illiterate, but they are not densely ignorant, as the
Commissioners would make them appear. On the contrary, the Porto
Ricans as a rule are intelligent, quite able to earn a living in agricultural pursuits, in the mechanical arts and many of these illiterates
are fitted to fulfil the duties of citizenship."

On the matter of concubinage, the two bishops found the report
exaggerated, since "there exist a true and valid marriage, according
to American law, between a couple who recognize each other publicly
as man and wife, and therefore from the point of view in which the
Commissioners should have placed themselves, such unions cannot
fairly be looked upon as concubinage." Moreover, they found it "a
matter of record . . . that the priests never refuse to marry the people
who are unable to pay the usual fees." It is further no matter of
wonder "if in an exclusively Catholic country the mere civil marriage
should not have been recognized." On the general subject of morality,
the bishops asserted that "the people of Porto Rico have had as high a
moral standard set before them as the people of the United States.
The very laws under which they live prove it, and the Commissioners
themselves in their report have acknowledged that crime is *not* more
prevalent in Porto Rico than in the United States."

In criticizing the report's treatment of education in Puerto Rico,
it is noted that "if schools were not more numerous, it was more likely
for reasons of just and unjust economy than for the purpose of keeping the people in subjection." They added that in some areas the
public schools were only open for three or four months "on account
of scarcity of funds." They found the Catholic system of education
"as progressive and complete as the best methods followed anywhere
in the United States." They pointed in particular to the Young
Ladies' Academy in Santurce "about which the Commissioners do
not deem it necessary to give any details." The bishops believed that
the Normal School should be improved not closed. They opposed the
idea of employing "mostly American teachers in Porto Rico,"

because the language problem would "necessarily tend to retard rather than to advance education in the island, and it would most probably meet with resentment on the part of the people." They favored a gradual change of language. In considering the question of education, the bishops urged "foresight, wisdom, fruitful experience, united with thorough insight into the race-characteristics." Their conviction was that:

> The Porto Ricans are intelligent; many of them are thoroughly educated and highly cultured; in view of these facts would it be wise policy on the part of our government to put them aside in this matter of education which must lie nearer to their hearts than to ours?
>
> Would it be in keeping with the traditions and principles of our own Country, to treat the inhabitants of Porto Rico, in the School question and in others, as mere helpless children, altogether incapable of contributing towards the regeneration and elevation of their country? With peoples as with individuals all development and growth, whether intellectual, social, or moral, must mainly come from within to be healthy and enduring.

The bishops were in favor of leaving education, in some measure, "to the deliberations and action of the Territorial government, if this form of government is to be granted to the island." On the subject of religious education, the bishops favored the Catholic Catechism in the schools, on the argument that "the reasons which make it necessary to keep religion out of the schoolroom in the United States do not exist in Porto Rico"; i.e., the whole community is Catholic." They added that "the people should have a voice in this matter."

In respect to Catholic schools, the bishops spoke particularly of the high school in Santurce, which was under the control of the Fathers of the Pious Schools who had contracted "not to maintain religion primarily, but to impart a sound commercial and classical education." They explained the decrease in the number of students by "a most unjust and arbitrary act," that is, the fathers had "for a time been expelled by the civil authorities under the sanction of the American Governor General." They denied that the lease to the school had expired at the time of the American occupation.

In closing their remonstrance to the secretary of war, Archbishop Chapelle and Bishop Blenk urged that the land laws should be changed without doing any injustice to present lawful owners. Congress could well establish a court of private lands claims, "such as

was established some years ago for Colorado, New Mexico and
Arizona.'' They mentioned the *ley hypotecaria,* the code of Spanish
land law that forbad the registering of churches in the same way that
it forbad the registering of public highways. This was ''not because
it did not acknowledge the church as a corporate body having ownership of them, but in order to secure more efficaciously the right of
what is called Royal Patronage.'' They noted that, with Puerto
Rico's passing under the jurisdiction of the United States, ''there has
been worked out a separation of Church and State which annuls said
Royal Patronage, and deprives the Church of the material support
by the State, and therefore the Church property should be granted a
legal title . . . as secure as that by which any other kind of property
is held or transferred.''

In respect to a full code of laws—proposed by the commission and
promulgated by the commander-in-chief—the bishops charged that it
would be ''unwise, impracticable and tyrannical.'' They believed
the members of the Insular Commission to be ''totally unfit to guage
the situation'':

> They know not the needs nor the character of the people.
> To force on Porto Rico a full code made *a priori,* would be to
> ride rough shod over a people who are well disposed towards
> us, but who, by such a measure, would become inevitably and
> forever alienated.
> The people undoubtedly eagerly desire good laws such as
> we have; but every state has its laws which like the federal
> laws are a system which has developed slowly. It would be
> folly at one stroke to change all laws or nearly all, now in
> vigor. The people have surely a right to take a hand in the
> making of the laws by which they are to be governed.
> Provisionally let the military authorities govern in accord-
> ance with the directions of our Constitution, with equity and
> the spirit of the common law. But in the name of justice let
> Congress give to these people, as soon as possible, the freedom
> of a Territorial form of government. . . . By granting it, the
> government of the United States is perfectly sure to direct the
> destinies of the island, since the President of the United States
> appoints the Governor, the judiciary and the Collectors of
> Revenue; and the laws of the Territorial legislature are sub-
> ject to revision by Congress.
> The territorial form of government will please the people
> of Porto Rico, and the granting of it to Porto Rico cannot
> but make a most favorable impression on the Cubans and on
> the Filipinos.[6]

The wisdom and practicality of this advice by these two bishops reveals that they had a far deeper insight into Puerto Rico and its peoples than the Insular Commission. We may well believe that their criticism had much to do with Secretary Root's decision to let the "proposed Code" of the commission rest in the war department archives. The people of Puerto Rico can well be thankful to the bishops for their influence in preventing a policy that could have brought calamity to the island.

At the beginning of the new year, Bishop Blenk, in a letter to Governor Davis, again raised the question of the Insular Commission. He recalled a conference that he and Archbishop Chapelle had had in the previous August with President McKinley. At that time, the bishop had protested against the commission's recommendation that "priests and others who have taken the vow of celibacy, may be permitted to renounce said vows and enter into marriage relations, the same as other persons." The president, he said, had "solemnly affirmed that he would pay absolutely no attention to this recommendation, and added that had he known the nature of this report, he would never have consented to the printing of it." Bishop Blenk stated that "on the strength of the President's solemn promise . . . I used my good offices with the Catholic press and secured silence on this subject."[7]

While this issue was under consideration, the vicar of the Diocese of San Juan, Reverend Juan Perpiñá y Pibernat, was warning his clergy that they were not to involve themselves in the political controversies then raging in the island. He made clear that this was an order and that failure to comply would bring penalties of suspension and privation of office.[8] Soon after this, Bishop Blenk arrived at San Juan, accompanied by the archbishop of Santiago de Cuba, and was welcomed by the pastors of the diocese, by the Vincentian and Redemptorist Fathers, by the mayor of San Juan, and by the Sisters of Charity. In the cathedral, the new bishop "gave a warm and paternal sermon in good Castilian, with short phrases in English for those from the United States."[9] The high esteem that Bishop Blenk soon merited was to be acknowledged years later, when, on the occasion of the four-hundredth anniversary of the church in Puerto Rico, he returned to his former post. Bishop Gunn of Natchez, in an interview at the time of this 1913 celebration, spoke of the reception tendered Archbishop Blenk:

The most cordial and enthusiastic ever given an American in a Spanish-speaking colony. The people who tolerated his arrival in 1899 learned in a short time to appreciate him as a man of unusual ability, of diplomatic qualities which they rarely associated with a churchman, and a successful bishop. . . .

The treaty of Paris made all church possessions safe in theory, his tact made them practical securities. He found America fair and square. He made the Porto Ricans recognize American fair play and justice and prepared them to accept that justice which America was prepared to give.[10]

Anticlericalism and Protestantism

Most Latin countries experience the influences of anticlericalism, and in this, Puerto Rico was no exception. Eduardo Newman Gandia, in 1899, wrote *Benefactores y Hombres Notables de Puerto Rico* (*The Benefactors and Prominent Men of Puerto Rico*), in which he mentions a strong movement in favor of Masonry in Ponce during the turbulent times of 1873. He says that there was an attempt "to check the influence of the Jesuits" and that Román Baldorioty de Castro mounted a barrel in Ponce's plaza in order to extoll the glories of Masonry. In the midst of his discourse, the bells of a nearby church began to toll. He interrupted his discourse with the comment: "Behold the last breathing of an idea that is about to die." It was the time of the Spanish Republic that Baldorioty founded the publication *El Derecho,* which carried articles of strident republicanism and sociological controversy.[11] This journal had anticlerical overtones and provoked an article in the *Boletín Eclesiástico,* entitled "The Profane Press." The latter pointed to the sarcasm and ridicule that was used against sacred things and showed the bad effect of this propaganda on youth. The writer charged that, under the disguise of philosophy, *El Derecho* was zealously laboring for the destruction of religion.[12]

Another prominent Puerto Rican, Salvador Brau, wrote a tribute to Victor Hugo in which he praised the French government for its invoking a decree of the Constituent Assembly of 1791 that legalized the secularization of a Catholic church. This temple was to be used as a pantheon for such distinguished patriots as Hugo and as a tribute to "the social progress of our century."[13] *La Democracia* also editorialized on the new role of religious emancipation that characterized the free-thinkers:

Religious festivals are on the way out. . . . We who remain estranged from the imposition of this blind faith, yet who are idealists and dreamers, visit the Catholic Church on feast days such as have ended today with the Mass of the Resurrection.

We do not go to these places from any deep conviction; rather, we are brought by the study of these phenomena and by our obligation as journalists to inform our readers of every event.

The writer saw the church driven into retreat, for "in every emergency it must appeal to a sickly propaganda in order to survive in the simple feelings of women. Thinking and intelligent men do not go to these affairs."[14] The church was well aware of this anti-Catholic movement, for during the summer of 1899 the vicar of the San Juan diocese reproved "the blasphemies and heretical statements of certain periodicals . . . of Ponce, Mayagüez and the capital," mentioning in particular a Masonic pamphlet that was widely circulated. He chided the dissensions of the political parties at a time when peace was most badly needed and pointed out the serious shortage of priestly vocations, attributing this to the home where, instead of fostering religious vocations and the spirit of piety, the parents sought to suffocate them. The minds of their youth were distracted, he said, by worldly pleasures that bring grave spiritual harm and rob the Church of God of vocations.[15]

While the forces of anticlericalism had known a long history in Puerto Rico, Protestantism had a relatively recent entrance. In 1867, the *Boletín Eclesiástico* reported the introduction into the island of two Protestant books from the United States: *El Protestantismo* and *El Retrato de la Virgen María en los Cielos*. The priests were urged to use their influence in preventing the circulation of these books attacking the Catholic faith.[16] In 1873, the Overseas Ministry of the Spanish government allowed the establishment in Vieques of a Protestant school for the children of foreign families.[17] The first non-Catholic church in Puerto Rico was that of the Holy and Ever Blessed Trinity, which was erected in Ponce in 1873. By decree of the archbishop of Canterbury, in 1898, the church and congregation were transferred to the American Episcopal church. After United States occupation, the Church of Jesus was founded at Quebrada Limón. Since then, according to Claudio Capó, "The work of the Protestant Church in the Island has been effectively progressive, the Evangelical Union and other denominations contributing in a great measure to the spiritual and mental uplift of their members, through their numerous churches, schools, charitable institutions, periodicals, etc. Today Protestantism is an active force in every town of Porto Rico."[18]

Another source of information on Protestantism in Puerto Rico is the *San Juan News* which, on January 3, 1900, announced the arrival of the Reverend J. Milton Greene of the Presbyterian church, whose "special mission here is to the native inhabitants of Puerto Rico. His plan includes, besides the regular preaching services, a medical mission and dispensary, as well as the establishment of a school." At the end of the month this paper informed its readers that mass was to be celebrated in jail by Bishop Blenk, and commented: "It is the intention to invite ministers of other denominations to officiate at future dates, but as all of the prisoners were born Catholics a deference was made in favor of the Bishop by first inviting him."[19] This American paper raised another highly sensitive issue in a Catholic country, namely, divorce. After announcing that there was no divorce law in Puerto Rico, it editorialized to the effect that "there are many just cases for divorce awaiting the laws"; though divorces should not be made easy, "it is recognized that the proceeding is necessary for the public welfare."[20]

A much more sensitive issue, however, developed from religious influences over the public school. The *Pittsburgh Observer* wrote a stinging editorial on the subject in the summer of 1900. It had printed long extracts from the official report of the United States commissioner of education on "the Protestantization of our public schools by means of the Protestant edition of the Bible, the Protestant version of the Lord's Prayer, Protestant hymns, and the Protestant religious opening exercises." It then wrote to the commissioner of education, asking why the public schools in Cuba, Puerto Rico, and the Philippines had been secularized. The *Observer* printed the reply of Acting Commissioner Lovick Pierce, in which he said that "the administration of the affairs of the public schools in the various States, territories, and our recently acquired islands, is entirely in the hands of the local authorities. The general government does not interfere in the matter in any way." The editor of the *Observer* replied:

> It is not true that the administration of the affairs of the public schools in our recently acquired islands is "entirely in the hands of the local authorities. . . ." Who appointed the Yankee Protestant Frye superintendent of schools in Cuba? Who appointed the Protestants Clark and Groff superinten-

dents of schools in Puerto Rico? Who appointed the Protestant superintendent of schools in the Philippines? The McKinley Administration.

We did not need to have Mr. Pierce tell us that "Each State and territory has its own school system." What we ask is, why, if they can make our public schools Protestant, religious, sectarian, the schools in Cuba, Puerto Rico and the Philippines must be made strictly secular and Godless, when not also anti-Catholic, by the American Government authorities.[21]

Though the editor did not seem willing to concede a difference between state regulation of education and federal control of education in a territory, he did reflect the sensitivity of Catholics to what seemed a policy of religious discrimination.

At the same time, Protestant groups in the United States were voicing a strong support of the position of separation of church and state in the new territories. The American Baptist Home Mission Society, "on behalf of four million Baptists," wrote to President McKinley, stating that "it is not to be expected that either the ecclesiastical leaders or the untrained peoples will be able at once to see the wisdom of our American idea of separating civil from ecclesiastical affairs." They reiterated the idea that "a great multitude of intelligent citizens of our country hold very sacredly the principle that any union of Church and State is wrong."[22]

Religious friction also appeared in the hospital system of the island. On January 8, 1901, María Díaz de Palmer and 215 other persons sponsored a petition, protesting the passage of a bill introduced in the House of Delegates of Puerto Rico that sought to dispense with the Sisters of Charity in the hospitals. This petition was originally submitted to the governor who transmitted it to the Executive Council.[23] Another petition, presented by Ramón Vega de Goenaga "with a great number of signatures" also asked that "the Sisters of Charity be continued in the service of the hospitals of Porto Rico."[24] The *San Juan News* publicized the dispute over the religious status of the Hospital Tricoche in Ponce, in which the Catholics maintained that it was Catholic, and the Protestants that it was nonsectarian. The City Council finally passed an act prohibiting any religious doctrine, except on petition of a patient. This issue came to a head when the medical director of the hospital, Dr. Aguerrevere, was requested to call a priest for a patient. The director made no direct reply, "but fifteen minutes later the practicant told the patient that he was well and might leave the hospital.'' Though weak, the patient left, and a complaint was made to the San Juan authorities.[25]

In the years that followed, there was a recurring bitterness between Catholics and Protestants. Sometimes it was friction over public demonstrations of religion; on other occasions, it was a matter of the transfer of public land for religious purposes. Catholics in the subsequent years also were sensitive to the fact that very few American Catholics or practising Puerto Rican Catholics obtained significant posts in government. It was stated that the anticlerical elements in the island and Protestant influences in the United States saw to it that the significant posts in the insular government and educational system went to non-Catholics.[26]

Church Property

Few matters aroused so much hostility during the first days of Puerto Rico's transfer from Spain to the United States as that of church property. When the United States took over the sovereignty, all state subsidies to the church instantly ceased. The title to church property, under the *patronato real* and by concordat with the Holy See, was held in the name of Spain, with the understanding that Spain would give financial support to the church. Because of this title the insular and municipal governments of Puerto Rico were ready to take over title to Catholic churches, convents, monasteries, rectories, and cemeteries. The church was reduced to a critical condition both because of its loss of revenue and the title to its property. It could, moreover, hope for little financial support from the impoverished population that had been made destitute by the hurricane of San Ciriaco in midsummer of 1899.

The condition of the church is expressed by Lieutenant A. C. Blunt of the United States 5th Artillery: ''The Roman Catholic Church, the established religion of Spain and her colonies, has had complete control at every point of the Island. All public charities have been controlled by it; the removal of Governmental financial support and its loss of political power have just now weakened and almost paralyzed the Church. . . . The buildings owned by the Church are fine large churches and several smaller chapels, a small hospital and two asylums, also a school for priests.''[27] The lieutenant's statement that the church was in a weakened condition was most certainly true. But, when he spoke of the church's "immense landed properties" and asserted that "the Church has been the government," he was quite wide of the mark. He undoubtedly had been victimized by hearsay evidence. The confusion that surrounded this point is reflected in the testimony given by General Davis before the Senate Committee on Puerto Rico. Part of this testimony is here transcribed:

PETTIGREW: Do religious orders hold much property?

DAVIS: The orthodox church—that is to say, the secular priests as distinct from the monastic orders—have control of the churches throughout the island and one or two other buildings. There are claims made by the church for property that formerly belonged to the monastic orders, and claims to certain revenues now collected by the State, and which have been transferred to the United States by Spain, with the churches, for which they claim restitution.

COCKRELL: On what ground do they base their claims?

DAVIS: On the ground that the sequestration of the property of the monastic orders by Spain in 1843 was illegal and a usurpation of power, and that by subsequent royal decree of the King restitution . . . was promised but was not carried into effect . . . and they wish to have that act of restitution completed. . . .

PETTIGREW: Does the church hold any property there now?

DAVIS: The church owned nothing in its own right there, as I understand. A priest of the Catholic Church was a part of the Government, and no landed property in Puerto Rico was ever registered in the name of the Government; there was nothing at all in shape of registered deeds to show that the Church owned an inch of land.

NELSON: It is a species of State property under the protection of the State, held as a sort of trust in the name of the State for religious purposes, which has come to the United States by transfer?

DAVIS: Yes, Sir; that is my understanding.

COCKRELL: How much is there of it?

DAVIS: In every town, every municipality, there is at least one church, and there may be more; some have three or four but the church properties are not considerable, amounting usually to simply the ground on which the building stands with a small plot of ground around it.

NELSON: The cemetery?

DAVIS: No, sir; that is usually detached, and not connected with the church. The cemeteries are usually owned by the municipality, although consecrated by the church, and under the supervision of the priest.

General Davis concluded his testimony on church properties by speaking of the property of the monastic orders seized by Spain and now held by the United States which was known as the San Franciscan and San José Barracks. These he believed to be worth some hundreds of thousands of dollars, and for these the church sought restitution. A last class of property, known as "pious foundations," was based on "bequests made by individuals for the benefit of monastic orders, and the payment made to the heads of these monastic orders during their continuance in the island, and then appropriated to the Government after the suppression of the orders." The general noted that these properties were a matter of dispute between the church and the local government in Puerto Rico.[28]

Very early in the period of the military government, the apostolic delegate, Archbishop Chapelle, directed a communication to General Guy V. Henry asking that the property rights of the Catholic diocese of Puerto Rico be respected. He mentioned that the Catholic church had been recognized as a body corporate and juridical by Spain, with the right to acquire and hold property; to this end, he cited the *patronato real* and the various concordats with the Holy See. The delegate made three specific requests: first, that "all churches, chapels, oratories, schools, colleges, academies, hospital, charitable and educational institutions of all kinds . . . and all real estate of which the Church . . . enjoyed a legitimate and peaceful possession . . . be vested . . . in a corporation representing the Catholic diocese of Puerto Rico"; second, that "titles of mortgages, legitimately belonging to this diocese, but now in the possession of the United States as coming from the Spanish government, be made over to said diocesan corporation . . ."; and, third, that "the convents and the real estate thereto pertaining adjoining the churches of San José and of San Francisco . . . be restored without unnecessary delay to their legitimate owners by the United States."[29]

The matter of church property soon developed into a serious discussion between Secretary of War Elihu Root and Bishop Blenk. The secretary of war requested of Bishop Blenk copies of the concordats entered into by Spain "with Pope Pius IX in 1851 and 1859 relating to seizure by Spain of properties belonging to religious orders." The bishop promised to send them and informed the secretary that Archbishop Chapelle would be in Washington soon and ready to furnish further information.[30] The documents were sent, and within two weeks, Archbishop Chapelle wrote a long letter, in the form of a statement of position, to Secretary Root. He first cited the second paragraph of Article VIII of the Treaty of Paris (1898), in which the property rights of ecclesiastical bodies were protected. He argued that the Roman Catholic church in the islands recently ceded by Spain to the United States is a ''juridical person, corporation or body incorporate . . . capable of acquiring rights and contracting obligations.'' He here quoted from the Spanish constitutions of 1812, 1845, and 1876 and referred to Articles 35, 38, and 746 of the Civil Code of Spain. These articles defined corporations and the rights of the church to inherit. The concordats of 1851 and 1859 made clear provision for the church legally to acquire and hold ownership of property. From this the apostolic delegate reasoned that

> If the Government of the United States finds itself at present in the possession of property which the Spanish Government was bound to release and return to the Church, under the Concordat of 1851, the obligation has devolved upon it of fulfilling in behalf of Spain the obligation assumed by the latter and still unfulfilled. That obligation becomes the more imperious when the most important fact is considered that Spain had to provide for the expenses of divine worship and the support of the clergy, while the Government of the United States determined at the close of the war not to pay subsidies of any kind to the Church.

The conclusion of the delegate was that Catholic church property and its use in Cuba, Puerto Rico, and the Philippines be guaranteed and that where property—which under Spanish agreement with the Holy See was to be restored to the church—was held by the United States Government, return be made to the church.[31] Secretary Root made a brief reply, asking Archbishop Chapelle to file with the War Department an itemized statement of the property claimed, its alleged ownership, and the facts substantiating the claims of the church.

The legal outcome of church property was not to be determined for some time. A step was taken by Senator Foraker in 1903 when he introduced a bill relative to church property in Puerto Rico. By it the United States government would relinquish all title to property received from Spain, which at the time of the United States military occupation was held by Spain ''for the use and benefit of the Holy Roman Catholic Church, under and by virtue of any law or of any concordat between said church and the Government of Spain then in force, together with all church buildings and other edifices, structures, and appurtenances which were then in the peaceable possession of said church under claim of title or beneficial use.''[32] In a letter to Senator Foraker, President Roosevelt expressed great interest in this question of church property:

> I have requested Bishop Blenk to call upon you and lay the whole matter before you. I have very great confidence in the Bishop's fairness and wisdom. He has done admirable work for good government and in upholding American principles and institutions in Porto Rico, and has very great difficulties to meet. Without pretending to familiarity with all the facts in the case it would seem to me that in principle the bill you have introduced meets the case. All that Bishop Blenk asks is an opportunity to lay his case before an impartial tribunal and abide by our final decision.

The president closed his letter by asking that Senator Foraker let him know if there was anything that he could do to help ''in getting your bill through.''[33]

By the end of the year, nothing had been done about the Foraker Bill, and Bishop Blenk complained to the president that ''the little property in possession of the government, without the shadow of a doubt belonging to the Church, has not yet been returned by the United States.'' He was convinced of the good intention of the president, but ''I have reasons to doubt the sincerity of Governor Hunt's promises to carry out the President's wishes.''[34] Bishop Blenk was known to all as a perfect gentleman, with much diplomatic poise in handling difficult questions, but there was a point beyond which he would not go. On this matter, he spoke bluntly. The bishop also reflected on the economic conditions of the island in this same letter: ''The misery and grinding, killing poverty, prevalent throughout the island are simply appalling. All that is being said about the prosperity of Porto Rico is a damnable lie. The pity of it; that this little island should be so unfortunate and wretched under our sway.'' The ability of the bishop to speak out when need warranted it was recognized and praised by the *Puerto Rico Herald,* the official organ of Luis Muñoz Rivera. In an editorial, a discourse of the bishop was cited in which he criticized the lack of prosperity, liberty, and justice in the island, adding that ''there are many who have no hope, and only see in the future the absorption, poverty and misery of the Puerto Rican.'' The bishop's solution was that, if Americanization was to be accomplished in Puerto Rico, it must be based on prosperity, peace, tranquillity, in a way that "becomes the character of the Puerto Ricans and the personality of Puerto Rico."[35] Despite this strong agitation, the measure of Senator Foraker which dealt with church property saw no further action. Solution was left to the courts.

In early 1906, Juan Hernández López, representing the bishop of Puerto Rico, presented his brief before the Supreme Court of Puerto Rico. He argued that "if through separation of Church and State by the United States Government, the needs of the Church were no longer cared for by the Government, then the property—given over by concordats with the Holy See—should be returned; moreover, all production of said property since October 1898 should be turned over." He then argued a precedent from Cuba, whose claims, he asserted, were identical. He also cited Article VIII of the Treaty of Paris, which protected private and ecclesiastical property rights. And lastly, he found that the people and government of Puerto Rico, "in bringing about this severance and *rescission* . . . are bound to return that which, on their part, the Government of Porto Rico and the 'Intendencia General' of the Island were under obligation to return." Introduced into the brief was an interesting statement of General Leonard Wood on the parallel condition existing in Cuba. The general found the position of the Catholic church "a trying one" because of the severance of church-state relations. He stated that the attitude of the church in Cuba had been "one of cooperation with the Military Government in the work it has had to perform . . . and the relations existing have always been harmonious and friendly."[36]

The decision of the Supreme Court of Puerto Rico was given on December 15, 1906, by the presiding judge, José S. Quiñones. In accord with the reasoning of the church's lawyer, the chief justice believed that it was reasonable and just that the church's property then in the possession of the government of Puerto Rico be returned to the church. The court cited extensively from the laws of the Spanish Cortes, royal decrees, and the concordats, and so it argued the right of the church to the properties of the Dominicans and Franciscans. The dissenting opinion was filed by Justice MacLeary on January 10, 1907, and concurred in by Justice Wolf. This opinion first raised the argument that the insular legislature of Puerto Rico had conferred by statute of March 10, 1904, original jurisdiction on the Supreme Court of Puerto Rico; whereas, the case had been raised under the old Code of Civil procedure, and so the statute of limitation favored the defendant. Secondly, it questioned the personality of the plaintiff, that is, the relation between the friars and the Roman Catholic church. To whom did the ground rents and annuities belong? This minority denied that the canons and the authority of the bishop represented the church. Lastly, it was contended that a mere case of ejectment should not pertain to the original jurisdiction of the Supreme Court of Puerto Rico.

On the same day, another case decision was handed down by the chief justice of Puerto Rico in reference to the Jesuit high school that had been erected by the Provincial Assembly at Stop 19 (Santurce) in 1884. It had been used as a church and school by the Jesuits until 1886 when it was leased to the Railroad Company of Puerto Rico. The chief justice dismissed this case on the grounds that the Provincial Assembly had never granted "a perpetual servitude of use" but that there had been a "reservation of rights contained in said resolution." It is to be noted that the case had been raised by the bishop of Puerto Rico, not by the Jesuits. The basis of his claim was the chapel that was continued in religious worship, at the time that the railroad lease was extended.[37]

Catholic Cemeteries

One of the sharpest controversies at the time of the American occupation of Puerto Rico was the secularization of the cemeteries which, attached to the church, had been under clerical control for almost four centuries. In the *Boletín Eclesiástico* of December 15, 1898, the vicar of the Diocese of Puerto Rico stated that reports had been sent in by various pastors of burials of non-Catholics, excommunicated persons, and suicides in the Catholic cemeteries. This action had been taken on authority of the town councils, which attributed their right to the recent annexation of Puerto Rico by the United States. The Council of Arecibo, for instance, proposed the secularization of the cemeteries, arguing that they had been constructed by municipal funds. The vicar answered these charges point by point. First, the municipalities were nothing more than administrative corporations within the organism of a Catholic state; and, since the vast majority of the state was Catholic, it was their funds that realized the cemeteries. The churches in the island had been constructed by state, provincial, municipal, and private funds. They and the cemeteries had been blessed and consecrated to Roman Catholic usage. To change this clear disposition would be a serious violation of religious liberty. He was certain that this was not the North American interpretation of religious liberty. If the insular government, moreover, did not consider the plots alongside the Catholic cemeteries as sufficient, then other sites should be sought where Catholic authority was not involved. He further argued from the canons of the church and from the civil legislation that was still in effect.[38]

This question was quickly handled by the American authorities. On January 9, 1899, General Henry published an order in the *Gaceta Oficial* to the effect that the Catholic cemeteries should continue as exclusive burial places for Catholics.[39] This matter was again clarified by General Henry on February 7, 1899, when he issued Order No. 13:

> Cemeteries which have been consecrated for use by Roman Catholics will be used only for the burial of those of that faith and will be administered according to the perpetual laws of that dedication. Burials subject to the order of parish priests may be allowed in portions of grounds not dedicated; for others, a suitable burial ground will be established by the municipalities.
>
> The existing habit of exhuming bodies in cemeteries and placing their bones in a corner of the cemetery or some other place, thus desecrating the dead, will be discontinued.[40]

It is interesting to note here the greater tolerance and consideration that was shown toward the traditional rights of the church in the action of such non-Catholics as General Guy V. Henry. He behaved as a more understanding person than many a nominal Catholic of Puerto Rico.

Summation

At the turn of the century an American author, William Dinwiddie, wrote his reflection on the conditions in Puerto Rico. In treating the church-state problem, he found that the "real weakness in the ecclesiastical system of the island, and the one which has led up to the discords of the past, and has fostered vice in the church—if it does exist—lay in the fact that the church and state leaned upon one another in close association, the state supporting the Church financially, and using her oftentimes as a political lever to further the ends of grasping civil officials." When we compare this statement with the material that we have already discussed, it seems that it cannot be denied that the church suffered for its financial and

administrative dependence on the state and that greater independence could have been productive of better spiritual results. In
respect to the effect of the church upon the laity, Dinwiddie believed
that, in 1899, "most of the population profess religious sentiments,
but church attendance is restricted to a few women and girls." At
this point, we may well counter that the scarcity of clergy had an
effect on the church attendance; but we can hardly deny the suspicion
that all was not as dynamic and zealous as the Christian ideal exacts.
The author concludes his observation with what may have been a
perceptive insight: "whether the opprobrium heaped upon the clergy
be deserved or not, the stigma cannot now be removed without a
complete remodeling of the organization, perhaps by the church of
America. Under the American regime which has set in, the church
appropriations have already been cut off, and reconstruction now
rests in the hands of the people themselves, as the future support of
the church is dependent upon the generous spirit of the populace."[41]
The church in its members—both lay and clerical—has ever known
periods of zeal and dynamic impact upon mankind. It has also seen
eras of decline into mediocre functioning by both the laity and the
clergy. Some of this was realized in the church at the time of the
invasion by the United States; that it was as serious as Dinwiddie has
suggested is debatable.

CONFLICTS IN EDUCATION

One of the first acts of Major General John R. Brooke was to
order the opening of the normal schools and to approve the educational regulations of the town councils. His successor, Brigadier
General Guy V. Henry, announced in the *Gaceta Oficial* of February
4, 1899, that General John Eaton was appointed superintendent of
public instruction and that all school officials were to report to him.
One of the first changes that appears is contained in a letter of
General Henry who informed General Eaton that he had no authority
to close the schools during Holy Week since "it is not an American
custom."

The new educational system met with many difficulties. Chief
among these were inadequate numbers of well-trained personnel, insufficient and poorly equipped schools, the poverty of the island, and
the linguistic and religious barriers. Dr. Victor S. Clark, in introducing his "Puerto Rican Papers" many years later, had this to say
of the first years of United States occupation: "The papers owe their

interest, if any, to the peep they give into some of the difficulties of initial contact between the two races—difficulties that have not yet vanished.'' In speaking of José E. Saldaña, a member of the insular Board of Education, he found that his complaints arose from the following points: first, a discontinuance of the Roman Catholic religious instruction in the public schools; second, the substitution of a strictly disciplined organization for the easy-going Spanish system ''where the teachers did much as they pleased''; and third, the low salaries paid and the strenuous character of teachers' duties, which prevented authorities from getting the best American teachers for supervisory positions.[42] Another vigorous criticism came from the wife of Governor General Henry. In reflecting on her first days in San Juan, Mrs. Henry wrote: ''The schools in old San Juan were of not much account—a fine system on paper, but no system in practice. . . . General Eaton was sent from Washington and undertook this arduous task. Months of work, filled with obstacles, awaited his patient, willing efforts, and developed the starting-point of a public school system.''[43] Another criticism comes from the pen of Dr. Clark who wrote to General Eaton: ''Whenever the General [Davis?] returns from one of his trips out into the Island, he usually has some account to give of a visit to one of the country or town schools. He was greatly disgusted to find a rural school and a wayside grocery and drinking shop in the same building at Cayey Saturday, and told me that such conditions should be remedied at once.'' The general was quoted as saying that there was much political interference with the quiet and effective running of schools on the local level.[44]

Much of the island's criticism of the new education arose from the regulations that General Eaton submitted to the secretary of interior, Dr. Carbonell, for approval. Some of the radical provisions were: first, all teachers now employed are expected to learn English; second, in the employing of new teachers, those who can speak English will be preferred; and third, all candidates for diplomas from the Higher School, the Normal School, and the Collegiate Institute are to be examined in English. Accordingly, Eaton recommended the purchase of ten thousand copies of Appleton's *First Reader in English*.[45] The new commissioner was set on the conversion of all instruction into English. He wrote to President McKinley that he was receiving weekly reports from ''our sixteen supervising teachers of English'' and that ''we are in direct correspondence with 500 regular teachers, all the Alcaldes, and the local Boards of Education.'' He, also, reported the aid of all local military commanders, American postmasters, and ''an Education Society distributed over the Island.'' The conclusion of his letter to the president asserted that ''we are embarrassed by the fact that Porto Ricans were not made to understand that the raising of the American flag meant the enforcement of American principles of government.'' He was convinced that, if we had been more firm in the beginning, many changes would have been accepted ''without a murmur.'' He spoke in particular of the exclusion of the church catechism from the schools, the ending of municipal payments to priests, and the lack of money for the repair of churches. He concluded that such evils, so long tolerated, can only be overcome by the ''most patient treatment.''[46]

From the beginning, political passions raged about the field of education. Typical of this is a letter of Miguel Rodríguez Sierras to President McKinley, asking that he be confirmed in his new post of superintendent of the high school in San Juan and charging that political feelings were endangering his job. In dealing with this case, Dr. Clark charged that he had been appointed by Secretary Carbonell although he was lacking in the legal requirements. Clark repeated his position that teachers ''are to be appointed by the municipal school boards and will serve under legal contracts, as in the States.''[47] It was such friction that produced the resignation of Dr. Carbonell, who soon thereafter wrote a strong letter to *La Democracia*: ''Like Egyptian plagues the orders on public education keep appearing in the *Gaceta*. . . . And, though these laws are good for the United States, they are not adapted to our climate, nor to our customs, and much less to our economic conditions. . . . With a stroke of the pen General Eaton . . . has destroyed the Institute of Secondary Education, the Normal School . . . and the honorable Secretary of the Interior approves this suppression of centers created by State laws.''[48] In June, the teachers of Puerto Rico were said to be organizing a large assembly in San Juan to protest the legislation of the United States. Among their complaints were the following: new examinations were required of the teachers and so reflected upon the competence of their ability; salaries were insufficient; because of compulsory vacations the school year was shortened; and the required language was English. The press report found that the intolerable conditions of the Spanish regime were being renewed under the American flag.[49]

In the meantime, General John Eaton was retired from Puerto

Rican affairs; his correspondence, however, with Commissioner Victor S. Clark gives an insight into the early reorganization of education. In early November, Eaton wrote that school matters should be separated from political action; the regulation of the size of barrios should meet necessary conditions; parental and social regard for children should be regarded as a means of improving the communities. The general saw in these matters an opportunity for the people "to try self-government in the simplest form and freest from complications." He finally commended Dr. Clark on his success in separating "the schools from residences in rented buildings" and in "adhering to the school laws as provided." He also asked if some of the $200,000 that had been allotted to the war department for the building of military roads might be used for educational purposes.[50] In reply to Eaton's letter, Dr. Clark wrote: "We have attempted the barrio organization, but it does not seem to me . . . that it is workable. The only people who can read and write in municipalities in many instances reside in the town and its immediate vicinity. There are barrios here in which the entire value of buildings and improvements is only a few hundred dollars and which do not contain a single frame building suitable for a school house." He then cited the supervisor of Guayama who wrote that he had been acting as mayor, municipal council, and school board for two months, as the majority of the elected members of the school board "are now in jail for election frauds and the board is therefore inactive." Dr. Clark concluded his letter by commenting on the teachers from the states, of which there are "several very poor ones among them. I wish we had some person in New York City who could pass upon our teachers as to qualifications for the work here before they come."[51] An example of Dr. Clark's analysis of his staff appears in an evaluation of Dr. Riopel who is described as "a very strong man . . . of a Calvinistic temperament and [who] hews pretty close to the line without much regard to policy or compromise." The director's conclusion was that this "may be needed in Ponce as their municipal authorities have been among the most lax and inefficient in the island."[52]

In the Clark-Eaton correspondence, there is the suggestion that an institution be established "upon the Indian school plan." Dr. Clark, however, reported an objection from congressmen who hold that "we have established Indian schools to educate the Indians to become self-supporting because we have taken their land and their hunting grounds," but "we are under no such obligations to the people of

Puerto Rico . . . [since] we have taken nothing away from them.''
Clark made much of the point that education of the young Puerto
Ricans would bring industrial and commercial advantages to the
United States:

> We have used the argument elsewhere, that technical and
> industrial education here will give us a corps of young Puerto
> Ricans, trained in both the English and Spanish language and
> in our industrial and commercial methods who will be valuable
> pioneers in extending our trade in South America. This is the
> most densely populated Spanish-American country. Many
> young men will seek fields of labor in South America, and in
> the other islands of the West Indies. If our government should
> interest itself in educating them so that they can become the
> industrial leaders of these countries they ought to accomplish
> much in extending our commerce and in creating markets for
> our manufactures.[53]

At the end of the month Dr. Clark was again writing to General
Eaton, telling of a long conversation with General Davis who recommended that the proceeds of the sale of public lands in Puerto Rico
be made a permanent school fund, that part of the proceeds of the
insular loan be devoted to the building of school buildings, and that
industrial and agricultural education be fostered. The personal view
of Victor S. Clark was that educational reforms will ''have to wait
upon social and economic reforms''; the work of many American
teachers ''is not more than half or one-third as effective as it might
be, because they work under conditions that prohibit success.'' He
believed that the federal government should support English and
industrial education in Puerto Rico until it was able to support a
system of schools from its own revenues; the money raised by the
island should go to the support of its native schools and to pay the
salaries of the native teachers. Twenty good schools that teach
English and industry should be located in the suburbs of the larger
towns ''where they can draw an attendance from pupils residing at
home.'' He suggested that land be attached to each school in order
that practical instruction in agriculture might be given. Clark concluded his recommendations with the observation that ''Puerto Rico
is over-populated'' and that there will be immigration to the less
populated countries of South America and the adjacent islands.
''This immigration will carry trade in its wake if a large enough
percent of the immigrants have the technical training necessary.''[54]

The Insular Board of Education

By order of General Davis on December 7, 1899, an insular Board of Education was established. It was to consist of nine members, "three of whom shall be residents of San Juan . . . and six shall be representatives of six districts of the Island defined in this Order, of which they shall be respectively residents. They shall be men conversant with educational affairs who are willing to serve without compensation." Victor S. Clark was appointed president.[55] Two of the problems that faced Dr. Clark were poor attendance at school and unsatisfactory teaching in English. His solution of the first was to request Colonel Hoff of the insular police to "secure attendance in rural districts wherever so requested by the board of trustees." At the same time, he realized that poor attendance was chiefly caused by lack of food and clothing. He found that the average school attendance in some schools was about twelve pupils, while there were towns in which the waiting list was seven or eight hundred. On the second point, he admitted little success in English where there were no American teachers, and he advised that the insular revenues devoted to public instruction "be expended upon schools largely under native teachers with English instruction optional or given only where the teacher is competent to teach in that language." This was a change from Clark's original position that Spanish in Puerto Rico was a patois with no literature and of little value as a cultural medium.[56]

Clark was again in fear of trouble from Dr. Saldaña who, as a member of the insular board, was charged with being a discordant element and misinformed. The president of the board consequently cabled General Davis, asking that he suggest that the Executive Council in the Foraker Bill be given direct control of the schools. He found that "Economic depression and race prejudices and the agitation of teacher politicians have created a hostile spirit to the American schools, and especially to the introduction of American teachers in the Island. Most of our teachers report difficulties of this kind. Education must be in strong hands for the present." He was certain that effective co-operation could be secured from the people, if they were dealt with sympathetically and with a regard "for their inherited prejudices and sentiments; but the initiative must be taken by the Americans until a habitual public school spirit is aroused." He regarded it as folly to leave public instruction to

Puerto Rican initiative.[57] At the same time, he was willing to admit that there has been an improvement in the public school system under the Spanish regime and that there was considerable ability and public spirit to be found among the people.

Again, in February and March of 1900, Dr. Clark mentioned the growing criticism that arose from Dr. Saldaña and the Federalist party. The people were annoyed with the delay of Congress and its failure to give full territorial government. He was able to understand their attitude, for "they are suffering from an acute economic crisis, worse than ours in 1893." He frequently overheard statements on the street corners that "the Spanish rule was the good old times that would never be seen in Puerto Rico again," and many letters from American teachers and supervisors in the island bore out this attitude. This, he said, had an effect upon the schools and upon the insular board. Here he cited the leader of the Republican party, Dr. José C. Barbosa who said: "You will never attain your object until you have your department entirely under the control of Americans, then you can go straight forward,—until then you will have to devote your main energy to reconciling the discordant elements with which you work."[58] It was Dr. Barbosa who worked, from his acceptance of the new regime in 1899 to his death in 1921, toward bringing Puerto Rico into United States statehood. He saw the modern world as one that demanded the formation of large social groups capable of balancing each other in the furtherance of peace, order, and progress. He saw the destiny of Puerto Rico as inevitably and beneficially associated with the United States.[59]

At this time, W. T. Harris, United States commissioner of education, in a personal letter to Dr. Clark, expressed his regret that "the teachers of English lessons in Puerto Rico had in some cases been indiscreet and that some reaction was making its appearance on the part of the Spanish population against the schools." The burden of his letter is that one must be careful of a reaction setting in: "The conservative people, namely the aged women and men, the grandparents, and the members of the priesthood will be alarmed at the appearance of a danger of wholesale educational transformation. An education that contemplates the change of the native language will involve a change of the religion and a change of the entire body of traditions of the people. This of course will be opposed by a dead weight of inertia which will be very difficult to lift."[60] After dismissing the aged and clerical elements with some calm superiority, the

American commissioner concluded that "in the presence of very much ambition for self-government, there is little ability for its actual realization," and "infinite patience must be exercised towards our new fellow citizens."[61]

At this time, Dr. Clark was becoming discouraged with the conditions of education in Puerto Rico. He saw a sharp rift in the insular Board of Education: the Republicans favoring his policy, and the Federals opposing. Opposition was still under the direction of Dr. Saldaña who tried to get a resolution requesting Clark's dismissal as president. The discouraged Clark saw the insular board as handicapping the enforcement of rules and regulations; in place of effective work, he saw continual change, criticism, and "a tendency to make the law one thing and the practice another." He was convinced that "if the present system continues, it will be impossible for the most partial investigator to render a favorable report upon the school system of Puerto Rico by the end of the year." He remarked that Dr. George E. Groff took a noncommittal stand in most of the board conflicts.[62] Within two days, on March 12, 1900, General Davis announced that, on the request of Dr. Clark, he was relieving him from the presidency of the Board of Education and appointing Dr. George E. Groff, acting assistant surgeon of the United States Army, in his place. Dr. Clark was appointed to the new post of assistant superintendent of public instruction.[63]

The discontent of the American teachers was bluntly expressed. A few days after Dr. Clark's resignation from the presidency of the board, he received a letter from an American teacher who expressed regret upon hearing the news. The teacher mentioned the joy of others over "the nearness of their departure, and I am gazing at them with envious eyes."[64] On the same day, the secretary of the American Teachers Association of Puerto Rico protested the treatment of American teachers by the local boards of education. The writer claimed that "ignorant Native Teachers are placed in authority over them and that Municipalities have not paid the additional salaries promised." Two copies of a resolution of the association were included; in these they asked to be placed directly under the control of the insular Board of Education and that the promises be fulfilled. After showing this letter to Dr. Groff, General Davis remarked that it had been impractical "to correct all the abuses existing in the Island. This matter will receive, no doubt, the attention of the Civil Governor, before whom it will be brought."[65]

On the first of May, 1900, Charles H. Allen was inaugurated as the first civil governor of Puerto Rico. On the recommendation of the governor-elect, General Davis had established an Executive Department and appointed the "acting officials." Dr. Groff was one of these acting officials. An official report gives us an insight into the educational setup on the island in June of 1900:[66]

Members of insular Board of Education	9
Number of teachers employed	628
Supervisors of schools	16
School boards of five members each	69
Mayors on the island	69
American teachers	70
Normal schools	1
Night schools	1

One of the first acts of Dr. Groff, in his role as commissioner of education, was to inform the local school boards that, if they were satisfied with their American public school teachers, they should renew their contracts, for soon the teachers would be returning to the United States. He also announced August 1 as the date on which examinations for teaching licenses would be held.[67] The term of Dr. Groff was coming to a rapid end, for Dr. M. G. Brumbaugh had been appointed as commissioner to take the acting commissioner's place. His brief term of office had not been without conflict, as is evidenced by a letter from a teacher in San Juan to Dr. Clark. The writer first found fault with Dr. Groff's arranging of a series of institutes in the larger towns; these were to be lectured to by a corps of instructors who were to be paid $100 a month and expenses. The institutes were to be held from July to mid-September when Dr. Groff would have to return for the opening of Bucknell University. A second sensitive point was Groff's arranging of an Assembly to Teachers, at which Dr. Saldaña was to speak and to which "too many priests" were invited. She reported: "Neither of the two political parties appeared to be willing to aid him. Dr. Barbosa refused, Mr. Muñoz Rivera refused. He invited the Secretary of State who also refused. He invited Governor Allen who accepted and then did not put in an appearance." The writer found that the trouble began with Dr. Saldaña who, "before an audience composed almost entirely of Roman Catholics," insisted upon "religious instruction being given in the schools, and that it be the Roman Catholic religion." As the writer describes it, the meeting broke up when the bishop and priests left in indignation, and the writer left upon realizing that "I was taking part in what appeared to me to be a Roman Catholic religious meeting and not an educational meeting."[68]

This conference brought out the religious issue in public education. As reported by *El País*, the Republican daily of Dr. Barbosa, the principal address was given by Dr. Saldaña, in which he opposed the "neutral, lay school" and urged the continuance of Catholic instruction in the public school. He was followed by Juan Vallmer who stated: "With the permission of the Catholic bishop and the priests who accompany him, I maintain that the backwardness which Brazil suffers, along with Spain, Portugal, Austria, and Italy, is due to the clergy." Thereupon, reported *El País*, the bishop struck the table and cried out, *"Mentira"* ["a lie"]. General confusion followed in which the Catholic party—after invoking the laws of the United States and giving a *viva* for religion—left the hall. The editor of *El País* reflected that the bishop will "by now have realized his error and repented of it."[69] The *Diario de Puerto Rico* gave a different presentation and interpretation of the facts. It reported Dr. Saldaña as having recommended that a religious basis be given to instruction in Puerto Rico and that the schools be used by the ministers of the different sects for those students that are of their belief. Vallmer was identified by the *Diario* as a minister. He was reported as having censured his own country (Brazil) and its culture, while attributing the backwardness of Austria, Spain, France, and Italy to the Catholic religion. Thereupon Bishop Blenk interrupted with some energetic words of protest, and most of those present felt injured by Vallmer's remarks. Father Hernández of the Cathedral Chapter protested in the name of American law that prohibits an attack on any religion in public acts of an official nature. The comment of the *Diario* was: "We respect all beliefs. Let each religion profess that which pleases it. But let us not give approval to acts such as that of yesterday, in order to attack Catholicism which is the belief of almost all the Insular population."[70] This meeting was a complete failure because it was boycotted by the leaders of the major parties and by the chief officials and because it brought out such sharp differences of opinion.

Adding to the internal difficulties over education was the caustic criticism of the *San Juan News*. On June 24, the *News* found serious deficiencies in the Charity School that had previously enrolled 223 boys from the age of five to fourteen but which was now reduced to 165 students. Some had been discharged and others had dropped out. The writer noted the insubordination of the boys and attributed it to the incompetence of the superintendent and the lack of harmony between the controlling Board of Charities and the Sisters of Charity, who had charge of the infirmary and the moral welfare of the boys. The boys were described by an employee as "mostly picked out of the gutter." The editorial continued that "too much religion and too little of that which is practical is being taught especially among the older boys." An American teacher of English was reported as saying that he had been reprimanded for inflicting corporal punishment on a boy, whereas "both the spirit and law of the regulation forbidding corporal punishment was being ignored every day by both the sisters of charity and the native teachers." He was convinced that "it is only when an American becomes involved in an act of discipline that notice is taken of it."[71]

By the end of August, the *News* was taking a more optimistic outlook on the future of education in the island. It saw the need of co-operation on the part of administrative officers, teachers, and parents in the interest of the Puerto Rican child who is "apt in acquiring knowledge." This American paper also praised the summer institutes that were staffed by American teachers who traveled over the whole island in order to instruct the teachers in modern school methods.[72] In the spirit of constructive growth, the *News* had appealed to American universities for a grant of free tuition to worthy Puerto Rican students. A generous response came from Georgetown, Yale, Cornell, Williams, Amherst, and others.[73]

The Brumbaugh Policy of Education

By mid-August, 1900, Dr. Brumbaugh had replaced Dr. Clark as commissioner of education in Puerto Rico. In a letter to Dr. Clark, he expressed appreciation for a letter of introduction to the Puerto Rican people. He remarked that he had taken over on August 4 and that Dr. Groff had sailed on August 6, "after being refused a request to be made Assistant Commissioner of Education." Brumbaugh reported that he was involved in a great deal of desk work and that he had already made visits to Fajardo, Ponce, Mayagüez, and Bayamón.[74] That Groff and Brumbaugh had not been in agreement is quite apparent from letters received by the secretary of interior in

Washington. In October, 1900, Governor Allen submitted Brumbaugh's report as commissioner of education to the secretary. After reading these documents, Dr. Groff informed the secretary of the interior that "Dr. Brumbaugh is very much mistaken in a large portion of his report. He absolutely refused any information from me in reference to the office, when he took charge. On almost every point concerning the work of the past year, his report is grossly incorrect and misleading. I may add that I believe Dr. V. S. Clark's reports to the military governor are very accurate. As correct as it was possible to make them.'' On the basis of these sources of information, Governor Allen reported to the Puerto Rican legislature on December 4, 1900, that 800 schools were then in operation and that this represented a gain of 184 over last year. The island had over 700 native teachers and fewer than 100 teachers from the United States. The schools were lacking in adequate buildings and sanitation. Finally, he stated, only 40,000 children could be accommodated, whereas 300,000 were unprovided for because of a lack of funds.[75]

The Brumbaugh Report was a very blunt statement of conditions as its author saw them. He first noted that a month before he took office a fire had destroyed the office and records of the Department of Education; that Dr. Groff had left no "oral statement of educational conditions in Puerto Rico"; and that he had been "obliged to begin . . . work without records or guidance.'' Dr. Brumbaugh also criticized the school laws of General Henry because they were modeled on the Massachusetts system and "not fitted to the conditions'' of Puerto Rico. He described the sixteen English supervisors appointed by General Eaton as former soldiers, packers, and teamsters—some of whom were heroic and others "mere adventurers.'' After this release of emotion, Dr. Brumbaugh recommended that the people should be taught both languages and that United States teachers receive $50.00 per month for nine months, while Spanish teachers be kept on salary all year along with the classes. Lastly, he recommended a normal school to be set up at Fajardo. In commenting on Brumbaugh's Report at a later date, Commissioner Harris found that the criticism of General Eaton's management of the schools was a "violation of etiquette.''[76]

The general policy of Brumbaugh has been described as the conservation of Spanish, along with the acquisition of English. The commissioner believed that, whereas Spanish should be the language of instruction in the elementary schools, English should be stressed in the secondary schools. His purpose was in accord with the instruction sent by President McKinley to Governor Allen in 1900 to Americanize the Puerto Ricans for the achievement of statehood. Dr. Brumbaugh returned to the United States in 1902 and was succeeded by Samuel McCune Lindsay who was ready to base the school system on English, when both teachers and pupils "can be trained sufficiently in the use of the English language."[77]

As the years passed, the initial problems that had arisen during the administrations of Clark, Groff, and Brumbaugh kept recurring. These problems were primarily the relative importance to be given to English and to Spanish, the continuing high percentage of illiteracy that resulted both from inadequate facilities and from the economic condition of the masses, the consistent political intrusion in educational matters, and the tradition of religious instruction in the public schools.

Some who favored "Americanization" of Puerto Rico were strongly opposed to any attempt to eradicate the Spanish language, since, as they argued, "its continuation would help in divulging American ideas and principles among 75 millions of Spanish-speaking people."[78] The small success in achieving a widespread mastery of English was remarked by a visitor to Puerto Rico in 1915. He found Spanish taught almost exclusively in the rural school, with fifteen minutes devoted to English.

It is unfortunate that we are unable to use the records of the teachers and students whose correspondence was "disposed of as useless during the period of formation of the files of the BIA."[79] These would give us a fuller view of the English-Spanish struggle. We do, however, have the acts of the House of Delegates that, in 1915, decreed under Section 5 "public instruction in the Normal School, in the Colleges of Liberal Arts . . . and in any other Departments of the University of Puerto Rico as well as in all High, Graded and Rural schools, shall be carried on in the Spanish language." This was a resolution that was presented by delegate De Diego and was supported by the *Boletín Mercantil*.[80] In 1922, the governor of Puerto Rico decreed that "Teachers in all grades above the fourth will use English as a medium of instruction in all subjects except physiology in the fifth grade and the Spanish language itself. Frequent complaints have reached the department to the effect that the teachers do not teach in English, to the detriment of the pupils."[81]

Associated with the language problem was the more serious problem of illiteracy. A report of 1914 stated that "practically two-thirds of the adult males of the island are illiterate and, if we exclude all males who do not belong to the wage-earning classes, this proportion will be greatly increased." It was noted in respect to the education of rural children that "only one-third of them could be enrolled in all the rural schools, and to do this required an average enrollment of 74 to each teacher." In 1915, Governor Yager reported that "as many as 150 and sometimes more pupils were enrolled under one teacher," and "it was thought wise . . . to attempt to do real educational work rather than make a show of numbers."[82] The fact of high enrollment is therefore no indication of great improvement in education over the period of Spanish sovereignty. On this point, the editor of *The Puerto Rico Eagle* wrote to the secretary of war in 1909 that "the whole effort of our educational force today is devoted to getting as many names as possible on the registers of our public schools, with little or no concern as to whether any results are obtained after the pupils are enrolled." He stated that forty of the eighty-nine schools erected in the past two years were $250 "shacks" (rural schools). He exposed the erection of school libraries in fifty-seven towns and twenty-three in the country as a collection of thirty thousand unused texts, stamped "school libraries of Porto Rico" and sent to teachers with the statement that they were "libraries." He cited the town of Lajas that had a "library" of 453 old text books and 12 other books. It was his conclusion that "the department no longer has the confidence of the people" and that good men were leaving the system in disgust.[83]

In summarizing the basic problems that faced the two peoples who sought to use education as an instrument in building cultural understanding, we have a keen analysis that was offered by José Padín, the commissioner of education in 1933. His analysis penetrates the major difficulties that occurred in those years of misunderstanding which followed United States seizure of Puerto Rico. He found the "Americanization" of Puerto Rico to be a living issue since 1898, and the department of education was being used as an instrument to this end. The commissioner had been charged with overemphasizing Spanish culture to the detriment of the Americanization of Puerto Rico. In counterattack, he charged that the "cloak of one hundred per cent Americanism" had been used by selfish politicians, in order to secure "larger shares of spoils." He recalled that the pioneer educators from the United States had carefully considered the "use of English as the sole medium of instruction in the public schools"; General Eaton and Victor Clark had favored it, while Doctor Brumbaugh decided to use both English and Spanish as the media of instruction. He considered the latter to be a wise policy. He with others was led to envision the possibility that "our Island may some day become the spiritual bridge spanning the gulf which separates the republics of Hispanic origin from those of Anglo-Saxon. To perform this service . . . the sons of Puerto Rico should master Spanish and English and drink deep in the fountainheads of the two cultures expressed through these languages. The school system should foster this noble ideal and help to bring it to fruition." With much vision Commissioner Padín espoused the "bilingual and bicultural policy of the Department of Education." He strongly decried the native politician who since 1898 had been waving the flag because it was "a profitable racket." He then deftly pointed to the "continental American" who in public service or in business "brings down with him his Americanism, takes it around, generally unaware of the fact, and lets it go at that. He propagates by example." The last type is the "native son" who has lived American ideals in the American environment, "whose life has been expanded and enriched by the experience and who yearns to share his good fortune with his fellow citizens."[84] If we read Padín correctly, it seems that he was determined to take the best from the Anglo-Saxon culture that had come to Puerto Rico, while not abandoning the great contributions of four centuries of Spanish culture. It was an ideal that aspired to the fashioning of a new culture that would represent the labor of his own people.

This chapter has not sought to give a detailed study of the educational institutions that were left by Spain and developed under the pressure of ideas from the United States. It merely attempts to indicate the differences and conflicts that arose from the change of sovereignty. We have suggested some analysis beyond the period with which this book is concerned, only because it is a reflection upon the problems that began in 1898.

VII

Trends in Puerto Rican Evolution

This final chapter proposes to express some elements of the stress that immediately preceded and climaxed the enacting of the Foraker Act and the complaints that grew into parties and institutional tendencies that have since characterized island mainland relations. It is with some trepidation that a foreigner seeks to portray these realities, and yet it is often true that a stranger can delineate a scene with less unconscious prejudice.

The most interesting study for a visitor to another country is its people. At the time of the change of sovereignty, much of the wealth of the island was concentrated in the hands of the conservatives (critically labeled "unconditional Spaniards") and a group of liberal reformists who were the more popular of the political leaders. These two groups—a very small percentage of the island's population—held the majority of the significant government posts and most of the financial control of the island. They constituted a paternalistic class and looked upon social legislation as an expression of socialism that was to be avoided at all cost. This class at heart still clings to the philosophy of *laissez-faire* capitalism but has been forced to accede

to reform legislation begotten of the principles of social justice. Their
social life is measured by extremes of party life. Parents with an
urge to place their children in the social merry-go-round bring them
to early debutante expression, and so they mature with difficulty into
a responsible part of society. Though all the wealthy do not deserve
this criticism, a great many do.

The middle class in Puerto Rico has been growing rapidly and
has contributed greatly to the development of the country. Through
intelligent industry and mature appreciation of insular problems, it
can boast a development in political, economic, and educational advance that few other countries have achieved in so short a time. It is
through this class that the dynamic growth of Puerto Rico will
continue. Its danger, as it amasses wealth, is an attempt to imitate
the social expression of the wealthy, and already some of these
families live far beyond their incomes.

The most interesting class in Puerto Rico is that of the *jíbaro*.
Generally speaking, he is a country dweller who wrests his livelihood
from the soil that he infrequently owns. Dr. Bailey K. Ashford,
writing during the early years of American occupation, described
him as follows:

> The jíbaro is respectful and obedient, fearful of the law and
> unconfiding in his superiors. He is generous in the extreme,
> and shares his last banana with the first person who comes.
> . . . If it is true that he has in many cases a type of existence
> distinct from the other classes, it is equally true that there
> is no masonry more powerful than that which exists among the
> jíbaros of Puerto Rico. Joined together by the most intimate
> bonds of kinship, and even more strongly by the eternal tie
> that the title of *compadre* represents; they share together their
> misfortunes. And they protect each other (*se sirven mutua-
> mente de escudos*) as if they pertained to one great family.[1]

The kindness and hospitality that characterizes this class is traditional in Puerto Rico. At the same time that the *jíbaro* has suffered
intensely from malnutrition, overwork, anemia, various tropical
diseases, and from such violent forces of nature as floods, earthquakes,
and hurricanes, he has ever maintained his patience and generosity.
One who knows the *jíbaro*, however, never confuses this with lack of
intelligence. He is often unaware of the world beyond his environment, but he is keen in evaluating people and shrewd in handling
them. It is no slight tribute to former Governor Luis Muñoz Marín

that he knows the *jíbaro,* knows how to talk to him, and, even more significant, has provided an administration that has worked for his social and economic betterment. Soon the word *jíbaro* will have to be relegated to history or re-defined for, through radio, television, and broadened education, he is being drawn into the middle class, though in a humbler economic bracket.

Lastly, there is the proletariat class that has grown with the industrialization of Puerto Rico. The beginnings of this class may be found in the first days of occupation by the United States when Santiago Iglesias began the organization of workers under the Socialist banner and sought to relate them to the laborers of the United States who had united under the AFL. Though much of this organization was among the workers in the farming industries in the early period, that history post-dates the period of this book.

Cutting across all classes in Puerto Rico, one finds a quiet and deep culture that expresses itself in many different ways, from the artistic expressions of the educated classes to the warm human expression of the *jíbaro.* From the earliest days of United States sovereignty to the present, but few mainlanders have appreciated this plurality in Puerto Rican life. Misunderstanding has developed into unjust criticism; it is unfortunate that there was small willingness to understand and to foster a policy of friendship. This failure aroused the sensitive Puerto Rican people. An instance of this is found in Llorens Torres who, in 1910, protested the memorial of the Puerto Rican Assembly that found "the people of Puerto Rico love the United States, while the people . . . do not love the people of the United States." He remarked: "there is no motive for a liking here for the people of the United States. There is no affinity of races, nor of speech, nor of religion, nor of customs, nor of other relations which engender gratitude. Porto Rico has no motive, particularly under the present circumstance, to be thankful to or care for the American people, who have done everything possible to keep us from caring for them."[2] This is not a solitary instance of misunderstanding, nor is it a mere expression of over-sensitivity. Anglo-Americans can often be too quick in judgment and consequently unintentionally unfair.

In turning to a consideration of the socio-economic relations that existed between the United States and Puerto Rico, we have already seen the vital problem of markets and tariffs. We have noted the great poverty that has characterized the island over a long period and have recorded the Puerto Rican criticism that the United States was slow to assist in the betterment of these conditions. This criticism was stated again later by Santiago Iglesias who bitterly scored the government of Governor Yager (1913-1921): "It was, and is the government of the insolent rich, of the corporations, of the oppressors, of the miserable judicial, political and religious bosses. . . . Under the regime of the 'graceful government' which has just terminated its first and only epoch, the rich have become richer and the poor, poorer." He further charged the leaders of the principal Puerto Rican parties, Muñoz Rivera and José Barbosa, with co-operating in maintaining the "physical and mental pauperism for the enormous mass of productive laborers of the fields, factories and shops."[3] Governor Yager admitted that the poverty of the masses was beyond dispute, adding: "Their dwellings are, for the most part, mere hovels, almost devoid of furniture and crowded beyond belief. Their food consists of rice, codfish and beans, supplemented by the native fruits which grow wild and practically all over the island. And their wages are, as a rule, barely sufficient to maintain their existence under these miserable conditions." He found that over-population was the principal problem and that, if any of the island's industries were to suffer a calamity, such as a hurricane destroying the coffee plantations, "the situation would become very critical." He believed that a large number of the population would have to migrate.[4]

While the labor and population problem has continued in Puerto Rico and must find its escape valve in migration to continental United States, there was an attempt to solve the problem of land ownership. On May 1, 1900, the United States Congress enacted a Joint Resolution No. 23 (S.R. 116), as a supplement to the Organic Act of April 12, 1900. By this act, corporations were restricted to the ownership of not more than five hundred acres of land. The House Committee on Insular Affairs had stated: "It would not be for the interest of a million people crowded upon a territory 100 by 40 miles in extent, to have one corporation own all, or substantially all, the land." The history of this legislation's effect is traced by Gilberto Concepción's remarks: "The written prohibition continued to be a 'dead letter' from 1910 to March 25, 1940, when the Supreme Court of the United States declared that the Legislature of Puerto Rico has a right to enforce the limitation and that the same was constitutional. During the period, concentration of land in the hands of absentee corporations steadily increased." The situation was finally improved, on

April 12, 1941, when the Legislature of Puerto Rico passed Act No. 26 that created the Puerto Rico Land Authority, a governmental instrument that set out to end the corporative latifundia in the name of the people of Puerto Rico.[5]

The thinking out of sound political principles and their expression in realistic institutions of government has been another ever-present problem for Puerto Rico. The age of political shock came at the turn of the century, when Puerto Rican leaders who had learned the strength and weakness of Spain's hegemony were presented with a new political milieu. If interpreted correctly, the leaders knew too little of the United States and tended to interpret our constitution too simply. When the United States set up its government by military rule, the Federals tendered their co-operation in the belief that Congress would quickly provide a better form of autonomy than Spain. When this was not forthcoming—especially during the governorship of General Henry—they withdrew embittered. Thereupon, the Republicans took a position and displayed a realistic attitude in trying to get along with the military government. When the civil government, under the Foraker Act of 1900, was set up, it was again the Republican party of Puerto Rico that co-operated with the Republicans in Washington. The Federals, meanwhile, sought to wed themselves to the Democratic party in the United States and to achieve some form of autonomy or independence. Their effort resulted in party divisions. It was not until 1904 with the formation of the Union party and the friendship of Governor Beekman Winthrop that their vitality as a party revived.

One of the first irritants in the period of disillusionment occurred in 1901 when Governor William H. Hunt attempted to restrict the right of speech in the public plaza. Much friction had developed with the Federación Libre de Trabajadores (Free Federation of Workers), a predecessor of the Socialist party and a product of Santiago Iglesias. The governor proposed a law restricting speech, on the basis of disturbing the peace, by the use of the "police powers." The first Legislative Assembly instead wrote a law that defined the rights of the people. Section 3 read: "Free speech shall not be restricted; and everyone shall have full freedom in the speaking, writing or publishing of that which pleases him upon any matter, while remaining responsible for any abuse in the use of this liberty."[6] Another measure in 1903 brought annoyance to the people of Puerto Rico. The Puerto Rican Assembly asked for a territorial form of govern-

ment and the extension of the United States Constitution to the
island. It was their hope to bring statehood closer through the intermediate step of an organized territory. The Executive Council—
which was in the majority composed of continental Americans—rejected this in its Judiciary Committee. The committee argued that it
saw no need of greater powers, since "those delegated to us under the
organic act are as ample as the powers of legislation enjoyed by any
state." Secondly, it stated that "a territory has no place of special
importance in the American system," nor is it a necessary step to
statehood.[7]

When the Union party of Puerto Rico was formed in 1904, Muñoz
Rivera—through the pages of *La Democracia*—stated the ideal of
the island: "We declare that the Puerto Rican people aspire unanimously to self-government."[8] This vigorous leader became disgusted with the island's relationship to the United States. After
praising Spain's policy of 1897-98, he added:

> They [the Americans] arrived, and our sympathetic friendship
> continued, because we thought that the freedom enjoyed by
> the United States would be extended to Porto Rico, no longer
> in the form of the Latin autonomy of Moret and Sagasta, but
> in the shape of Anglo-Saxon autonomy prevailing in the
> British colonies. Instead of that we had the military govern-
> ment first and afterwards the civil government, with the
> Foraker Act, within which we see its autonomic and indepen-
> dent petty kings arising.[9]

As the years passed, new political parties were formed, but es-
sentially the same political question remained: should Puerto Rico
strive for independence, statehood, or some form of autonomy? A
majority of the Puerto Ricans believed that, in the island's present
condition, independence would offer serious difficulties. Problems
of population, trade, politics, and protection from aggression, they
say, urge some form of union with the United States. Statehood, it is
argued, presents its economic and cultural problems that must be
resolved before any decision on the part of the people of Puerto Rico.
The commonwealth status (*estado libre asociado*) or some variation
upon it is regarded by most Puerto Ricans as the most practical at
present. This means a wide form of autonomy that retains essential
association with the United States. They also consider the growing
concept of the twentieth century to be extensive local autonomy within

an ambient of interdependence. Ever-growing mutual dependence is seen in regional blocs of ideology, culture, defense, and economic relations. The United States itself is in the process of evolution regarding essential dependence upon other peoples. The degree to which she relates to other Latin American countries will have its effect on the status of Puerto Rico.

Abbreviations

AR 1901—*First Annual Report of Governor Charles H. Allen*, Puerto Rico, May 1, 1901
BIA—Bureau of Insular Affairs, War Department, National Archives, Washington, D.C.
Bol. Ecl.—*Boletín Eclesiástico*, San Juan, Puerto Rico
Bol. Hist.—*Boletín Histórico de Puerto Rico*
Bol. Mer.—*Boletín Mercantil*, San Juan, Puerto Rico
Congr. R.—*Congressional Record*
CR Report of Dr. Henry K. Carroll, 1899
DIPR Department of the Interior, Puerto Rico
El. Lib.—*El Liberal*, San Juan, Puerto Rico
Gac. Ofic.—*Gaceta Oficial de Puerto Rico*
GPO—Government Printing Office, Washington, D.C.
HAHR—*Hispanic American Historical Review*
HSPA—Historical Society of Pennsylvania
IC—Insular Commission of 1899, appointed to Puerto Rico by President McKinley
La. Corr.—*La Correspondencia*, San Juan, Puerto Rico
La. Dem.—*La Democracia*, Ponce, Puerto Rico
L.C.—Library of Congress, Washington, D.C.
NAPR—National Archives of Puerto Rico
NAUS—National Archives of the United States, Washington, D.C.
PSQ—*Political Science Quarterly*
RDC 1899—*Report of General Davis: Civil Affairs, 1899*, Washington, 1900
RMGC 1899-1900—*Report of Military Governor [Davis] of Puerto Rico on Civilian Affairs, 1899-1900*, Washington, 1902
SJN—*San Juan News*
UPR—University of Puerto Rico
USIC—*United States Insular Commission Report*, June 9, 1899

Notes

CHAPTER I

1. *Peninsulares*—Spaniards who, born in Spain, came to the colonies to direct their political, economic, and religious life. *Criollos*—born in the colonies, but of European blood. *Mestizos*—a mixture of Indian and European blood.

2. William Dinwiddie, *Puerto Rico: Its Conditions and Possibilities* (New York, 1899), p. 101.

3. *Re* Francisco Vitoria and Francisco Suárez, see James Brown Scott (ed.), *The Classics of International Law* (London, 1944, Carnegie Endowment for International Peace).

4. John Tate Lanning, "The Reception of the Enlightenment in Latin America," in *Latin America and the Enlightenment* (New York: 1942), pp. 72-89, and Holand D. Hussey, "Traces of French Enlightenment in Colonial Hispanic America," in *ibid.*, pp. 23-37.

5. Salvador Brau, *Historia de Puerto Rico* (New York, 1904), p. 225. In the Carnegie Library (San Juan), the collection of the writings of the Real Sociedad Económica de los Amigos del País is incomplete. They deal with matters of government, public administration, accounting, treasury, city councils, public works, war, and the church. The volumes in the collection reflect little of politics and philosophy.

6. In 1511, the Diocese of Puerto Rico was created, and Alonso Manso was consecrated its first bishop; he died at his post in 1539. His episcopal charge was initiated and evolved under the protection of the Spanish crown, for on July 28, 1508, Pope Julius II had granted to the rulers of Spain and their successors the

privilege of royal patronage. This grant obliged the crown to establish, endow, and defend the Catholic religion in the Americas, and so unity was achieved in the spread of religion and in defense against intervention by foreign nations. In return, the Pope conceded certain privileges to the king, such as the presentation of candidates for episcopal consecration, the designation of the site, and the determination of the budget in the building of monasteries and churches.

The church, under the guidance of the crown, was faced with the conversion and education of the indigenous population of Puerto Rico, along with the spiritual care of the Spaniards. The Indians had a religion with many superstitious overtones. Many Spaniards were either religiously indifferent or lax in religious practice. The church had to contend with both the country-folk who clung to their pagan superstitions and with the "intellectuals" who were nominal Catholics but ignored religious practice and often displayed a bitter anticlericalism.

One of the constant problems in Puerto Rico was a shortage of clergy. This lack was most serious in the country areas where the landholders were unable to secure priests for their people. Though parishes were set up in the principal concentrations of population, the greater part of the population was scattered over the island. Bishop Solís, writing in 1636, stated: "I have found that a great part of the population of this land is in the country which they call stations [*estancias*]." Besides, Bishop Bastidas had complained in the mid-sixteenth century that "we have a great need of clerics in these Islands, and because of our sins few come from among these people" (Antonio Cuesta Mendoza, *Historia Eclesiástica del Puerto Rico Colonial, 1508-1700* (República Dominicana, 1948), I, 189-93, 214-15).

In the sixteenth and seventeenth centuries, many chapels were built but were destroyed by the fierce Carib Indians. Other churches and monasteries were despoiled by the French in 1528 and by the English under Drake in 1595 and Cumberland in 1598. Further depredations were committed by the Dutch in 1625. Even greater damage was done by the periodical hurricanes that leveled chapels and homes and upset the island's economy.

7. *Bol. Hist.*, II (Jan.-Feb. 1815), 3-8.

8. Lidio Cruz Monclova, *Historia de Puerto Rico* (Santurce, 1952), I, 49-51. Text: "Este pueblo, bastante dócil para obedecer a las autoridades que tiene conocidas no sufrirá jamás que se saque de la Isla un solo americano para llevarlo a pelear contra sus hermano los caraqueños." The translation in the text and all subsequent translations are the author's unless otherwise indicated.

9. *Ibid.*, I, 66-67. Also Brau, *Historia*, p. 225.

10. Cruz Monclova, *Historia*, I, 69, 88, 107, 112-14, 94, 137. Consult also D. Vicente de la Fuente, *Historia de las Sociedades Antiguas y Modernas en España* (Barcelona, 1933), I, 241-44.

11. The first steps in education in Puerto Rico were taken in the teaching of religion. King Ferdinand of Spain had ordered the agents of the kingdom—in accord with the terms of the royal patronage—to provide for the teaching of the Indians in Christian doctrine (*Recopilación de Leyes de los Reynos de las Indias*, etc., II, libro VI, tit. VIII, 249). This decree of 1503 required that the children be gathered together twice a day in a house near the village church, in order that the chaplain might teach them to read, write, and pray. A cathedral-school in San Juan also provided for the instruction of the children (Alejandro Tapia y Rivera, *Biblioteca Histórica de Puerto Rico* [San Juan, 1945], pp. 102, 114). Bishop Alonso Manso, in his message of 1512, concerned himself with the building of a cathedral in his diocese of San Juan and spoke of the intent of the Catholic Kings in the New World "to bring the inhabitants to a reverence of Our Lord

. . . and to the profession of the Catholic Faith.'' His purpose, then, was to supervise instruction in the Christian religion, and he created the ''office of school master who was to teach.'' (*Ibid.*, pp. 371-77).

A royal decree of 1513 ordered special care of the Indian children, forbidding that those under fourteen years of age be obliged to work. Children over fourteen were left under the control of their parents until they reached the legal age; and those left orphans were to be cared for by ''persons of good morals who are to see that they are taught the truths of our Holy Faith'' (*Ibid.*, p. 207). The concern of Spain in educating the inhabitants of the New World was primarily to see that they were formed in Christian life. There was no divorce of education from the life of faith, and the priests were to carry the burden of formation. Since there were few priests, education was necessarily limited to the most essential religious duties. It was the Dominican monastery that provided the education to the priesthood; and in 1529 the Bishop of La Española, on a trip to Puerto Rico, reported that there were twenty-five students in this newly founded monastery (Juan José Osuna, *A History of Education in Puerto Rico* [Río Piedras, 1949], pp. 12-13). But in 1548, the bishop of Puerto Rico wrote to Emperor Charles V, complaining that ''we have a great need of priests in these islands, for few [vocations] come from here, and those from Spain manage to move elsewhere'' (Tapia y Rivera, *Biblioteca*, p. 344).

In 1554, Charles V made clear that the purpose of the landed estates was a means of providing for the spiritual and temporal care of the Indians, their instruction in the faith, and the defense of their persons. Philip II repeated this idea in 1500 and inquired into how his orders were being fulfilled, whether the people were free or oppressed, and if they were receiving instruction. Philip III, in 1619, was concerned with the use of funds for the missions not merely to extirpate idolatry, but also to educate the sons of the Indian chief in schools (*Recopil. de Leyes*, p. 218). The minutiae of the *Laws of the Indies*, in both positive legislation and in demands for the checking of abuses, give testimony to the serious purpose of the Spanish crown in educating the peoples of the Americas.

In the seventeenth century, Puerto Rico suffered invasions from French, British, Dutch, and pirate fleets, and was forced to expend large sums on defense, while the ravages of epidemics and hurricanes prevented the island's economic progress. In the face of such evils, education was put aside for better days. Nevertheless, in 1644, the bishop of Puerto Rico reported to the king that in the cathedral school of San Juan there were two dozen grammar students; in the San Juan convent of the Dominicans there were thirty students; and six students in the Franciscan convent (Osuna, *History*, pp. 12-13). A lawyer named Diego de Torres Vargas who was also a canon of the San Juan Cathedral wrote, in 1647, of the teaching of grammar at the cathedral to the neighboring children. He also mentioned the Dominican convent that had thirty in training for the religious life (Tapia y Rivera, *Biblioteca*, pp. 463-65, 526-30). This report has been criticized by such authors as José Julián Acosta, Cayetano Coll y Toste, and Antonio Cuesta Mendoza. Cf. Osuna, *History*, pp. 13-21. Since it was an official report to the crown, it cannot be lightly discounted. In the year preceding O'Reilly's visit, Bishop Mariano Martí had made a visit to Bayamón and had ordered the establishment of schools in Bayamón and Guaynabo. He also ordered the teaching of reading, writing, grammar, and formation in citizenship.

12. Cayetano Coll y Toste, *Reseña del Estado Social, Económico, e Industrial de la Isla de Puerto Rico* . . . (San Juan, 1899), p. 27. Also Cuesta Mendoza, *Historia*, pp. 19, 25-28.

13. Osuna, *History*, pp. 21-22. From 1821 to 1898, the control of public schools passed successively from the Sociedad Económica to the Academy of Belles

Lettres, and then to the Municipal Councils of Primary Instruction. On the establishment of the Autonomous Charter of 1897, the Secretariat of Public Instruction took charge of education.

14. Monclova, *Historia*, I, 132-33, 212-13.
15. *Ibid.*
16. *Ibid.*, I, 141-58, 170-81, 191-93, 231-33, 244-47.
17. Brau, *Historia*, p. 238.
18. *Ibid.*, pp. 239-40.
19. Cruz Monclova, *Historia*, I, 187-88.
20. William R. Manning (ed.), *Diplomatic Correspondence of the United States Concerning the Independence of the Latin American Nations* (New York, 1925), I, 266, 272, 279, 314; II, 1290, 1297.
21. Luis M. Díaz Soler, *Historia de la Esclavitud Negra en Puerto Rico, 1493-1890* (Madrid, 1949), pp. 213-17. The *audiencia*, in Spanish law, is a judicial body that also produces many legislative and administrative acts.
22. Osuna, *History*, pp. 103-9.
23. Cruz Monclova, *Historia*, I, 277-83, 298-301, 310-13, 317, 333, 363-68, 372-81, 385-90. Also, Don Modesto Lafuente y Zamalloa *Historia General de España* (Barcelona, 1922), XXI, 209.
24. Samuel F. Bemis, *A Diplomatic History of the United States* (New York, 1953), pp. 320-21. The Spanish ambassador also tried to have the United States modify the tariffs of 1842 that were troublesome for Spain and her colonies.
25. Cruz Monclova, *Historia*, I, 348-50, 416-20.
26. *Ibid.*, I, 313.
27. *Ibid.*, I, 417-19, 422-31.
28. Brau, *Historia*, p. 249.
29. Cruz Monclova, *Historia*, I, 446, 462.
30. Brau, *Historia*, pp. 259-61.
31. Cruz Monclova, *Historia*, I, 486-94.
32. *Ibid.*, I, 514-53, 557-80, 492-514, 588-608.
33. E. Fernandez Garcia (ed.), *The Book of Porto Rico* (San Juan, 1923), pp. 877-79; Pilar Barbosa de Rosario (ed.), "De Baldorioty a Barbosa" in *La Obra de José Celso Barbosa* (San Juan, 1957), V, 17.
34. Cruz Monclova, *Historia*, I, 643-45. Masonic lodges are said to have been in operation in Puerto Rico as early as 1805.
35. *Ibid.*
36. Leopoldo Zea, *Dos Etapas del Pensamiento en Hispano-América* (México, D.F., 1949), pp. 31-33, 39, 43-47.
37. James Collins, *A History of Modern European Philosophy* (Milwaukee, 1954), p. 703.
38. Antonio S. Pedreira, *Hostos: Ciudadano de América* (Madrid, 1932), p. 143.
39. *Ibid.*, pp. 153, 165, 169.
40. *Ibid.*, p. 53.
41. *Ibid.*, pp. 55-56.
42. Angel Acosta Quintero, *José Julián Acosta y Su Tiempo* (San Juan, 1899), pp. 36-51.
43. *Ibid.*, pp. 79-87, 60-61, 56, xi.
44. Arturo Córdova Landrón, *Salvador Brau: Su Vida, Su Obra, Su Epoca* (Río Piedras, 1949), pp. 22-38.
45. Salvador Brau, *Ecos de la Batalla* (Puerto Rico, 1886), p. 9.
46. Salvador Brau, *Lo Que Dice la Historia* (Madrid, 1893).

47. Córdoba Landrón, *Brau*, p. 81.

48. Brau, *Ecos*, p. 216.

49. Jaime Balmes, *Obras Completas*, Vol. V of *Biblioteca de Autores Cristianos* (Madrid, 1949). This volume gives a good insight into Balmes' treatment of modern philosophy and Catholicism.

50. Brau, *Ecos*, p. 27. Written in periodical *El Agente*, Nov. 5, 1881.

51. *Bol. Ecl.*, June 15, 1864.

52. *Ibid.*, Oct. 15, Dec. 15, 1865.

53. *Ibid.*, Dec. 1, 1866. This speech was given by Felix, Bishop of Orleans, on October 9, 1866, and is quoted from the *Correo de la Gironda*.

54. *Bol. Ecl.*, Jan. 15, 1867.

55. *Ibid.*, Dec. 15, 1870.

56. *Ibid.*, pp. 37-42.

57. Cuesta Mendoza, *Historia de la Educación en el Puerto Rico Colonial* (República Dominicana, 1948), I, 48-51.

58. Cruz Monclova, *Historia*, I, 374. Text: ''. . . que la instrucción había perdido las Américas y que, con ella, era materia que debía manejarse con sumo tacto, convenía que los que quisieran estudiar fuesen a España . . . que los pobres tenían bastante con aprender a leer, a escribir, bastante doctrina cristiana y un oficio; pues España, quería sus colonias, para su gloria y no para su perdición.''

59. *Ibid.*, I, 477-78. Text: ''Puertorriqueños: Por más de tres siglos nos ha estado oprimiendo el despotismo español, sin que hasta ahora ningún hijo del país se haya visto llamado a ocupar un puesto de distinción. . . . Los jíbaros son pobres e ignorantes por culpa del Gobierno que prohibe las escuelas, los periódicos y los libros, y hace poco, acaba de negar que se funde una Universidad, para que los pobres, que no pueden mandar sus hijos fuera de Puerto Rico.''

60. Osuna, *History*, pp. 62, 73, 69-72, 77-82, 92. This material is well presented in Chapter V of Dean Osuna's history of education.

61. *Bol. Ecl.*, Oct. 15, 1860.

62. Cruz Monclova, *Historia*, II, Pt. I (Puerto Rico, 1957), 17-30, 56-61. Also, Manuel Fraga Iribarne, *Las Constituciones de Puerto Rico* (Madrid, 1953), pp. 15-16; and Barbosa de Rosario, ''De Baldorioty,'' pp. 25-34.

63. Cruz Monclova, *Historia*, II, Pt. I, 106, 227, 268-75, 330-55. At the time of this economic problem, United States relations with Spain were tense. On June 29, 1869, Secretary of State Hamilton Fish had instructed Daniel Sickles (U.S. minister to Spain) to urge the Spanish government to pass a law abolishing slavery in Puerto Rico. In mid-December, the secretary renewed his request that Spain emancipate all those born of slave mothers and those who had reached the age of fourteen. On December 24, 1872, the Spanish overseas minister presented a resolution that slavery be immediately abolished in Puerto Rico. The decree abolishing slavery was published in the *Gaceta Oficial* of Puerto Rico on March 30, 1873, by order of Governor General Martínez Plowes.

Relations between Spain and the United States, however, took a serious turn at the end of the year in the ''*Virginius* Incident.'' The *Virginius* was a Cuban revolutionary ship that was sailing under the flag of the United States. Seized by a Spanish warship, the captain and fifty-two sailors—mostly Americans—were executed on deck; and only through the intervention of the British warship, *Niobe*, were ninety-six more saved from the same fate; the war spirit was enkindled in the United States, and Puerto Rico prepared itself against invasion. Both Conservatives and Reformist Liberals protested their defense of Spain. Despite the aroused press of the United States and the determination of President Grant and many of his Cabinet, Secretary Fish was able to prevent an armed conflict. Cf. Thomas A. Bailey, *A Diplomatic History of the American People*, (New York, 1958), pp. 380-81.

64. Brau, *Historia*, pp. 274-76. Also, Antonio S. Pedreira, *El Año Terrible del '87* (México, D.F., 1948), pp. 20-24; Barbosa de Rosario, "De Baldorioty," pp. 30-32, 92; and Lidio Cruz Monclova, *Historia del Año de 1887* (Río Piedras, Puerto Rico, 1958), pp. 49-80.

65. Cruz Monclova, *Historia*, II, Pt. 2, 413-78, 523-24, 490-500, 653-73, 685-86, 761-63. Rafael María de Labra was born in Cuba, elected as deputy to the Cortes from Infiesto, Asturias (Spain). He represented the cause of the Antilles in the Cortes and was elected "leader" of the Reformist Liberal cause of Puerto Rico in the Cortes. Text: (Art. 89, Spanish Constitution of 1876): "Las provincias de Ultramar serán gobernadas por leyes especiales pero el Gobierno queda autorizado para aplicar a las mismas, con las modificaciones que juzgue convenientes y dando cuenta a las Cortes, las leyes promulgadas o que se promulguen para la Península."

66. Cruz Monclova, *Historia*, II, Pt. 2, 681-93. Also Pedreira, *El Año*, pp. 30-35, 123-35; and Barbosa de Rosario, "De Baldorioty," pp. 39-42, 58-64. Text: (Art. 7, Constitution of the Autonomist party, 1887): "Dado el carácter local de la unión o partido autonomista se deja a cada uno de los afiliados en completa libertad para ingresar en los partidos políticos de la Metrópoli, que acepten o defiendan la Autonomía de las Antillas; de sustentar sus ideas particulares respecto de la forma del gobierno."

67. Barbosa de Rosario, "De Baldorioty," pp. 107-21. Also, Pedreira, *El Año*, pp. 36-45. At this time, a secret organization named La Boycatizadora (also, La Torre del Viejo or Los Secos o Mojados) was founded. It boycotted the commerce of the *incondicionales* who stood for peninsular dominance in Puerto Rico and set up co-operatives in the benefit of the members of its party. This pressure was soon felt; and during the months of May and June, 1887, the Conservative elements sent petitions to Madrid, while their press—*El Boletín Mercantil*, *La Bandera Española*, and *La Integridad*—charged the Autonomists with illegal action. The Conservative press identified the boycotters with the Autonomists. Spain feared that this movement might be a conspiracy, since it occurred at a time when rumors of filibustering expeditions from Santo Domingo were rampant. Barbosa del Rosario, "De Baldorioty," pp. 117-66; Pedreira, *El Año*, pp. 43-63; and Brau, *Historia*, pp. 286-87.

68. *Bol. Ecl.*, June 1, 1871.

69. *Ibid.*, May 1, 1879.

70. Cuesta Mendoza, *Historia de la Educación*, II, 135-40. Also, Antonio López de Santa Ana, *Los Jesuitas en Puerto Rico de 1858 a 1886* (Santander [España], 1958), Chapter 15.

71. *Bol. Ecl.*, March 15, April, June 1, 1881.

72. This lecture can be found in the Colección Puertorriqueña, UPR, under the title, "Discurso por Don Juan Perpiñá y Pibernat" (San Juan, 1887). Text: "El mundo moderno adolece de . . . la falta de conocimientos sólidos y verdaderos en las ciencias metafísicas, de ideas estables y verdaderamente filosóficas. . . . La enciclopedia francesa de últimos del siglo pasado y principios del actual, y las ideas malamente llamadas filosóficas de las escuelas alemanas . . . que, bien que admirables en su método de exposición, lo contienen todo, menos la verdad, ejercen todavía su perniciosa influencia en todos los ramos del saber humano y en las fibras más recónditas de los estados sociales. . . . La razón humana se independiza de Dios."

73. Cuesta Mendoza, *Historia de la Educación*, II, 138-40. Also, De Santa Ana, *Los Jesuitas*, pp. 120-27; Gabriel Ferrer Hernández, *La Instrucción Pública*

en Puerto Rico (Puerto Rico, 1885), pp. 71-75; José Pablo Morales Miranda, *Misceláneas Históricas* (San Juan, 1924), p. 84; "Solemne Distribución de Premios en Seminario-Colegio" (San Juan, 1872), in Colección Puertorriqueña, UPR; "Solemne Distribución de Premios en Colegio San Ignacio de Loyola" (Santurce, 1883-84), in Colección Puertorriqueña, UPR; Martín Travieso y Quijano, *Memoria sobre el Estado Actual de la Instrucción Pública* (Mayagüez, 1885), p. 20; Osuna, *History*, pp. 113-16.

74. Osuna, *History*, pp. 105-9. Cuesta Mendoza, *Historia de la Educación*, II, 39-44, 88, 138-40, 141-57. Father Rufo was a distinguished professor of the natural sciences and fosterer of advanced studies (*Bol. Ecl.*, Dec. 5, 1899).

CHAPTER II

1. Obras Públicas, DIPR, Leg. 181, exp. 56.

2. Rudolph A. Van Middeldyk, *The History of Porto Rico* (New York, 1903), pp. 178-79, 228-29.

3. Salvador Brau, *Ecos de la Batalla* (Puerto Rico, 1886), p. 28. Text: "La economia política es una ciencia que abarca el estudio de los importantes intereses sociales, no solo con relación al capital acumulado, si que también con los principios generadores de ese capital, tendiendo a la destrucción de todo antagonismo entre el proletario y el propietario y tratando de levantar el nivel social por medio de esta suprema formula: Trabajo y ahorro, justicia y libertad."

4. Salvador Brau, *Lo que Dice la Historia* (Madrid, 1893).

5. Obras Municipales, DIPR, 1890, Isabela, Puerto Rico. Another insight into the warmth of Puerto Rican life appears in the notices from Lares on July 25, 1890. A celebration in honor of Don Isaac Peral, "inventor of the submarine," was announced. The day began with a solemn *Te Deum* and the singing of the National Anthem. All civil, military, religious, judicial, and educational officials were in attendance. Dances followed. At the celebration, Señora Isabel Rivera y Esclusa, clothed in the national colors, represented the nation, and a child, Salvador Juan y Carbonell, was dressed as a sailor. A procession of children carried wreaths of flowers to the altar of the nation, in honor of Spain and Peral. Alms of bread and meat were given to the poor, and the day ended with races and dances. Cf. Obras Municipales, DIPR, 1890, Lares, Puerto Rico.

6. Cayetano Coll y Toste (ed.), *Reseña del Estado* (Puerto Rico, 1899), p. 370.

7. Cruz Monclova, *Historia de Puerto Rico* (Madrid, 1957), II, Pt. 2, 440-41.

8. Antonio Cánovas del Castillo, *El Solitario y su Tiempo* (Madrid, 1883), II, 132. Quoted from Enrique Pineyro, *Como Acabó la Dominación de España en America* (Paris, 1908), p. 55.

9. Pineyro, *Como Acabó*, pp. 58-60.

10. Pilar Barbosa de Rosario (ed.), "De Baldorioty a Barbosa," in *La Obra de José Celso Barbosa* (San Juan, 1957), pp. 167-88.

Text: 1—". . . los partidos políticos son dentro de este regimen, los mas eficaces instrumentos de Gobierno.

2—". . . el Gobierno de Su Majestad considere como del más alto interés político el procurar que los partidos que viven y se desenvuelven bajo una misma legalidad constitucional, tengan puntos de acuerdo y soluciones de armonía y que, jamás encuentren en los actos de la administración motivos o pretensos para disidencias ni para desmayos.

3—". . . que los ciudadanos españoles de Cuba y Puerto Rico gocen de los mismos derechos y cumplan con los mismos deberes que los ciudadanos españoles de la Peninsula: por eso desea que los partidos se muevan con toda libertad, que ejercitan los derechos de reunión, de asociación y de propaganda por medio de la prensa . . . La prensa ha de ser libre, si ha de reflejar el juicio de la opinión, que es la base de los gobiernos parlamentarios, pero el respeto a esta libertad no escluye ni siquiera debilita el rigor con que los tribunales de Justicia y las Autoridades gubernativas deben reprimir los delitos y las faltas que se cometan por medio de la imprenta.

4—''. . . mejorar el sistema tributario para que los impuestos respondan en su base a la justa proporción entre las fuerzas del país y el sacrificio del contribuyente.

5—''. . . reformar los servicios de la Hacienda para que la imposición y la recaudación obedezcan a principios de justicia y de equidad. . . .

''Aliviar los presupuestos de todo gasto que no represente un servicio del Estado indispensable para la seguridad y bienestar del país.

6—''. . . formentar la agricultura, la industria, y todos los elementos de la riqueza general; estimular la instrucción; dar impulso a las obras públicas; cumplir las obligaciones que pesan sobre el Estado, alguna de ellas tan sagrada, como los haberes de los que han defendido con su sangre la integridad de la patria.

7—''. . . protejer la seguridad de la personas y el respeto a la propiedad. . . .

''depurar la administración civil y económica para que la ilustración y la probidad sean las garantías del empleado y los títulos que más le recomienden a la consideración del país y del Gobierno de Su Majestad.''

11. *Ibid.*, 167-88.

Text: ''No creo conveniente que siga Puerto Rico la buena o mala suerte de Cuba. . . . Tenemos diferentes inclinaciones . . . y otras aspiraciones. . . . Vivamos en amistosa separación. Yo que no quiero mi isla colonia de España, sino provincia española, no querría verla nunca colonia de Cuba. El esclavo más infeliz es el esclavo del liberto.'' (Vizcarrondo)

''La diferencia entre Puerto Rico y Cuba es inmensa. Aquí no tenemos un solo hombre de talla y ellos tienen muchos. Aquí nos conformaríamos con una vida municipal medianamente racional y ellos aspiran o son empujados . . . a la vida del Canadá o de la Australia. Ellos quieren una patria cubana dentro o fuera de la unidad nacional y nosotros nos conformamos con desear la vida de una Provincia secundaria.'' (Baldorioty de Castro)

12. Luis Muñoz Rivera, ''Campañas Políticas,'' in *Obras Completas,* ed., Luis Muñoz Marín (Madrid, 1925), I, xxxii; also, ''Apuntes para un Libro,'' in *Obras Completas,* III, 1. Text: ''La anexión de los Estados Unidos, simpática en el concepto de muchos insulares, me pareció siempre absurda, por la incompatibilidad de las razas latina y anglo-sajona, por el obstáculo inmenso del idioma, por el carácter absorbente de los políticos de Washington y por la anemia de nuestro pueblo, tan apto para ser rápidamente absorbido.''

13. Muñoz Rivera, ''Campañas Políticas,'' in *Obras Completas,* I, 34-47. Text: ''Carecemos de fuerzas populares por la ignorancia de la población campesina; carecemos de juventud militante por la apatía y el *laissez faire* de nuestros jóvenes; carecemos de personalidades ricas, porque esas temen mucho a la política romántica, y se inspiran en un egoísmo imperdonable; es necesario educar a las primeras, vigorizar a las segundas y atraer a la tercera de esas clases.''

14. Barbosa de Rosario, ''De Baldorioty,'' p. 205.

15. *Ibid.*, pp. 207-44, 247-78, 280-83, 287-90. Text: (Art. 7 of Autonomist meeting, Mayagüez, May 15-18, 1891) ''La Delegación, de acuerdo con el *Leader* del Partido, y por medio de los comisionados que designe . . . quedan facultados para acordar y realizar inteligencias o alianzas del Partido Autonomista porto-

rriqueño con los demócratas peninsulares que acepten o defiendan el sistema autonómico-administrativo de las Antillas.''

16. *Ibid.*, pp. 292-95. Also, Jorge Mañach, *Martí el Apóstol* (Madrid, 1933), p. 281. Dr. Ramón E. Betances, delegate general; Dr. J. J. Henna, president; Juan de Mata Terreforte, Manuel Besosa, and Sotero Figueroa, voting directors; Gumersindo Rivas, secretary of proceedings; and Gerardo Forrest, secretary of correspondence. In September, 1896, the last two offices were combined into one, under the control of Roberto H. Todd.

17. Roberto H. Todd, *Estampas Coloniales* (San Juan, 1946), pp. 46-47. Todd also gives a brief biography of the leaders of the Puerto Rican junta in New York, pp. 49-62.

18. Barbosa de Rosario, ''De Baldorioty,'' pp. 294-95, 298-304. The letter of Dr. Barbosa is dated January 23, 1896. Text of Muñoz Rivera's statement: ''Mi situación es ésta, señor Forrest: soy partidario de la independencia, como ideal. Todos los pueblos han de ser libres. Considero sin embargo, absolutamente imposible la independencia de mi patria. Nuestras masas carecen aún de una educación cívica completa. No pelearon nunca y no pelearán con el empuje de las masas cubanas. Intentar el esfuerzo equivale a realizar un sacrificio inútil. Cuba no ha podido vencer tras 25 años de titánicas proezas. Puerto Rico sucumbiría sin éxito y sin gloria. . . . No se lo que ellos harán; pero de mi puedo asegurarle, bajo mi palabra que volveré a Puerto Rico por Nueva York y volveré con ustedes, amigo Forrest, y volveré con las armas en la mano para libertar a nuestra tierra o morir en la demanda.''

19. *Ibid.*, pp. 323-37. Also Antonio S. Pedreira, *El Año Terrible del '87* (México, D.F., 1948), pp. 123-35. These instructions were soon to show grounds for difference of interpretation, and the understanding of the word *alianza* as a mere ''pact'' was to conflict with its interpretation as a ''fusion with a Spanish party.'' The difference split the Autonomist party into two camps: the Ortodoxos (Puros) and the Fusionistas (Pactistas).

20. Barbosa de Rosario (ed.), ''La Comisión Autonomista de 1896,'' in *La Obra de José Celso Barbosa* (Venezuela, 1957, San Juan, 1957), VI, 3-50, 57-75. Text: (Memo of Gómez Brioso *re* conversation of commissioners with Sagasta, Nov. 30, 1896. *Cf.* ''La Comisión,'' p. 74) ''Quedan ustedes autorizados para declarar que el partido liberal que presido implantará en la isla de Puerto Rico tan pronto sea poder la ley de reformas votadas por las Cortes en el sentido de la más amplia descentralización administrativa en aquella provincia española y hará extensiva a ella todos los derechos políticos que se gozan en la península.''

21. Barbosa de Rosario, ''La Comisión,'' pp. 88-20, 121-33. Also, Manuel Fraga Iribarne, *Las Constituciones de Puerto Rico* (Madrid, 1953), pp. 139-61, 163-82. Also, Lidio Cruz Monclova, *Luis Muñoz Rivera* (San Juan, 1959), pp. 310-13, 329, 336-37. Text: (Gómez Brioso formula, Cf. Barbosa de Rosario, ''La Comisión,'' p. 118).

''La comisión del partido autonomista de Puerto Rico, a nombre de la Delegación del mismo y a virtud de las facultades de que se haya investida, declara que prestará su apoyo al partido liberal que preside Don Práxedes Mateo Sagasta, tanto en su política general como local 'visto que los ideales que contiene el programa de Ponce de 1887 habrán de ser realizados por dicha colectividad'.''

Text: (Sagasta formula, Cf. Barbosa de Rosario, ''La Comisión,'' pp. 118-20. ''Visto que este partido al desenvolver las Bases de reformas . . . otorgará a las Antillas . . . la mayor descentralización posible dentro de la unidad nacional, en el cuidado y gestión de sus intereses municipales y provinciales, y dará satisfacción a los principios democráticos, siempre en la tendencia del ideal de la perfecta igualdad de derechos entre los ciudadanos Antillanos y sus hermanos peninsulares, todos igualmente españoles.''

Text: (Final formula, Cf. Barbosa de Rosario, ''La Comisión,'' signed Jan. 12, 1897, p. 132-33). ''La Comisión del partido autonomista de Puerto Rico . . . declara que prestará su apoyo al partido liberal que preside don Práxedes M. Sagasta, tanto en su política general como antillana, visto que este partido, al desenvolver las bases de reformas con el espíritu más expansivo y el criterio más liberal, otorgará a las Antillas . . . la mayor descentralización posible dentro de la unidad nacional, de suerte que la iniciativa y gestión de sus intereses locales (municipales y provinciales) les corresponda y pertenezca por completo, como solicitan los liberales puertorriqueños; y que cesando toda distinción entre españoles, los habitantes de Puerto Rico gocen de los mismos derechos que los peninsulares, como medio el más seguro de dar satisfacción a los principios democráticos por todos proclamados.

''Y como para la debida unificación en el procedimiento es necesaria la incorporación a las filas liberales de los autonomistas de Puerto Rico la Comisión someterá a la asamblea general del partido la indicada incorporación para constituir en la isla un solo partido liberal sometido a la disciplina del de la Península, como prolongación suya en aquella provincia ultramarina.''

22. Barbosa de Rosario, ''La Comisión,'' pp. 140-62. The various names, such as ''Pactistas,'' ''Ortodoxos,'' etc., have a tendencious meaning, but were commonly used in the battle of the press of the differing factious.

23. *Bol Hist.*, V, 349-54. In this letter of Luis Muñoz Rivera to Don Antonio Maura (Madrid), June 14, 1897, he noted that the governor general of Puerto Rico was ultra-conservative and was using every pretext to inform Madrid against his party.

24. *Ibid.*, V, 354. Luis Muñoz Rivera to Don Germán Gamazo (Madrid), June 14, 1897.

25. Fraga Iribarne, *Las Constituciones*, pp. 221-25. This charter for the ''Government and Civil Administration in the Island of Puerto Rico'' was issued, under a royal decree, by María Cristina, Queen Regent of Spain, on November 25, 1897.

26. *Gac. Ofic.*, Jan. 12, 1898.

27. Salvador Brau, *Historia de Puerto Rico* (New York, 1904), p. 293. Also, *RDC 1899*, p. 9; and *El Lib.*, Feb. 11, 1898, to March 25, 1898. This daily newspaper was founded on Jan. 10, 1898, in San Juan and was dedicated to the Liberal party ideas of Luis Muñoz Rivera.

28. *El Lib.*, Jan. 10, 20, 25, 1898; April 6, 1898.

29. *El Lib.*, March 29, 1898.

30. *Gac. Ofic.*, April 5, 15, 17, 21-24, 27, 1898. Also, *El Lib.*, April 22, 1898.

31. Edward J. Berbusse, S. J. ''The Origins of the McLane-Ocampo Treaty of 1859,'' in *The Americas* (Jan., 1958), pp. 223-45.

32. Richard Hofstadter, ''Manifest Destiny in the Philippines,'' in Theodore P. Greene (ed.), *American Imperialism in 1898* (Boston, 1955), pp. 54-70.

33. Charles A. Beard, ''Territorial Expansion Connected with Commerce,'' in Greene (ed.), *American Imperialism in 1898*, pp. 21-26.

34. Julius W. Pratt, ''American Business in the Spanish-American War,'' *HAHR*, XIV (May, 1934), 163-201.

35. Joseph E. Wisan, ''The Cuban Crisis as Reflected in the New York Press,'' in Greene, *Amer. Imper. in 1898*, pp. 43-54.

36. Olney to Spanish Minister Dupuy de Lome, *Papers Relating to the Foreign Relations of the United States* (1897), pp. 540-44.

Notes to pages 61–80

37. Hofstadter, ''Manifest Destiny,'' pp. 60-67.

38. Roberto H. Todd, *José Julio Henna, 1848-1924* (San Juan, 1930), pp. 18-21.

39. Antonio Rivera, *El Laborantismo o la Liquidación del Régimen Español en Puerto Rico* (México, D.F., 1943), p. 157.

40. Todd, *Henna*, pp. 23-30.

41. *Gac. Ofic.*, July 5, 19, 21-22, 1898.

42. *El Lib.*, July 22, 1898.

43. *El Lib.*, May 30, June 2, 9, 18, 1898.

44. Angel Rivero Méndez, *Crónica de la Guerra Hispano-Americana en Puerto Rico* (Madrid, 1922), pp. 17-19, 162, 218, vii.

45. *Gac. Ofic.*, Aug. 21, 28; Sept. 10, 14; Oct. 1, 2, 4, 11, 13, 1898.

46. Official Order of Governor Macías, signed by Francisco Acosta, of the Audiencia Territorial, Tribunal Pleno, NAPR, Instituto de Cultura Puertorriqueña.

47. Antonio S. Pedreira, *Insularismo* (Puerto Rico, 1942), p. 99.

48. *Bol. Hist.*, II, pp. 134-40. Speech given by Coll y Toste, on Aug. 12, 1908.

49. Pedro Capó Rodríguez, ''Some Historical and Political Aspects of the Government of Puerto Rico,'' *HAHR*, II, No. 4 (Nov., 1919), 548-53.

50. Enrique Calderón, *El Dolor de un Pueblo Esclavo* (New York, 1950), pp. 31, 39.

51. *La Dem.*, June 24, 1898.

52. *La Corr.*, June 28; July 24, 1898.

53. *Bol. Ecl.*, March 15; May 26; Aug. 6, 1898. It is to be noted that the church's contribution to the National Subscription was 994 pesos.

54. This lecture can be found in the Colección Puertorriqueña, UPR, under the title, ''Discurso de Inauguración del Colegio de los Escolapios'' (San Juan, 1896).

55. *Bol. Ecl.*, Nov. 15, 1894; March 1, 1895; May 1, 1897; Sept. 1, 1897; April 15, 1898. Bishop Mingüella was a man of literary ability, a member of the Royal Academy of History in Madrid and of the Overseas Council of Spain (Consejo de Ultramar). He had a good knowledge of oriental languages and had written a Tagalog Grammar in 1878, along with a book entitled *The Unity of the Human Species, as Proved by Philosophy*.

56. *Bol. Ecl.*, May 1, 1896; June 15, 1897.

57. *Bol. Ecl.*, Jan. 1, 1881. The towns listed as having priests were seventy-three in all. *Gac. Ofic.*, Jan. 4, 1897, Feb. 25, 1897, May 5, 1897.

58. Cf. footnote 55.

59. *La Dem.*, Feb. 27, 1899.

60. Henry K. Carroll (ed.), *Report on the Island of Porto Rico* (''Carroll Report'') (Washington, 1899), pp. 683, 687-88, 693, 653, 668.

CHAPTER III

1. Juan B. Nieves, *La Anexión de Puerto Rico a los Estados Unidos* (Ponce, 1898).

2. *RMGC 1899-1900*, pp. 19-25.

3. Cayetano Coll y Cuchi, *La Ley Foraker* (San Juan, 1904), p. 117.

4. *RMGC 1899-1900*, p. 20.

5. *Ibid.*, pp. 20-22, 295, 350. See also a letter of the Reverend Thomas E. Sherman, S.J., to General Brooke, Dec. 30, 1898, MS., NAUS, BIA, No. 124.

6. Tomás Blanco, *Prontuario Histórico de Puerto Rico* (5th ed.: San Juan, 1955), pp. 118-19.

7. *RMGC 1899-1900*, p. 45.

8. Roberto T. Todd, *Desfile de Gobernadores de Puerto Rico* (San Juan, 1943), pp. 2-4.

9. Carbonell to Brooke, Oct. 15, 1898, Brooke Papers, 1898, MS, HSPA.

10. *Gac. Ofic.*, Oct. 20-22, 26, 1898.

11. *RDC 1899*, pp. 89-91. Also, *Gac. Ofic.*, Oct. 28, 1898.

12. General H. C. Corbin (Adjutant General's Office, War Department) to General Brooke, Nov. 16, 1898, Brooke Papers, 1898, MS, HSPA.

13. *RDC 1899*, pp. 91-92. Also, *RMGC 1899-1900*, p. 72. Other significant officials were: Ramón Méndez Cardona, assistant secretary of finance; Francisco de Paula Acuña, attorney of the Supreme Court; Manuel Camuñas, assistant secretary of state.

14. Brooke to Gen. H. C. Corbin, Nov. 30, 1898; and C. W. Wadsworth to Brooke, Nov. 28, 1898, Brooke Papers, 1898, MS., HSPA.

15. *RMGC 1899-1900*, pp. 73-74.

16. Henry K. Carroll (ed.), *Report on the Island of Porto Rico* (Washington, 1899), p. 234.

17. *La Corr.*, Sept. 20, 1898.

18. *La Dem.*, Nov. 2, 9, 1898.

19. *La Dem.*, Nov. 12, 15, 17, 1898. The Reverend Aderson (*sic*) got a permit to continue his preaching but after the Newman incident decided not to preach in the public plaza.

20. *La Dem.*, Nov. 24, 1898; Dec. 5, 1898. *La Nueva Era* was the organ of the Ortodoxos (Puros) and had used the name of *El Autonomista* in the period before the United States occupation. *La Democracia* was the periodical of Luis Muñoz Rivera.

21. *SJN*, Jan. 23, 1900. See also *SJN*, Vol. V, 116, 119, 135, 148; and Vol. VI, 86, and others.

22. *La Dem.*, Dec. 5, 1898.

23. *La Corr.*, Nov. 14, 15, 1898.

24. *La Corr.*, Nov. 20, 1898.

25. *La Corr.*, Nov. 21; Oct. 29, 1898.

26. E. G. Rathbone (director general of posts) to General Brooke, undated (probably early 1899), Brooke Papers, MS, HSPA.

27. Todd, *Desfile*, pp. 6-8.

28. General Henry to Adjutant General of San Juan, Ponce, Dec. 3, 1898, Brooke Papers, 1898, MS, HSPA.

29. *La Dem.*, Dec. 6, 8, 15, 1898.

30. Brigadier General Guy V. Henry to Adjutant General, Washington, Dec. 8, 1898, MS, NAUS, BIA, 81.

31. *Gac. Ofic.*, Dec. 14, 17, 25, 1898.

32. *RDC 1899*, p. 93.

33. As quoted by Martin G. Brumbaugh, in Rudolph A. Van Middeldyk, *The History of Puerto Rico* (New York, 1903), p. viii.

34. *RDC 1899*, pp. 94-95.

35. *La Dem.*, Dec. 29-31, 1898.

36. *La Corr.*, Dec. 31, 1898.

37. *La Dem.*, Jan 2, 9, 12, 1899.

38. *RDC 1899*, pp. 96-98; also, *Gac. Ofic.*, Jan. 26, 31; Feb. 3, 4, 9, 1899.

39. *RDC 1899*, pp. 98-99; also, *La Dem.*, Jan. 20, Feb. 6, 1899, and the *Gac. Ofic.*, Feb. 8, 12, 1899.

40. *Gac. Ofic.*, March 23, 1899; also, *RDC 1899*, p. 99.

41. *La Dem.*, Feb. 9, 1899.

42. *RDC 1899*, pp. 100-1.

43. John G. Meyers, July 11, 1899, MS, NAUS, BIA, 333-3.

44. W. S. H. Lathrop, Dec. 14, 1899, MS, NAUS, BIA, 333-3.

45. Henry K. Carroll to Attorney General John W. Griggs, Plainfield, N.J., MS, NAUS, BIA, 33-4.

46. *La Dem.*, Feb. 13, 1899.

47. *RDC 1899*, p. 103.

48. *La Dem.*, Feb. 13, 28, 1899.

49. Obras Públicas, DIPR, Leg. 182, exp. 74.

50. *La Dem.*, Feb. 27; March 14, 21, 23, 1899.

Text: ''Es un hombre de gran capacidad natural, nacido para jefe, aunque representa esto falsamente; es egoísta y poco escrupuloso.

''Antes autonomista, se le acusa por sus antiguos correligionarios de haber vendido su causa a Sagasta, y de que por el favor del último Gobernador General, aunque entonces no ejercía cargo oficial, condujo las elecciones para las primeras cámaras autonomistas, de una manera violenta y engañosa. . . .

''Se dice que este político autócrata vendrá pronto a Washington a interponer su influencia para relevar al General Henry. Nosotros creemos que su misión fracasará.''

51. *Gac Ofic.*, April 14, 1899.

52. *Ibid.*, Jan. 15, 20; Feb. 2, 1899.

53. *RDC 1899*, p. 102.

54. *Gac. Ofic.*, March 25; April 16, 25, 30; May 3, 5-7, 24, 1899. SPCA, Society for the Prevention of Cruelty to Animals.

55. Roberto H. Todd, *Estampas Coloniales* (San Juan, 1946), pp. 29-31.

56. *La Dem.*, May 13, 16, 1899.

57. *AR 1901*, p. 14.

58. *La Dem.*, May 25, 1899. Within a month, *La Democracia* (June 27, 1899) was opposing Davis for attempting to form a council that represented both parties. The editors charged that it would not work, as it had not worked under Governor Macías and General Henry.

59. George W. Davis, ''Porto Rico: Its Present and Its Future,'' in the *Proceedings of the Lake Mohonk Conference* (Oct., 1909), p. 11. Italics mine.

60. G. W. Davis to Adjutant General, U.S. Army, Oct. 13, 1899, MS, NAUS, BIA, 295-26.

61. *RMGC 1899-1900*, p. 57-64, 265-67.

62. *RDC 1899*, pp. 111-27, 154-55. A ''judge of instruction'' (*juez de instrucción*) was one who, in a court of first instance summarized the facts of the case and passed them on to the *audiencia*. Note also that ''the United States provisional court'' existed for a period of ten months and handled a great number of cases.

63. *RDC 1899*, pp. 128, 131.

64. *RMGC 1899-1900*, pp. 60-62, 27-30. Italics mine.

65. *Senate Document No. 147*, 56th Congr., 1st. sess. See MS, NAUS, BIA, 834-12.

66. MS, NAUS, BIA, 437-8.

67. ''*Notes on Puerto Rico*,'' prepared by Brigadier General Frank R. McIntyre, chief of the Bureau of Insular Affairs, MS, NAUS, BIA, 4231-28.

68. *La Dem.*, April 22, 1899.

69. *RMGC 1899-1900*, pp. 210-11; also, *Gac. Ofic.*, Aug. 12, 1899.

70. MS, DIPR, Leg. 205, exp. 13, Aug. 30, 1899.

71. *RMGC 1899-1900*, pp. 213-18.

72. *RDC 1899*, pp. 132, 143.

73. McIntyre, ''Notes on Puerto Rico,'' MS, NAUS, BIA, 4231-28.

74. *RMGC 1899-1900*, p. 116.

75. Major Francis W. Mansfield, 11th Infantry (collector at Ponce), to Adjutant General, U.S. Army (Washington), Sept. 15, 1899, MS, NAUS, BIA, 295-21.

76. *RDC 1899*, pp. 22, 112, 145. *RMGC 1899-1900*, pp. 269, 291.

77. McIntyre, ''Notes on Puerto Rico,'' MS, NAUS, BIA, 4231-281.

78. *RDC 1899*, pp. 22, 112, 145. *RMGC 1899-1900*, pp. 269, 291.

79. Letter of WCTU forwarded by Senator McBride to Assistant Secretary of War Meiklejohn, April 13, 1900, MS, NAUS, BIA, 1512-5.

80. This opinion is dated December 7, 1899, MS, NAUS, BIA, 834-5.

81. *RMGC 1899-1900*, pp. 125-29; *RDC 1899*, pp. 126, 119.

82. *RDC 1899*, pp. 119, 112, 123-24.

CHAPTER IV

1. Reverend Thomas E. Sherman to General Brooke, Dec. 30, 1898, MS, NAUS, BIA, 124.

2. Henry K. Carroll (ed.), *Report on the Island of Porto Rico* (Washington, 1899), pp. 55-57, 63-65.

3. *Ibid.*, pp. 37-38, 231-32, 340-43.

4. Philip C. Hanna to J. B. Moore, Nov. 25, 1898, MS, NAUS, BIA, 50-1; 50-2, Dec. 13, 1898.

5. Order of General Henry, March 7, 1899. MS, NAUS, BIA, 661-2.

6. *USIC*. Report addressed to the Secretary of War, June 9, 1899 (Washington, 1899), pp. 60-62.

7. C. H. Watkins to Secretary of War Alger, June, 1899, MS, NAUS, BIA, 661-6.

8. General Davis, Hearings: House Committee on Insular Affairs, Jan. 8, 10, 1900, MS, NAUS, BIA, 295-19.

9. George W. Davis, ''Our Policy Toward Porto Rico,'' *The Independent* (Jan. 18, 1900) p. 161.

10. Davis to Secretary of War, April 19, 1900, MS, NAUS, BIA, 856-72.

11. F. D. Grant to Adjutant General, March 19, 1899, MS, NAUS, BIA, 295-2.

12. *La Dem.*, May 8, 9, 11, 1899. Note especially Mariano Abril's letter to *La Democracia*.

13. J. J. Henna and M. Zeno Gandía, *The Case of Puerto Rico* (Washington, 1899), pp. 12, 14-17.

14. *CR*, pp. 61-63, 235-36.

15. General Davis, Hearings: House Committee on Insular Affairs, Jan. 8, 10, MS, NAUS, BIA, 295-19.

16. Guy V. Henry, ''Our Duty in Porto Rico,'' *Munsey's Magazine* (Nov. 1899), p. 236.

17. *CR*, pp. 23-27, 285-89, 302.

18. *CR*, pp. 284-93, 306.

19. Philip C. Hanna to J. B. Moore, Dec. 13, 1898, MS, NAUS, BIA, 50-2.

20. *CR*, pp. 53-65.

21. *USIC*, June 8, 1899, MS, NAUS, BIA, 661-2.

22. Letter of Insular Commissioners to Secretary of War, Aug. 1, 1899, MS, NAUS, BIA, 661-9.

23. *USIC*, pp. 34-41, 63-66. The facts of the commission were based on the report of Major A. C. Sharpe, the judge-advocate of the governor general's staff, and that of Gabriel Anciaux, the inspector of prisons.

24. Roberto H. Todd to General Kennedy, July 20, 1899, MS, NAUS, BIA, 661-8.

25. Horatio S. Rubens to Roberto H. Todd, July 29, 1899, MS, NAUS, BIA, "P"—Roberto H. Todd.

26. Herminio Díaz to General Henry, undated, MS, NAUS, BIA, 613-4; also, the protest of Herminio Díaz and other prominent Puerto Ricans, sent to the President of the United States, April 19, 1899, MS, NAUS, BIA, 613-10.

27. Statement of the Insular Commission, May 19, 1899, MS, NAUS, BIA, 613-10.

28. W. H. West to General Kennedy, Bellefontaine, Ohio, Sept. 1, 1899, MS, NAUS, BIA, 661-12.

29. Guy V. Henry to Major Pershing, Capron Springs, W. Virginia, July 5, 1899, MS, NAUS, BIA, 613-11. The italicized word "useless" is almost illegible.

30. *USIC*, p. 7.

31. Father Sherman Report, Dec. 30, 1898, MS, NAUS, BIA, 124.

32. General Davis, Hearings: House Committee on Insular Affairs, Jan. 8, 10, 1900, MS, NAUS, BIA, 295-19.

33. General Davis to Secretary of War, April 19, 1900, MS, NAUS, BIA, 856-72.

34. Davis to Secretary of War, Feb. 16, 1900, MS, NAUS, BIA, 856-77.

35. Charles E. Buel to George B. Cortelyou (secretary of President McKinley), Sept. 24, 1899, MS, NAUS, BIA, 856-28, 29.

36. *CR*, pp. 48-49, 51, 726.

37. General Davis, Hearings: House Committee on Insular Affairs, Jan. 8, 10, 1900, MS, NAUS, BIA, 295-19.

38. *USIC*, pp. 28-29.

39. *CR*, pp. 20-22, 380; also, *USIC*, p. 29.

40. Puerto Rican Commission, 1899, p. 49. This is entitled *The Case of Puerto Rico*, written by J. J. Henna and M. Zeno Gandía, the commissioners from Puerto Rico (Washington, 1899).

41. *CR*, pp. 371-84.

42. Guy V. Henry to Major Pershing, July 5, 1899, MS, NAUS, BIA, 613-11.

43. *USIC*, pp. 8-15.

44. General Davis, Hearings: House Committee on Insular Affairs, Jan. 8, 10, 1900, MS, NAUS, BIA, 295-19.

45. *Ibid.*; also, *RDC 1899*, pp. 33-34. *CR*, 42-43, 121, 134.

46. *CR*, pp. 43-47.

47. *USIC*, p. 58; also, General Davis, Hearings: House Committee on Insular Affairs, Jan. 8, 10, 1900, MS, NAUS, BIA, 295-19; also, *RDC 1899*, p. 101.

48. *USIC*, pp. 30-32.

49. Henna and Zeno Gandía, *The Case of Puerto Rico*, pp. 12, 18, 25-27, 52-64.

50. *La Dem.*, May 9, 1899.

51. General F. D. Grant to Adjutant General, War Department, March 19, 1899, MS, NAUS, BIA, 295-2.

52. *USIC*, pp. 74-76.

53. H. S. Rubens to Roberto H. Todd, July 29, 1930, MS, NAUS, BIA, "P"—Roberto H. Todd.

54. Henna and Zeno Gandía, *The Case of Puerto Rico*, pp. 60-61.

55. Henry, "Our Duty in Porto Rico," *Munsey's Magazine*, p. 240.

56. *CR*, pp. 59-60, 390, 393, 400, 447.

57. General Davis to Secretary of War, Oct. 17, 1899, MS, NAUS, BIA, 856-36.

58. Davis, "Our Policy Toward Porto Rico," *The Independent*, p. 162.

59. General Davis to Secretary of War, March 31, 1900, MS, NAUS, BIA, 856-73.

60. *USIC*, p. 72.

61. Henna and Zeno Gandía, *The Case of Puerto Rico*, pp. 13, 45-47.

62. *CR*, pp. 52-53.

63. *CR*, pp. 450-52, Dec. 25, 1898.

64. Henna and Zeno Gandía, *The Case of Puerto Rico*, pp. 41-44.

65. *USIC*, pp. 17-18, 72.

66. Nicolás Oyanguren, Hearings: House Committee on Insular Affairs, Jan. 29, 1900, MS, NAUS, BIA, 1239-36-1/2. He added: ''Of course I recognize that the intrinsic value of our dollar is not up to 38 cents, more or less, and that there is a deficit. . . .''

67. *USIC*, pp. 73, 36.

68. Reverend Thomas E. Sherman to General Brooke, Dec. 30, 1898, MS, NAUS, BIA, 124.

69. *USIC*, June 8, 1899, MS, NAUS, BIA, 661-2.

70. Reverend Thomas E. Sherman to General Brooke, Dec. 30, 1898, MS, NAUS, BIA, 124.

71. Henry K. Carroll, ''Puerto Rico as a Mission Field,'' *The Missionary Review of the World* (Aug., 1900), p. 584-91.

72. *CR*, pp. 654-55, 693-700, 711.

73. Reverend Thomas E. Sherman to General Brooke, Dec. 30, 1898, MS, NAUS, BIA, 124.

74. *USIC*, pp. 66, 68, 73. Italics mine.

75. Guy V. Henry to Major Pershing, July 5, 1899, MS, NAUS, BIA, 613-11.

76. George A. Stanley to President McKinley, Sept. 6, 1899, MS, NAUS, BIA, 613-13.

77. H. K. Carroll, ''The Religious Question in Puerto Rico,'' *The Independent* (Nov. 2, 9, 1899), p. 2935-37.

78. This is a manuscript in Bureau of Insular Affairs files, NAUS, 965-152. See, also, *Report of Census of Porto Rico, 1899* (Washington, 1900), pp. 72-86.

79. Reverend Thomas E. Sherman to General Brooke, Dec. 30, 1898, MS, NAUS, BIA, 124.

80. *USIC*, p. 51.

81. *CR*, p. 33.

82. Henry, ''Our Duty in Porto Rico,'' *Munsey's Magazine*, p. 238.

83. *USIC*, pp. 51-52.

84. *CR*, pp. 32-33, 65.

85. H. K. Carroll, ''Puerto Rico as a Mission Field,'' *The Missionary Review of the World*, p. 591.

86. *CR*, pp. 616-24, 643-46.

87. *USIC*, p. 53.

88. Henna and Zeno Gandía, *The Case of Puerto Rico*, pp. 50-51.

89. General Davis, Hearings: House Committee on Insular Affairs, Jan. 8, 10, 1900, MS, NAUS, BIA, 295-19.

90. Victor S. Clark, ''Education in Puerto Rico,'' *The Forum* (Oct., 1900), pp. 228-30.

91. Reverend Thomas E. Sherman to General Brooke, Dec. 30, 1898, MS, NAUS, BIA, 124.

92. *USIC*, pp. 55-56, 74.

93. General Davis to Secretary of War, April 19, 1900, MS, NAUS, BIA, 856-72.

94. *CR*, pp. 38-41, 206-16.
95. *USIC*, pp. 56-57.

CHAPTER V

1. Worthington C. Ford, ''Trade Policy with the Colonies,'' *Harper's*, 590 (July, 1899), pp. 293-303.
2. Memorandum of Chief Clerk of War Department, Sept. 21, 1928, MS, NAUS, BIA, 856-79-A.
3. Pedro Capó Rodríguez, ''Some Historical and Political Aspects of the Government of Porto Rico,'' *HAHR* (Nov., 1919), p. 555.
4. *Congr. R.*, 56th Congr., 1st sess., pp. 702, 1010. Payne was chairman of the House Ways and Means Committee.
5. Hearings: House Committee on Insular Affairs, Jan. 8, 10, 1900, MS, NAUS, BIA, 295-19, pp. 3-52.
6. *Ibid.*, Jan. 17, 1900, pp. 76-85.
7. *Ibid.*, Jan. 19, 1900, pp. 99-103.
8. *Ibid.*, pp. 107-9, 145-50, 157, 163.
9. *Ibid.*, pp. 134-43, 167-68, 176-78; *ibid.*, Jan. 26, 1900, pp. 233-44.
10. Hearings: Senate Committee on Pacific Islands, 56th Congr., 1st sess., Doc. No. 147. Jan. 20, 1900.
11. *Ibid.*, Jan. 22, 1900. Italics mine.
12. *Ibid.*, Jan. 20, 1900.
13. *Ibid.*, Feb. 5, 1900.
14. Senate Report No. 249, 56th Congr. 1st sess., Feb. 5, 1900.
15. House Report No. 249, 56th Congr., 1st sess., Feb. 8, 1900.
16. Speech in H. R. by R. L. Henry, Feb. 21, 1900, 56th Congr. 1st sess.
17. Speech in H. R. by R. W. Parker, Feb. 22, 1900, 56th Congr., 1st sess.
18. Speech of J. B. Foraker in Senate, Jan. 11, 1899, in *Speeches of J. B. Foraker*, II. See L.C. No. E 660. F69.
19. Joseph B. Foraker, *Notes of a Busy Life* (Cincinnati, 1916), II, 67, 77-84.
20. J. D. Richardson, ''Is Porto Rico a Part of the United States?'' *The Independent* (Feb. 22, 1900), pp. 467-69.
21. Editorial in *The Independent*, March 1, 1900.
22. Azel Ames, ''The Effect of the Proposed Porto Rican Tariff,'' *The Independent* (March 15, 1900).
23. Speech of J. B. Foraker in Senate, March 8, 1900. See *Speeches of J. B. Foraker*, III.
24. *Congr. R.*, 56th Congr., 1st sess., pp. 702, 1486, 3077, 3084, 3269, March 20, 1900.
25. *Ibid.*, pp. 3279-83, March 24, 1900.
26. *Speeches of J. B. Foraker*, III. A reprint from an article in *Leslie's Weekly*.
27. 31 Stat. 77 (1900). 48 U.S.C. No. 40 (1946). Also, in *Documents on the Constitutional History of Puerto Rico* (Washington, D.C.), pp. 64-80.
28. 182 U.S. 244 (1901). Also confer Paul P. Harbrecht, S.J., ''What Are the Liberties of Citizens of Puerto Rico Under the Constitution?'' *Georgetown Law Journal*, XXXVIII, No. 3 (March, 1950), 471-84.
29. Foraker, *Notes*, II, p. 68.
30. P. Capó Rodríguez, ''Colonial Representation in the American Empire,'' in *American Journal of International Law*, XV, No. 4 (Oct., 1921). Attached to this article in the Bureau of Insular Affairs is a penned note, signed by ''FMT''

(probably General Frank McIntyre, the chief of the bureau). It reads: "Not true—The Legislature may provide these. They were not imposed."

31. *Ibid.*

32. G. W. Davis, "Porto Rico Its Present and Future," a reprint from the *Proceedings of Lake Mohonk Conference* (Oct., 1909). See L.C. No. F 1965. D 26.

33. *La Dem.*, Sept. 7, 1899.

34. *La Dem.*, Oct. 5, 1899.

35. *Diario de Puerto Rico.*

36. *Diario de P.R.*, April 17, 19, 1900.

37. *Diario de P.R.*, July 6, 1900.

38. *AR 1901*, pp. 13, 407-10.

39. *Ibid.*, pp. 413-18.

40. *Ibid.*, pp. 16-17.

41. Roberto H. Todd, *Desfile de Gobernadores de Puerto Rico* (San Juan, 1943), pp. 14-18.

42. Governor Allen to Secretary Root, May 5, 1900, Root Papers, Box 139, MS Div., L.C.

43. *Ibid.*, June 14, 1900.

44. *AR 1901*, pp. 16-18.

45. *SJN*, Sept. 5, 1900.

46. *SJN*, Sept. 8, 1900.

47. G. Anxiaux to Commissioner Elliott, Aug. 30, 1900, MS, DIPR, Obras Públicas, Leg. 192.

48. *SJN*, Sept. 16-20, 1900.

49. G. Anciaux to Commissioner Elliott, MS, DIPR, Obras Públicas, Leg. 192. Sept. 19, 1900.

50. J. A. Gautier Dapena, "Nacimiento de los Partidos Políticos bajo la Soberanía de los Estados Unidos Programas y Tendencias," *Historia*, III, No. 2 (Oct., 1953), 153-78.

51. *SJN*, Oct. 3, 18, 25, 29, 1900.

52. *SJN*, Nov. 7, 1900.

53. *AR 1901*, pp. 19-20.

54. *SJN*, Dec. 15, 1900. In his study of political science, he admitted indebtedness to Professor Burgess of Columbia University: "I must go and shake Professor Burgess by the hand. He has helped me greatly."

55. *SJN*, Dec. 18, 1900.

56. G. Anciaux to Commissioner Elliott, Dec. 23, 1900, MS, DIPR, Obras Públicas, Leg. 192.

57. *SJN*, Jan. 20, 1901.

58. *AR 1901*, pp. 23-24, 420-23.

59. *AR 1901*, pp. 423-31.

60. *AR 1901*, pp. 25-26. Also, House of Delegates of Puerto Rico, *Journal*, 1st Leglisl. sess., Dec. 3, 1900, to Jan. 31, 1901, in General Records, State Dept., MS, NAUS.

61. *SJN*, Jan. 22, 1901.

62. G. Anciaux to Commissioner Elliott, Dec. 4, 1900, MS, DIPR, Obras Públicas, Leg. 192.

63. *Ibid.*

64. William F. Willoughby, "Municipal Government in Puerto Rico," *PSQ*, XXIV, No. 3 (Sept., 1909), pp. 420-32. The "legal commission" report is found in House Doc. No. 52, 57th Congr., 1st sess., 1900, 2 vols.

65. *SJN*, March 27, 1901.

66. *SJN*, June 18, 1901.

67. *SJN*, Sept. 29, 1901.

68. Ramón B. López, ''The Needs of Porto Rico,'' *The Independent*, No. 29, 1900.

69. *La Dem.*, Nov. 27, 1900.

70. Governor Allen to Secretary Root, May 25, 1901, Root Papers, Box 139, MS, Div., L.C.; also, Allen to Root, May 28, 1901, *ibid.*

71. *Puerto Rico Herald*, July 13, 27, 1901.

72. Letter of the former delegates to General Henry, San Juan, April 26, 1899, MS, NAUS, BIA, 168-13.

73. *SJN*, Aug. 9, 1900.

74. *SJN*, Aug. 15, 1900.

75. *SJN*, Sept. 5, 1900.

76. *SJN*, Jan. 23, and Aug. 15, 1900. General Roy Stone's speech to Bayard Taylor Library Association, Kenneth Square, Penna., July 25, 1900.

77. *SJN*, May 28, 1901.

78. *SJN*, July 27, 1901.

79. *AR 1901*, pp. 63-65.

80. *SJN*, Aug. 1, 1901.

81. *SJN*, Aug. 21, 1901.

82. *SJN*, Sept. 4, 1901.

83. *SJN*, Dec. 17, 1901.

CHAPTER VI

1. *Bol. Ecl.*, Sept. 8, 1898. Dr. Henry K. Carroll sent a letter of introduction to General Brooke in behalf of Monsignor Perpiñá. Dr. Carroll had met the Monsignor with Father Sherman and spoke of him as ''a very pleasant gentleman.'' Carroll to Brooke, Oct. 24, 1898, Brooke Papers, 1898, MS, HSPA.

2. *Bol. Ecl.*, Jan. 20, 1899.

3. *Ibid.*, April 30, 1899.

4. *Ibid.*, Feb. 28, 1899.

5. *Ibid.*, Sept. 30, 1899.

6. Letter of Archbishop Chapelle and Bishop Blenk to Secretary of War Root (no date of mailing; date of receipt, Sept. 8, 1899), MS, NAUS, BIA, 613-12.

7. Bishop Blenk to Governor Davis, San Juan, Feb. 6, 1900, MS, NAUS, BIA, 834-16. I have been unable to find further papers on this matter.

8. *Bol. Ecl.*, Oct. 30, 1899.

9. *Ibid.*, Dec. 31, 1899.

10. Date of interview is only given as 1913, MS, NAUS, BIA, 26504-4. The bishop of Nátchez described the people as ''honest, thrifty, hard-working, frugal, sober and religious.'' He found that ''there is neither legalized nor tolerated vice. Drunkenness is unknown and religion is a recognized and honored factor in social relations.'' He added: ''The religion of the people is Catholic and there is no eagerness to change. There is no such thing as a priest-ridden community, and there is only one priest to every 8,000 baptized and confirmed Porto Ricans. Before the arrival of the Americans, common law marriages were not uncommon, but it is not true that people were forced into that relationship by exorbitant church charges. All marriages were free from 6 A.M. to noon, and charges were only made for those who wanted a fashionable wedding, which custom placed in the 'wee sma' hours' of the morning, between 1 and 4 A.M. Those who wanted a lighted church, a choir, altar boys and clergyman at 2 P.M. were asked to pay, with the option of a free marriage when the sun did the illuminating.''

The sources of information on the church are handicapped during this transitional period by the suspension of the *Boletín Eclesiástico* at the end of 1899 because of the pastors' failure to pay the back dues for the paper. This bulletin had been started in 1861; it was revived for a brief period (1914-20) and then allowed to expire.

11. Eduardo Neumann Gandía, *Benefactores y Hombres Notables de Puerto Rico* (Ponce, 1899), II, 200-5. This author mentions that Baldorioty de Castro left unedited a translation of John Stuart Mills' *Liberty.*

12. *Bol. Ecl.*, Oct. 15, 1884.

13. Salvador Brau, *Ecos de la Battalla* (Puerto Rico, 1886).

14. *La Dem.*, April 1, 1899.

15. *Bol. Ecl.*, Aug. 31, 1899.

16. *Ibid.*, Nov. 15, 1867.

17. *Bol. Hist.*, Vol. II, No. 3, May-June, 1915, pp. 161-62.

18. Claudio Capó, ''The Island of Porto Rico,'' MS, NAUS, BIA, 20247-8.

19. *SJN*, Jan. 3, 7, 28, 1900.

20. *SJN*, March 14, 1900.

21. *Pittsburgh Observer*, July 19, 1900, MS, NAUS, BIA, 580-5.

22. W. C. P. Rhoades, chairman of American Baptist Home Mission Society to President McKinley, Jan. 14, 1901, MS, NAUS, BIA, 2396-11. The Bureau of Insular Affairs files contains many other informative letters that opposed use of public schools for religious purposes, the Faribault System of education, and any violation of the ''time-honored law touching separation of church and state.'' Cf. *ibid.*, 2396-11, 2316-12.

23. *Journal*, 1st Legisl. Assembly of Puerto Rico, Jan. 8, 1901, H. R. Doc., 57th Congr., 1st sess., MS, NAUS, BIA, 295-36.

24. *Ibid.*, Jan. 9, 1901.

25. *SJN*, April 20, 1901.

26. Instances of religious friction can be found in *La Verdad*, Aug. 19, 1905. Also in the Bureau of Insular Affairs files; cf. MS, NAUS, BIA, 942-441 21063, 23076, 20247-3, 858-25. A highly contested point was the free transportation on army transports of YMCA personnel and the sale for $1.00 to the YMCA of six thousand square meters of land in San Juan.

27. Lieutenant A. C. Blunt, San Juan, May 12, 1899, MS, NAUS, BIA, 295-14.

28. General Davis, Hearings: Sen. Committee on Puerto Rico, Sen. Doc. 147, 56th Congr., 1st sess., MS, NAUS, BIA, 834-12.

29. Archbishop Chapelle to Major General Guy V. Henry, Feb. 9, 1899, MS, NAUS, BIA, 580-7.

30. Secretary Root to Bishop Blenk, Oct. 17, 1899, MS, NAUS, BIA, 580-8.

31. Chapelle to Root, Oct. 30, 1899, MS, NAUS, BIA, 580-2.

32. Senate Bill No. S.7056, 57th Congr., 2nd sess., Jan. 21, 1903, MS, NAUS, BIA, 580-9.

33. Roosevelt to Foraker, Feb. 19, 1903, Foraker Papers, MS Div., L.C.

34. Blenk to Roosevelt, Dec. 2, 1903, Root Papers, Box 207, MS Div., L.C.

35. *Puerto Rico Herald*, July 18, 1903.

36. Brief of Hernández López, DIPR, Obras Públicas, Feb. 24, 1906. Leg. 153. The excerpt from General Wood is from his report of Jan. 1, to Dec. 31, 1901. See Edward J. Berbusse, ''Aspects in Church-State Relations in Puerto Rico, 1898-1900,'' *The Americas* (Jan., 1963), pp. 291-304.

37. Decision of Supreme Court of Puerto Rico, Dec. 15, 1906, MS, NAUS, BIA, 580-30.

38. *Bol. Ecl.*, Dec. 15, 1898.

39. *Ibid.*, Jan. 20, 1899.

40. Major General Guy V. Henry, General Orders No. 13, Feb. 7, 1899, MS, NAUS, BIA, 1604.

41. William Dinwiddie, *Puerto Rico: Its Conditions and Possibilities* (New York, 1899), pp. 166-205.

42. General Henry to General Eaton, undated, MS, V. S. Clark Collection, MS Div., L.C. However, General Davis, at the request of the people allowed a public holiday on June 24, the Feast of San Juan Bautista. See also *Gac. Ofic.*, June 24, 1899.

43. Mrs. Guy V. Henry, ''San Juan,'' *The Outlook*, LXVII, No. 14 (April 6, 1901).

44. Clark to Eaton, undated, MS, V. S. Clark Collection, MS Div., L.C.

45. Eaton to Carbonell, Jan. 16, 19, 1899, V. S. Clark Collection, MS Div., L.C.

46. Commissioner John Eaton to President McKinley, April 12, 1899, MS, NAUS, BIA, 451-3.

47. Report of Victor S. Clark, sub-director of education, May 5, 1899, MS, NAUS, BIA, 561-1.

48. *La Dem.*, May 10, 1899.

49. *La Dem.*, June 12, 1899.

50. Eaton to Clark, Nov. 3, 1899. V. S. Clark Collection, MS Div., L.C.

51. Clark to Eaton, Nov. 16, 1899, *ibid.*

52. *Ibid.*, Dec. 5, 1899.

53. *Ibid.*, Dec. 11, 1899.

54. *Ibid.*, Dec. 30, 1899.

55. General Davis, General Orders, No. 205, Dec. 7, 1899. The other members of this board were: George G. Groff, M.D. (San Juan), José E. Saldaña, M.D. (San Juan), Roberto H. Todd (San Juan), George Bird y Arias (Fajardo), Professor Henry Huyke (Arroyo), Rosendo Matienzo Cintrón (Ponce), Bartolomé Esteva (Mayagüez), and J. Ruiz de Sagrado (Arecibo).

56. Clark to Eaton, Jan. 6, 1900, V. S. Clark Collection, MS Div., L.C.; also, Pedro A. Cebollero, *A School Language Policy for Puerto Rico* (San Juan, 1945), p. 6.

57. Clark to Eaton, Jan. 30, 1900. V. S. Clark Collection, MS Div., L.C.

58. *Ibid.*, Feb. 10, March 10, 1900.

59. Pilar Barbosa de Rosario (ed.), ''Orientando al Pueblo, 1900-1921,'' in *La Obra de José Celso Barbosa* (San Juan, 1939), IV, 17, 33, 40, 59-83.

60. W. T. Harris to Clark, March 7, 1900, V. S. Clark Collection, MS Div., L.C.

61. *Ibid.*

62. Clark to Eaton, March 10, 1900. It is noteworthy that at this time General John Eaton was president of Sheldon Jackson College in Salt Lake City, Utah; the other college officials were Protestant ministers.

63. General Davis, General Orders, No. 53, March 12, 1900, MS, NAUS, BIA, 451-21.

64. Edith V. Hollobaugh to Clark, March 15, 1900, V. S. Clark Collection, MS Div., L.C.

65. Secretary of Treasury Dawes to President McKinley, March 27, 1900, MS, NAUS, BIA, 43-41.

66. Dr. Groff to Secretary of War, June 16, 1900, MS, NAUS, BIA, 451-32.

67. *Gac. Ofic.*, June 8, 16, 1900.

68. Margaret D. Hernández to Victor S. Clark, June 23, 1900, MS, V. S. Clark Collection, MS Div., L.C.

69. *El País*, June 27, 1900.

70. *Diario de Puerto Rico*, June 27, 1900.

71. *SJN*, June 24, 1900.

72. *SJN*, Aug. 26, Sept. 2, 1900.

73. *SJN*, Oct. 4, 1900. Other schools included Syracuse, Haverford, Lehigh, Hobart, Hampden-Sydney, and Virginia Polytechnic.

74. Brumbaugh to Clark, Aug. 24, 1900, V. S. Clark Collection, MS Div., L.C.

75. Letters received by U.S. Secretary of Interior from Governor Allen, Oct. 15, 1900, and George E. Groff, Nov. 23, 1900, MS, NAUS, BIA, Box 291, Doc. Nos. 3395, 3847.

76. Brumbaugh Report, Oct. 15, 1900; Commissioner Harris to U.S. Secretary of Interior, Dec. 4, 1901, MS, NAUS, BIA, Box 291.

77. Cebollero, *A School Language Policy*, pp. 8-10.

78. B. Vélez (Manatí, P. R.) to Secretary of War, Dec. 31, 1909, MS, NAUS, BIA, 50-16.

79. J. C. Muerman to U.S. Commissioner of Education, MS, NAUS, BIA, 451-101. Mr. Maxwell, who is a member of the National Archives staff (research section), has written an unpublished manuscript on ''The Teaching of English in the Schools of Puerto Rico, 1899-1945.'' He says in part: ''In spite of all the orders, circulars and instructions, Spanish was always the medium of instruction in the schools.''

80. Act, House of Delegates, Puerto Rico, 8th Ass., 1st sess., Jan. 11, 1915, MS, NAUS, BIA, 1043-7; also, *Bol. Mer.*, Feb. 20, 1915.

81. Government of Puerto Rico, Department of Education, ''Professional Bulletin for the Public Schools of Puerto Rico,'' 1922, MS, NAUS, BIA, 42-542-13.

82. Second Annual Report of Bureau of Labor of Puerto Rico, 1914, p. 112. MS, NAUS, BIA, 26770-5, 8, 4.

83. R. R. Lutz to Secretary of War, Dec. 28, 1909, MS, NAUS, BIA, 451-53.

84. José Padín to General Cox, Sept. 27, 1933; Padín to Secretary of War Dern, Oct. 23, 1933, MS, NAUS, BIA, 20324.

CHAPTER VII

1. Bailey K. Ashford, *Uncinariasis en Puerto Rico: Un Problema Médico y Económico* (San Juan, 1916), pp. 19-20.

2. Llorens Torres, in *Pica Pica* (San Juan), Feb. 26, 1910, NAUS, BIA, 50-28.

3. Supplement to *La Justicia*, Sept. 18, 1915, NAUS, BIA, 975-102.

4. Address of Governor Yager to Lake Mohonk Conference, Oct. 22, 1915, NAUS, BIA, 975-101. The friction between Governor Yager and Santiago Iglesias grew, with the governor only interfering where there was danger of riot and disorder. At this time, Samuel Gompers of the AFL was writing to President Wilson in defense of the actions of Iglesias: ''There is calm there, but it is a calm that results from hunger, fear, and lethargy. The fact that the workers are no longer clubbed, that their meetings are not disbanded, that they no longer make protests against violation of constitutional rights, does not mean that justice prevails now in Puerto Rico, but it means that these oppressed human beings are living in terror if not despair.'' Samuel Gompers to President Wilson, July 29, 1915, MS, NAUS, BIA, 975-94-2.

5. Gilberto Concepción de García, ''The Land Authority of Puerto Rico,'' *George Washington Law Review*, XII, No. 3 (April, 1944), 303-28.

6. Roberto H. Todd, *Desfile de Gobernadores de Puerto Rico* (San Juan, 1943), pp. 20-25.

7. Report of the Judiciary Committee of the Executive Council of Puerto Rico on House Memorial No. 4, March 11, 1903. The writer also believed that the attorney general of Puerto Rico was independent of the attorney general of the

United States; that Puerto Rico was independent of the United States federal taxation, since only the federal court in Puerto Rico came out of the Puerto Rican budget; and, lastly, that territorial government would mean a jury trial in criminal cases and in civil cases exceeding $20.00, whereas jury trial required wider literacy.

8. *La Dem.*, Feb. 22, 1904.

9. Speech of Muñoz Rivera in the House of Delegates, Puerto Rico, May 8, 1908.

Bibliography

I. MANUSCRIPT SOURCES: OFFICIAL AND
PRIVATE PAPERS

1. OFFICIAL—UNITED STATES

Department of Interior Archives, 1897-1905.
Department of State Archives, 1898-1900.
Department of War Archives, Bureau of Insular Affairs, 1897-1905.

2. OFFICIAL—PUERTO RICO

Archivo General (San Juan): Records of Audiencia, Corte Suprema, and the Diputación Provincial.
Obras Municipales, Department of Interior, Puerto Rico.
Obras Municipales, Department of Interior, Puerto Rico.

3. PRIVATE—UNITED STATES AND PUERTO RICO

Acta de la Real Sociedad Económica de Amigos del País, Carnegie Library, San Juan, Puerto Rico.
Acta del Ateneo Puertorriqueño, San Juan, Puerto Rico.

Ashford, Bailey K. Collection in Georgetown University, Washington, D. C.

Brooke, John R. Collection in Historical Society of Pennsylvania.

Clark, Victor S. Collection in Division of Manuscripts, Library of Congress.

Foraker, Joseph Benson. Collection in Division of Manuscripts, Library of Congress.

Hoes, Roswell Randell. Collection in Division of Manuscripts, Library of Congress.

McKinley, William. Collection in Division of Manuscripts, Library of Congress.

Roosevelt, Theodore. Collection in Division of Manuscripts, Library of Congress.

Root, Elihu. Collection in Division of Manuscripts, Library of Congress.

II. PRINTED SOURCES: OFFICIAL DOCUMENTS, ETC.

1. THE UNITED STATES

(a) Department of State:
Commercial Relations of the United States with Foreign Countries, 1897-1900.
Papers Relating to the Foreign Relations of the United States, 1897-1900.

(b) Military and Civil Governments in Puerto Rico:
Code Commission, 1901: Puerto Rico, Informe de la Comisión Codificadora de Puerto Rico. San Juan, 1902.
First Annual Report (Governor Allen). Puerto Rico, 1900-1.
General Regulations for the Execution of the Mortgage Law for Cuba, Puerto Rico, and the Philippines, 1893. Washington, 1899.
Military Government of Porto Rico: October 18, 1898, to April 30, 1900 (Appendices). Washington, 1901.
Puerto Rico: Embracing the Reports of Brigadier General George W. Davis, Military Governor. Washington, 1900.
Report of the Insular Commission to Secretary of War on Investigations into Civil Affairs of the Island of Porto Rico, with Recommendations. Washington, 1899.
Reports for Brigadier General George W. Davis on Industrial and Economic Conditions of Puerto Rico. Washington, 1900.
Report of Brigadier General George W. Davis, U.S.A., on Civil Affairs of Puerto Rico. Washington, 1900.

*Report of the Military Governor of Porto Rico on Civil Affairs,
1899-1900.* Washington, 1902.

Second Annual Report (Governor Hunt). Puerto Rico, 1901-2.

Supreme Court of Puerto Rico. *Roman Catholic Apostolic Church
of Porto Rico vs. The People of Porto Rico.* Washington,
1901.

Third Annual Report (Governor Hunt), Puerto Rico, 1902-3.

War Department. *Census of Porto Rico.* Washington, 1899.

(c) Senate Documents:

56th Cong., 1st sess., No. 147. Hearings before Committee on
Pacific Islands and Puerto Rico, on Senate Bill 2264, *To
Provide a Government for the Island of Puerto Rico and for
other Purposes.* Washington, 1900.

56th Cong., 1st sess., Senate Report 249. To accompany Senate
Bill No. 2264. Washington, 1900.

61st Cong., 1st sess., No. 40. *Message of President Relating to
Affairs in Puerto Rico.* Washington, 1909.

(d) House Documents:

56th Cong., 1st sess., No. 2. Annual Reports of the War Department for the Fiscal Year ended June 30, 1899, vol. 1, Pt. 6.
*Report of Brigadier General George W. Davis on Civil Affairs
in Porto Rico.* Washington, 1900.

56th Cong., 1st sess., No. 6883 & 8245. Hearings before Committee on Insular Affairs, *To Provide a Government for the
Island of Puerto Rico.* Washington, 1900.

56th Cong., 1st sess., House Report No. 249, on House Bill No.
6883. Washington, 1900.

56th Cong., 1st sess., House Report No. 986, on House Bill No.
8245. Washington, 1900.

56th Cong., 1st & 2nd sess., Hearings and Reports before Committee on Insular Affairs, 1900-1901 (compiled by R. B.
Horton). Washington, 1904.

57th Cong., 1st sess., Hearing, April 12, 1902. Committee on
Insular Affairs, Public Lands. Washington, 1902.

61st Cong., 2nd sess., House Report No. 750, on House Bill No.
615. *Conditions in Puerto Rico.* Washington, 1910.

The Congressional Record:

56th Cong., 1st sess., through the 61st Cong., 2nd sess.

2. SPAIN

Arecco y Torres, Domingo (ed.). *Recopilación de Disposiciones
Oficiales.* Las Leyes, Reales Ordenes etc., publicadas en la *Gaceta*

Oficial, desde el 1st de Enero de 1878 hasta fin de Diciembre de 1887. Mayagüez, 1889.

3. PUERTO RICO

Cámara de Delegados: La Asamblea Legislativa, la sesión 3 Diciembre 1900 a 31 Enero 1901.

Documents on the Constitutional History of Puerto Rico. Washington.

Gaceta Oficial (San Juan), 1897-1901.

La Nueva Constitución de Puerto Rico. Informes a la Convención Constituyente preparados por la Escuela de Administración Pública. Río Piedras, 1954.

4. MISCELLANEOUS

Carroll, Henry K. *Report on the Island of Porto Rico: Its Population, Civil Government, Commerce, Industries, Productions, Roads, Tariff, and Currency with Recommendations.* Washington, 1899.

III. BIOGRAPHIES, HISTORIES, SPECIAL STUDIES, ARTICLES

Abbad y Lasierra, Fray Iñigo. *Historia Geográfica: Civil y Natural de la Isla de San Juan Bautista de Puerto Rico.* Puerto Rico, 1866.

Abril, Mariano. *Un Héroe de la Independencia de España y América.* Puerto Rico, 1936.

Acosta, José Julián. *Apuntes para la Historia de Puerto Rico.* Puerto Rico, 1879.

Acosta Quintero, Angel. *José Julián Acosta y su Tiempo.* San Juan, 1899.

Alegría, Ricardo E. *La Fiesta de Santiago Apóstol en Loiza Aldea.* Madrid, 1954.

Allen, Charles H. "The Government of Porto Rico," *Independent,* 52 (July 19, 1900).

Alonso, Manuel A. *"El Gíbaro."* Puerto Rico, 1883.

Amadeo, Santos P. *El Habeas Corpus en Puerto Rico, 1899-1948.* Puerto Rico, 1948.

Arciniegas, Germán. *Caribbean Sea of the New World.* New York, 1946.

De Armas y Céspedes, Francisco. *Régimen Político de las Antillas Españolas.* Palma, Spain, 1882.

Asenjo Arteaga, Federico. *Efemérides de la Isla de Puerto Rico.* San Juan, 1886.

Ashford, Bailey K. *Uncinariasis en Puerto Rico: Un Problema Médico y Económico.* San Juan, 1916.

Bacon, Robert, and Scott, John Brown (eds.). *The Military and Colonial Policy of the United States.* Cambridge, Mass., 1916.

Balbas Capó, Vicente. *Puerto Rico a los Diez Años de Americanización.* San Juan, 1910.

Baldorioty de Castro, Román. *Las Facultades Omnímodas en 1811 y los Diputados de Puerto Rico en 1869.* Madrid, 1869.

Baldwin, James. *Our New Possessions: Cuba, Puerto Rico, Hawaii, Philippines.* New York, 1899.

Barbosa de Rosario, Pilar (ed.). "De Baldorioty a Barbosa: Historia del Autonomismo Puertorriqueño, 1887-1896," in *La Obra de José Celso Barbosa*, Vol. V. San Juan, 1957.

———— (ed.). "La Comisión Autonomista de 1896: Historia del Autonomismo Puertorriqueño," in *La Obra de José Celso Barbosa*, Vol. VI. San Juan, 1957.

———— (ed.). "Post Umbra," in *La Obra de José Celso Barbosa*, Vol. II. San Juan, 1937.

———— (ed.). "Orientando al Pueblo, 1900-1921," in *La Obra de José Celso Barbosa*, Vol. IV. San Juan, 1939.

———— (ed.). "Problema de Razas," in *La Obra de José Celso Barbosa*, Vol. III. San Juan, 1937.

Becker, Jerónimo. *Historia de las Relaciones Exteriores de España durante el Siglo XIX.* Madrid, 1924.

————. *La Independencia de América.* Madrid, 1922.

Belmonte, Federico. *Análisis Ideológico.* Santurce, Puerto Rico, 1953.

Berbusse, Edward J. "Aspects in Church-State Relations in Puerto Rico," *The Americas* (Jan., 1963), pp. 291-304.

Bird Piñero, Enrique. "The Politics of Puerto Rican Land Reform: A Study in the Dynamics of Legislation," M.A. thesis, University of Chicago, 1950.

Blanco, Tomás. *El Prejuicio Racial en Puerto Rico.* San Juan, 1942.

————. *Prontuario Histórico de Puerto Rico.* San Juan, 1955.

Blanco Fernández, Antonio. *España y Puerto Rico, 1820-1930.* San Juan, 1930.

Blanco Fombona, R. *Grandes Escritores de América.* Madrid, 1917.

Blanco y Sosa, Julián E. *Enmiendas a la Constitución Orgánica del Partido Autonomista Puertorriqueño Presentadas a la Asamblea de Mayagüez que Deberá Celebrarse el Primero de Abril.* Ponce, 1891.

Brau, Salvador. *Ecos de la Batalla.* Puerto Rico, 1886.

————. *Historia de Puerto Rico.* New York, 1904.

————. *Las Clases Jornaleras de Puerto Rico.* Puerto Rico, 1882.

————. *Puerto Rico y Su Historia.* Valencia, 1894.

————. *Lo Que Dice La Historia.* Madrid, 1893.

Canales, Nemesio R. *Paliques.* Río Piedras, 1952.

Capó Rodríguez, Pedro. "Colonial Representation in the American Empire," *American Journal of International Law*, XV, 530-51.

———. "The Relations between the United States and Porto Rico: Juridical aspects," *American Journal of International Law*, XIII, July, 1919.

———. "Some Historical and Political Aspects of the Government of Porto Rico," *Hispanic American Historical Review*, II, No. 4 (Nov., 1919).

Carroll, Henry K. "General Henry's Policy in Porto Rico," *The Independent*, XXI (Mar. 2, 1899) p. 643-44.

———. "How Shall Puerto Rico be Governed?" *Forum*, XXVIII (Nov., 1899).

———. "Puerto Rico as a Mission Field," *Missionary Review*, XXIII (Aug., 1900).

———. "The Religious Question in Porto Rico," *The Independent*, XXI (Nov. 2, 9 1899) pp. 2935-37, 3001-3.

———. "Report of Doctor Carroll on Porto Rico," *The Independent*, XXII (Jan. 4, 1900).

———. "What Has Been Done for Porto Rico under Military Rule," *American Review of Reviews*, XX (Dec., 1899).

Cebollero, Pedro A. *A School Language Policy for Puerto Rico.* San Juan, 1945.

Chaves, Antonio F. *La Distribución de la Población en Puerto Rico.* Río Piedras, 1949.

Clark, Victor S. (and others). *Porto Rico and Its Problems.* Washington, 1930.

Coll y Cuchi, Cayetano. *Notas Políticas.* San Juan, 1909.

———. *Pro Patria.* San Juan, 1909.

Coll y Toste, Cayetano. *Historia de la Instrucción Pública en Puerto Rico hasta el Año de 1898.* San Juan, 1910.

——— (ed.). *Repertorio Histórico de Puerto Rico.* Puerto Rico, 1896.

——— (ed.). *Reseña del Estado Social, Económico e Industrial de la Isla de Puerto Rico al Tomar Posesión de Ella los Estados Unidos.* San Juan, 1899.

Concepción de García, Gilberto. "The Land Authority of Puerto Rico," *George Washington Law Review*, XII, No. 3 (April, 1944).

De Córdoba, Pedro Tomás. *Memorias Geográficas, Históricas, Económicas y Estadísticas de la Isla de Puerto Rico.* San Juan, 1831-33.

Córdova Dávila, Félix. *Empire or Democracy?* Washington, 1928.

Córdova Landrón, Arturo. *Salvador Brau: Su Vida, Su Obra, Su Epoca.* Río Piedras, 1949.

Crawford, William Rex. *A Century of Latin-American Thought.* Cambridge, 1944.

Cruz Monclova, Lidio. *Historia del Año de 1887.* Río Piedras, Puerto Rico, 1958.

———. *Historia de Puerto Rico: Siglo XIX.* Vol. I (1808-68). Santurce, Puerto Rico, 1952.

———. *Historia de Puerto Rico: Siglo XIX.* Vol. II, Part 1 (1868-74). Madrid, 1957.

———. *Historia de Puerto Rico: Siglo XIX.* Vol. II, Part 2 (1875-85). Madrid, 1957.

Cuesta, J. Enamorado. *El Imperialismo Yanqui y la Revolución en el Caribe.* Puerto Rico, 1936.

Cuesta Mendoza, Antonio. *Historia de la Educación en el Puerto Rico Colonial, 1821-98.* República Dominicana, 1948.

———. *Historia Eclesiástica del Puerto Rico Colonial, 1508-1700.* República Dominicana, 1948.

Dana, Arnold G. *Puerto Rico's Case: Outcome of American Sovereignty, 1898-1928.* New Haven, 1928.

Davis, Richard Harding. *The Cuban and Porto Rican Campaigns.* New York, 1898.

Descartes, Sol L. (ed.). *Basic Statistics on Puerto Rico.* Washington, 1946.

Díaz Caneja, Ignacio. *La Autonomía de las Antillas.* Puerto Rico, 1887.

———. *La Cuestión Ultramarina.* Puerto Rico, 1885.

———. *Waterloo Político: Examen Crítico de las Principales Teorías sobre que Descansa el Edificio Político Moderno.* Puerto Rico, 1891.

Díaz Soler, Luis M. *Historia de la Esclavitud Negra en Puerto Rico, 1493-1890.* Madrid, 1949.

———. *Rosendo Matienzo Cintrón.* 2 vols. Puerto Rico, 1960.

De Diego, José. *Cantos de Rebeldía.* Barcelona, 1916.

———. "Nuevas Campanas," *Biblioteca de la Unión Antillana.* Barcelona, 1916.

Diffie, Bailey W., and Whitfield, Justine. *Porto Rico: A Broken Pledge.* New York, 1931.

Dinwiddie, William. *Puerto Rico: Its Conditions and Possibilities.* New York, 1899.

Discurso de la Inauguración del Colegio de la 1a. y 2a. Enseñanza en Santurce, dirigido por los RR.PP. Escolapios ... por el R. P. Esteban Calonje. Puerto Rico, 1896.

Discurso por Don Juan Perpiñá y Pibernat en la Solemne Distribución de Premios de la Casa de Caridad . . . de San Juan. Puerto Rico, 1887.

Education in Puerto Rico, "A Survey of the Public Educational System of Porto Rico" by International Institute of Teachers College, Columbia University. New York, 1926.

Enamorado-Cuesta, José. *Porto Rico, Past and Present: The Island after Thirty Years of American Rule.* New York, 1929.

Estatutos del Ateneo Puertorriqueño. Puerto Rico, 1885.

Fernández García, E. (ed.). *The Book of Porto Rico.* San Juan, 1923.

Ferrer Hernández, Gabriel. *La Instrucción Pública en Puerto Rico.* Puerto Rico, 1885.

Figueroa, Sotero. *Ensayo Biográfico de los que más Han Contribuído al Progreso de Puerto Rico.* Ponce, 1888.

Foraker, Joseph Benson. *Notes of a Busy Life.* 2 vols. Cincinnati, 1916.

———. *The Speeches of Joseph B. Foraker.* 7 vols. Library of Congress, Washington (undated).

———. "The United States and Porto Rico," *North American Review,* CLXX (April, 1900).

Ford, Worthington C. "Trade Policy with the Colonies," *Harper's,* 590 (July, 1899).

García Samudio, Nicolás. *La Independencia de Hispanoamérica.* México, D.F., 1945.

Gautier Dapena, José A. "Nacimiento de los Partidos Políticos bajo la Soberanía de los Estados Unidos: Programas y Tendencias," *Historia,* III, No. 2 (Oct., 1953).

González-Ginorio, José. *Luis Muñoz Rivera.* New York, 1919.

Greene, Theodore P. (ed.). *American Imperialism in 1898.* Boston, 1955.

Groff, George G. "After Two Years' Work in Porto Rico," *Independent,* XXII (Aug. 9, 1900).

———. "Colonial Government for Porto Rico," *Independent,* XXII (Jan. 11, 1900).

Gutiérrez del Arroyo, Isabel. *El Reformismo Ilustrado en Puerto Rico.* México, D.F., 1951.

Hagedorn, Hermann (ed.). *The Works of Theodore Roosevelt.* 25 vols. New York, 1926.

Hanson, Earl Parker. *Transformation: The Story of Modern Puerto Rico.* New York, 1955.

Harbrecht, Paul P. "What are the Liberties of Citizens of Puerto Rico under the Constitution?" *Georgetown Law Journal,* XXXVIII (March, 1950).

Harrington, M. W. "Porto Rico and the Portoricans," *Catholic World*, LXX (Nov., 1899).

Hayden, Sherman S., and Rivlin, Benjamin. *Non-Self Governing Territories: Status of Puerto Rico.* New York, 1954.

Henna, J. J., and Zeno Gandía, M. *The Case of Puerto Rico.* Washington, 1899.

Henry, Guy V. "Our Duty in Porto Rico," *Munsey*, XXII (Nov., 1899).

Henry, Mrs. Guy V. "San Juan," *The Outlook*, LXVII, No. 14 (April 6, 1901).

Hernández Usera, Rafael. *Semillas a Voleo.* Madrid, 1925.

De Hostos, Adolfo. *Ciudad Murada, 1521-1898.* La Habana, 1948.

———. "La Peregrinación de Bayoán," *Obras Completas.* Madrid, 1863.

———. *Tesauro de Datos Históricos.* San Juan, 1948-51.

De Hostos, E. M. *Madre Isla: Campaña Política por Puerto Rico, 1898.* Habana, 1939.

Iglesias Pantín, Santiago. *Luchas Emancipadoras.* San Juan, 1929.

Instituto Civil de Segunda Enseñanza de Puerto Rico. *Programa de Psicología, Lógica y Filosofía Moral.* Puerto Rico, 1874.

Jackson, F. E. (ed.). *The Representative Men of Porto Rico.* New York, 1910.

Lebrón Rodríguez, Ramón. *La Vida del Prócer.* San Juan, 1954.

López Landrón, Rafael. *La Ciencia y El Arte de la Filosofía.* San Juan, 1915.

Macho Moreno, Juan. *Compilación Legislativa de Primera Enseñanza de la Isla de Puerto Rico.* Madrid, 1895.

McKee, S. S. "Bishop Blenk in Porto Rico: The Carnival," *Harper's Weekly*, XLIV (March 10, 1900).

De Madariaga, Salvador. *The Fall of the Spanish American Empire.* New York, 1948.

Medina Ramírez, Ramón. *El Movimiento Libertador en la Historia de Puerto Rico.* San Juan, 1950.

Miller, Paul Gerard. *Historia de Puerto Rico.* New York, 1946.

Morales Carrión, Arturo. "Orígenes de Las Relaciones entre los Estados Unidos y Puerto Rico (1700-1815)," *Historia*, II, No. 1 (April, 1952).

———. *Puerto Rico and the Non-Hispanic Caribbean: A Study in Spanish Exclusivism.* Río Piedras, 1952.

Morales Miranda, José Pablo. *Misceláneas Históricas.* San Juan, 1924.

Muñoz Amato, Pedro. "Major Trends in the Constitutional History of

Puerto Rico,'' in *Revista de Derecho, Legislación y Jurisprudencia del Colegio de Abogados de Puerto Rico*, 12 (1949), 242-99.

Muñoz Rivera, Luis. *Are the Porto Rican People Prepared for Self-Government*. Washington, 1908.

———. ''Campañas Políticas'' (1890-1916), in Luis Muñoz Marín (ed.), *Obras Completas*. Madrid, 1925.

———. ''Apuntes para un Libro'' (1896-1900), in Luis Muñoz Marín (ed.), *Obras Completas*. Madrid, 1925.

Neumann Gandía, Eduardo. *Benefactores y Hombres Notables de Puerto Rico*. Ponce, 1896.

Nieves, Juan B. *La Anexión de Puerto Rico a los Estados Unidos*. Ponce, 1898.

Nolasco, Sócrates. *Escritores de Puerto Rico*. Manzanillo, Cuba, 1953.

Osuna, Juan José. *A History of Education in Puerto Rico*. Río Piedras, Puerto Rico, 1949.

Ots Capdequi, José María. *Manual de Historia del Derecho Español en las Indias*. Buenos Aires, 1943.

Pedreira, Antonio S. *El Año Terrible del '87*. México, D. F., 1948.

———. *Bibliografía Puertorriqueña, 1493-1930*. Madrid, 1932.

———. ''Un Hombre del Pueblo: José Celso Barbosa,'' in *La Obra de José Celso Barbosa*, Vol. I. San Juan, 1937.

———. *Hostos: Ciudadano de América*. Madrid, 1932.

———. *Insularismo: Ensayos de Interpretación Puertorriqueña*. Puerto Rico, 1942.

Bird, Augusto (ed.). *Bibliografía Puertorriqueña, 1930-1945*. Río Piedras, 1947.

Pérez Moris, José. *Historia de la Insurrección de Lares*. Barcelona, 1872.

Perloff, Harvey S. *Puerto Rico's Economic Future*. Chicago, 1950.

Petrullo, Vincenzo. *Puerto Rican Paradox*. Philadelphia, 1947.

Portell Vilá, Herminio. *Historia de Cuba en sus Relaciones con los Estados Unidos y España*. Havana, 1938.

Post Regis H. ''What's Wrong in Porto Rico?'' *The World's Work* (Jan., 1922).

Puerto Rico. *Gratitud y Progreso: Cuatro Centenario de la Colonización Cristiana de Puerto Rico*. San Juan, 1908.

Puerto Rico. *Insular Government of Porto Rico with Roster of Employees*. San Juan, 1902.

Puerto Rico. ''Porto Rico and the United States,'' in *Catholic Association for International Peace*. Washington, 1931.

Rippy, J. Fred. *Historical Evolution of Hispanic America*. New York, 1940.

———. *Latin America in World Politics*. New York, 1942.

Rivera, Antonio. *El Laborantismo o la Liquidación del Régimen Español en Puerto Rico.* México, D.F., 1943.

―――, and Morales Carrión, Arturo. *La Enseñanza de la Historia en Puerto Rico.* México, D.F., 1953.

Rivero, Angel. *Crónica de la Guerra Hispano-Americana.* Madrid, 1922.

Rodríguez Ramos, Manuel. "Interaction of Civil Law and Anglo-American Law in the Legal Method in Puerto Rico," *Tulane Law Review,* XXIII (Oct., 1948).

Roehm, Pauline K. *"Some Aspects of Recent Puerto Rican History,"* unpublished M.A. Thesis, University of Arizona, 1945.

Rosario, José C. *The Development of the Puerto Rican Jíbaro and His Present Attitude Towards Society.* Río Piedras, 1935.

Rotkin, Charles E., and Richardson, Lewis C. *Puerto Rico: Caribbean Crossroads.* New York, 1947.

Rowe, Leo Stanton. *The United States and Porto Rico.* New York, 1904.

De Santa Ana, S. J., Antonio López. *Los Jesuitas en Puerto Rico de 1858 a 1886.* Santander, Spain, 1958.

Salinas, Pedro. *Aprecio y Defensa del Lenguaje.* Río Piedras, Puerto Rico, 1948.

Sánchez Reulet, Anibal (ed.). "La Filosofía Latinoamericana Contemporanea," in the series *Pensamiento de América.* Washington, 1949.

Sinodo Diocesano del Obispado de Puerto Rico. Puerto Rico, 1917.

Solemne Distribución de Premios: Colegio de San Ignacio en Santurce, bajo la Dirección de la Compañía de Jesus. Puerto Rico, 1884.

Soto, Juan B. *Causas y Consecuencias Antecedentes Diplomáticos y Efectos de la Guerra Hispano-Americano.* San Juan, 1922.

Tapia y Rivera, Alejandro. *Mis Memorias o Puerto Rico como lo Encontré y como lo Dejó.* New York, 1927.

―――― (ed.). *Biblioteca Histórica de Puerto Rico.* San Juan, 1945.

Todd, Roberto H. *Desfile de Gobernadores de Puerto Rico.* San Juan, 1943.

―――. *José Julio Henna, 1848-1924.* San Juan, 1930.

―――. *Nuestro Status Político y su Concepto Jurídico.* San Juan, 1919.

Del Toro, Emilio. *The Future of Porto Rico.* San Juan, 1914.

Tous Soto, Manuel. *Puerto Rico, Posesión de los Estados Unidos de América.* San Juan, 1940.

Travieso y Quijano, Martín. *Memoria sobre el Estado Actual de la*

Instrucción Pública, su Pasado, y Medios para su Mejoramiento Futuro. Mayagüez, 1885.

Tribunal de Exámenes para Maestros Elementales y Superiores de Puerto Rico. San Juan, 1882.

Del Valle Atiles, Francisco. *El Campesino Puertorriqueño, sus Condiciones Físicas, Intelectuales y Morales.* Puerto Rico, 1887.

Vance, John Thomas. *The Background of Hispanic American Law.* New York, 1943.

Van Middledyk, Rudolph A. *The History of Porto Rico: From the Spanish Discovery to the American Occupation.* New York, 1903.

Vega Morales, Arturo. *Notas Pedagógicas.* Puerto Rico, 1899.

Venegas Castro, Luis. *Status Político de Puerto Rico desde el Punto de Vista Económico.* San Juan, 1922.

Whitaker, Arthur P. *Latin America and the Enlightenment.* New York, 1942.

Zeno de Matos, Elena. *Manuel Zeno Gandía.* San Juan, 1955.

IV. PERIODICALS AND NEWSPAPERS

1. PERIODICALS

Almanaque Puertorriqueño Asenjo.

Boletín Eclesiástico de la Diocesis de Puerto Rico, 1859-99, 1914-20 (July).

Boletín Histórico de Puerto Rico. Edited by Cayetano Coll y Toste. 13 vols. San Juan, Puerto Rico.

Boletín de Historia Puertorriqueña.

Boletín de la Gran Logia Soberana de Puerto Rico, 1907.

Cosmos (Yauco, Puerto Rico).

Historia (publication of National Honorary Society of History).

2. NEWSPAPERS

El Boletín Mercantil

La Correspondencia

La Democracia

El Ideal Católico (Ponce, Puerto Rico), 1900-14.

San Juan News

El Liberal

El País

Puerto Rico Herald (New York), 1901-3.

La Verdad, 1905-7.

Pomarrosa (Guayama, Puerto Rico), 1918.

Revista de la Antillas (San Juan, Puerto Rico), 1913.

Index